News scoops!   Exclusive beats!   Stop-press stories!

From Moscow to Rome . . . from Mexico to China . . . he traveled to get them.

Dramatic episodes in the lives of statesmen. Close-ups written behind the scenes in Government conflicts. A War crisis. Intrigue. Adventure. Romance.

Hurriedly he'd file the cables. And then . . .

The same old story. YOU CANT PRINT THAT!

Lenin expelled him from Russia! Musso-lini deported him from Italy! D'Annunzio drove him from Fiume! Bratianu sent the police to arrest him in Rumania! Pilsudski said "NO!" French Generals charged him with fomenting mutiny in the Foreign Legion! The President of Mexico held up his telegrams! Twenty countries cen-sored him!

But at last, George Seldes, reporter extra-ordinary, HAS PRINTED THEM.

He has told these vivid, graphic stories in the wonderful collection of uncensored material bound between the covers of this vital book.

If you enjoy movement, color, the reckless disregard for consequences that only a great newsman is born with, your atten-tion will be held from start to finish.

You Can't Print That!

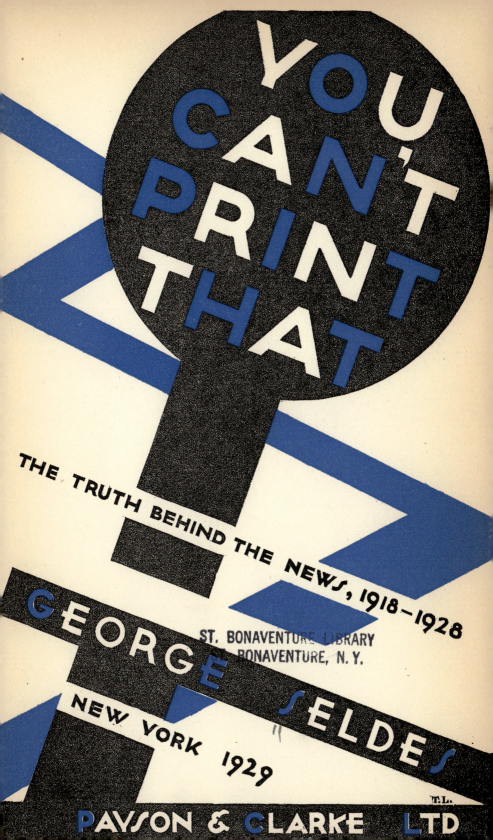

YOU CAN'T PRINT THAT

THE TRUTH BEHIND THE NEWS, 1918–1928

GEORGE SELDES

NEW YORK 1929

PAYSON & CLARKE LTD

To my father
GEORGE S. SELDES
Libertarian

Contents

Contents

Introduction

"All men were created free, and now they are everywhere in chains."

J. J. Rousseau

Introduction — Billions and Bunkum

". . . True opinions can prevail only if the facts to which they refer are known; if they are not known, false ideas are just as effective as true ones, if not a little more effective" . . .
Walter Lippmann, *— " Liberty and the News."*

IN his search for facts the newspaperman on foreign service contends with more censorship, propaganda, intimidation and frequently terrorism in Continental Europe nowadays than in that supposedly dark journalistic age which preceded the world war. Progress has been made in the past ten years but of all the liberties which were outlawed and debased during the great conflict that of the press seems to have recovered least.

For many and mighty reasons all governmental agencies of suppression in many countries continue to function with unrelenting thoroughness. They are directed against public opinion in the United States and England because these are the dominant nations. So long as Lombard Street ruled the money market the Continent sought to influence British public opinion; now that the United States has increased its foreign investments to $15,000,000,000, European chancelleries are dividing their effort, but they are also increasing it because they realize how much depends on the loans they raise and the moral support they obtain from their creditors.

The British investment has always been conservative; the fifteen billion dollars which America has spent has been plunged with a sometimes reckless, frequently ignorant hand into the rehabilitation of Europe. Some of this money has been used to raise wheat, some to build submarines and perfect poison gases; billions may be safe and at work for material progress and peace, but billions are unsafe because they prepare for new wars.

The presidents, kings and dictators of Continental Europe have been taught the full power of the press but recently, yet they are making extreme use of their knowledge. They have their friendly or their purchased press in Great Britain; toward America, which knows so pathetically little about the numerous lands over which it has cast its billions, the foreign offices have exercised a refined, more subtle, sometimes Machiavelian system of propaganda and censorship.

In one country the bankers' and manufacturers' associations have assumed arbitrary power, in another a perverted philosophy is in control of human fate; in a third an egomaniac rules and in a fourth medieval corruption has temporarily crushed all liberal resistance; therefore the word is spread throughout the dominant nations, America and Britain, that democracy is unsuitable for most of Continental Europe, that it has proven a fraud and a failure, that parliaments are a drag on the efficient expression of the will of a people, freedom is a modern delusion, truth is a false god and liberty nothing but a chimaera. The new propaganda reigns.

It boasts material progress. It points to trains running on time, to roads built, to budgets balanced, to efficiency in mines and factories. It says nothing of the fear of death and the fear of violence which are crushing the last remnants of those fighting for individual and mass liberty in many lands. Anyone can see the trains running on time, but who is willing to open his eyes to see the hidden terror which is holding many millions of civilized people captive? The international bankers and all their agencies of publicity, the foreign offices with their intimidation of journalists and their censorships and all the silly tourists who travel by the hundred thousand nowadays, all report to the holders of billions of bonds that the sun is shining brightly in all the 7 and 8 per cent. lands, that God's in his heaven and all's well with the postbellum world.

*   *   *   *

I believe with Mr. Lippmann that false ideas are frequently more effective than true ones and I know that there is a world of a difference between the mistakes which journalists make frequently but honestly and the official propaganda, the half truths, the *ballons d'essai,* the *canards,* and, to drop euphemism, the official lies of many dictators and premiers of Continental Europe. I also cling to that very old-fashioned belief that the press is the most powerful estate and that the journalist is (or should be) the great moulder of public opinion. Yet for twenty years I have heard again and again the layman's question: Why don't the papers print the truth; why don't the reporters write the truth?

Many answers have been written concerning national journalism; this book, by incident and adventure and the presentation of documents and facts, is an attempt to illustrate the foreign situation. There are many reasons behind the failure of the press to present the whole truth about Europe.

For one, there is censorship. In time of crisis almost every nation establishes a censor bureau; in all dictatorships such bureaus function continually, some openly, some secretly.

There are the bond issues of many billions. News must be suppressed when unfavorable, otherwise the market will crash; news must be perverted at all times, otherwise new loans will be more difficult, and rates will be too high. The foreign offices and the bankers combine in this attack on a free press and both are powerful and effective.

There is the political terrorism which still prevails in many lands and which touches the pen of the foreign correspondent as well as the lives of the suppressed citizens and subjects. You can't do much free writing when you know there is a detective outside your door (as in Russia) or a secret agent in your office (as frequently in Italy) or squads of police officials detailed to watch you (as in Roumania and many other countries).

And, finally, there are so few great newspapers in America and England brave enough to disregard the wishes of certain foreign offices and the "business at any price" international bond houses and the tourist and steamship organizations which spend large sums advertising, that when the truth is published it reaches so small a public that it is ineffective beside the half-truth which the majority of newspapers publish.

Almost always the foreign correspondent works honestly, but he is no modern Prometheus to defy the gods of European *Real Politik* by waving an iconoclastic torch over their conferences and their plans, their secret plots and their open betrayals. Against governmental systems the journalist can do little. He can, as witness a letter from one who had to submit to Mussolini's terrorism, "break his heart" and remain silent.

Or, being all too human and able to distinguish the buttered side, and finding encouragement in American editorial offices for a policy of suppression, and being also susceptible to worldly flattery and the delights of social advancement, the American journalist, once having found it doesn't get him anywhere to be an iconoclast, may adapt himself to the desired compromises. What Professor Salvemini says of the situation in

Italy may be read with a few necessary changes, for Russia, Poland, Hungary, Roumania, Spain, Bulgaria, Greece, Portugal and several other nations and still hold its truth. Salvemini says:

The difficulty of understanding the present situation of the Italian people is increased by the fact that French, English or American journalists, as soon as they arrive in Italy, are immediately surrounded by agents of Fascist propaganda and are introduced into aristocratic and high Fascist bourgeois circles; here they are flattered by every possible kindness and loaded down with statistics, information, interpretations, explanations *ad usum delphini*. Often they are salaried for translating and sending to their papers articles and news concocted in the offices of Fascist propaganda. A few intelligent and honest foreign journalists succeed little by little in seeing the light but their letters must omit much that they know and if they wire their papers accurate information, their telegrams are intercepted: they themselves are expelled from Italy. The most enthusiastic are forced to send unsigned articles to their papers and magazines, resorting to a thousand expediencies in order not to be discovered. Telegraphed news, which is most likely to impress the reading public, is ruthlessly controlled by the government censorship if it does not coincide with the taste of the Mussolini government.

Or with the taste of the Soviet government, or the Primo de Rivera government, or that of Horthy, Pangalos, Waldemiras, Bratianu I and Bratianu II, Pilsudski, Kemal Pasha, or that of the French in Syria and Morocco, the British in Mesopotamia and other protectorates, the Italians in Libya, or the dictators of many other lands.

* * * *

The American foreign correspondent who succumbs to flattery and the ribbons of various legions of honor, to occasional meetings with princes and marquesas, to handshakes with

13

various Mussolinis and Stalins, to bows and smiles from the Great of Our Age, usually finds many of the complexities of everyday life removed and receives praise from New York and Chicago for his diplomatic progress.

He who would be a man and a nonconformist may find himself in jail.

Of the hundred or more American journalists abroad whom I know well, so many have been imprisoned, so many have been expelled from countries and so many have just evaded either imprisonment or deportation by hook or by crook, usually by both, that it is only fair to emphasize their integrity and to do considerable pointing with pride. Newspapers as a rule do not fuss over the troubles of their representatives because editors believe the public is not interested in newspaper men. Yet correspondents' troubles illustrate better than anything else I know the vicious situation in many places.

Almost half of Europe today is governed by violence and terrorism. Proclaim liberty tomorrow and you would have revolutions in twenty countries. Almost half of Europe's population does not enjoy the fundamental rights of the days before the so-called war of liberation. It is not true that the people of Soviet Russia are happy or that the people of Italy are happy with their dictatorships, or that the parliamentary system has failed. Suppression by force does not mean failure. For corroboration of these statements I can refer to ninety or more of the hundred American and British journalists I know, who are working in Europe, who have investigated and who have the real knowledge. The bond dealers and the tourists and the noted magazine writers who make two-week visits (with half their articles written in advance in accordance with the views and instructions of their editors) may tell you differently, but the resident reporters know it is not so.

But it is too difficult to say the opposite when political police systems hang around the office doors, and American ambassadors, most of whom cringe before dictators, offer no protection, and when, after all, the editor frequently is on the side of the tourists and bankers and the noted magazine journalists. And what, let me ask, dare an American write about the success or failure of the League of Nations when 48 per cent. of the American papers for political party reasons are blindly opposed to it and another 48 per cent. for the same reasons, are blindly in favor of it, and not one of the 96 per cent. wants an impartial and objective cablegram?

I defied anyone to challenge the statement that Roumania was the most politically corrupt state in Europe in 1928 and that a loan would be a considerable risk for American pocket-books. Dictatorial terrorism, unrest and the danger of revolution prevailed under Vintila as under Jon Bratianu. Yet when M. Quesnay and M. Rist of the Bank of France came to New York to speak about an $80,000,000 loan (which is really a $200,000,-000 French political manœuvre to outwit Italian intrigue in Bucharest), certain American journals began a campaign in favor of Roumania, aiming to hide the truth about terrorism at a time when important minorities and the whole peasantry threatened a revolt which would endanger the American dollar investments.

In what position does such a loan campaign place the American correspondent in a capital such as Bucharest?

1. If his paper is supporting the loan, he is silenced. (If Queen Marie has already visited his editor and let him kiss her hand, he is already journalistically impotent.)

2. If the bankers favor the loan and are using the reporter's newspaper, he is again silenced.

3. If neither 1 nor 2 is true, and he tries to write or cable an honest warning, thereby doing a great service to thousands of Americans who might be foolishly attracted by the 7 or 8 per cent. which such a speculative loan must pay, he will be arrested or expelled, the frontiers permanently closed to him, and his future usefulness curtailed.

The same holds for Russia, Italy, Poland, Spain, and other despotic lands.

* * * *

Billions and bunkum. Billions of dollars, at home and abroad, are able to control or hide the international truth, while bunkum, thanks to censorship of facts, frequently replaces them entirely. If America or England had known the whole truth about the Continental European system, and there had been no propaganda, would the necessary emotions have been aroused to bring either into war?

If America were allowed by its editors to know the whole truth about Mexico, would we ever engage in warfare there?

If America and England — the public not the politicians — had known the facts of March 1917, could they not have insured a Russian democratic revolution without Bolshevism?

If America knew the whole truth about Italy today, would it float the Italian bonds? Likewise the Polish bonds? Or the bonds of other terroristic countries?

If America had known the truth about Queen Marie, would not the royal farce of 1927 have been different?

These are typical questions the American journalist abroad, who cannot for the life of him tell the whole truth, is asking pertinently.

He sees Continental Europe drifting towards new wars; dates are being mentioned. He sees American relations with free England frequently grow cold and distant, while our relationship with despotic regimes suddenly grow warm and friendly, thanks to no sound reasons, but to efficient propaganda. Misunderstandings undermine solid foundations. Solid foundations are frequently replaced by dangerous golden ones. Billions and bunkum more and more order our relationship to foreign nations. The journalist sees passions pass for realism. He sees propaganda overwhelming truth. He sees the race for armament continuing. American dollars frequently encourage it. False frontiers and injustices more cruel than any before 1914 give cause for bigger and better world wars. Many say the future of western white civilization is endangered. Some believe only America, now the moral and financial supernation, can save it. And yet our portion is so much bunkum and propaganda that in ten years we have done almost nothing to further international relations with the free nations.

If ever there was a voice crying in a political wilderness, it is that of the American journalist on foreign service. Cassandra had a larger audience despite the thunder and waves on the rocks of the Mediterranean. She at least was close to the national ear. But the American correspondent does not seem able to penetrate the curtain covered with $15,000,000,000 of gold on one side and on the other the thickest veils of censorship that have ever existed.

Peacetime censorship exists for one reason only: to hide rotten affairs of state. Wartime censorship alone is justifiable — but we who were in the press section of the American Army in France may doubt if even then it has any value, inasmuch as General Pershing always gave us the fullest information about the enemy and, as we later learned, the enemy knew everything there was to know about our side. (Three days before our attack the Germans moved out of the St. Mihiel salient because they knew almost as much as Pershing did about the plans for that battle.)

In the chapters which follow I have begun with wartime and armistice censorship incidents; followed by experiences in those parallel despotisms, Italy and Russia; the League of Nations mandated terrorities which should be free from the domination of any European country but which are not; a visit to Mexico where censorship exists from time to time, but which is not a tenth as stupid or vicious as that practised in American newspaper offices where owners and editors have policies of war and interventions which force their editorial writers and reporters to prostitute themselves; and I have concluded with side trips to several European countries, including the most corrupt of all, Roumania, where censorship exists to cover not only political terrorism as in other countries, but also moral corruption which begins in the royal palaces.

I have given only my own experiences. Every one of a hundred colleagues, many of whom I thank for aiding me in gathering the facts and bringing them up to 1929, could supplement this book, and a score could, if they were free, easily surpass both in number and significance the episodes of censorship, foreign office intimidation and the frequent national terrorisms here recorded.

What I have tried to do is realize the hope of every one of my colleagues who says: " Some day I am going to take a holiday and write THE TRUTH BEHIND THE NEWS."

PARIS—NEW YORK, 1928–1929.

Part I — War

Chapter I

Marching Back to the Trenches Again

THE Rainbow Division. Wallowing in the mud of the Luneville training sector. Learning to hate like men, the night the enemy threw a shell into our line which made a dugout the tomb for twelve. Raids and little encounters to take the godawful fear out of our bellies.

Standing up before a moving wall of flame and hot iron and blinding gas and whirling infernos of the sand of Champagne. The first two lines given up to the enemy. The artillery smashing hell out of them, foe and comrade alike, there in the first two lines, where irresistibly wave after wave, five inhuman times, the ugly gray surf had broken, subsided, and left only blood and broken bodies on the dazzling chalk of Champagne.

St. Mihiel!

Days of anxious preparations, days of building up courage, all numbed in one universal roar of barrage fire. Finally the zero silence. Finally release of all emotions. Finally the command, let's go, come on you, and over the top comes the unleashed bound of ten thousand men, and — nothing! Nothing. No enemy. No sound.

Victory!

And then the Argonne.

And now, marching back to the trenches again.

Where were the old men of the Rainbow, eager youths of six months ago? Scattered. In hospital. Dead. Over all the fields of France, from down there near the neutral border, to up here on the road to Sedan. "Replacements" forever arriving. The Rainbow Division forever marching back to the trenches. A little rest — rest? — and marching back to the trenches. Then fire and flame and blood, and a little rest, and again marching back to the trenches. This war was never going to end. This war was never going to end.

* * * * *

They sang their moods.
Sometimes they sang:

> K-k-k-k-katy, beautiful k-k-k-katy,
> You're the only girl that I adore. . . .

Sometimes they sang lugubriously, but with humor, a macabre folk-song, jerking the words to their step:

> The worms — crawl in
> The worms — crawl out
> They crawl — in your eyes
> And they crawl — in your mouth. . . .
>
> And I some — times think
> When I'm — dead and gone. . . .

Dead? Death? Why think of it? Why think of anything? Close your eyes and erase your mind and think nothing. Until the first shell falls into your hiding place and a white fear and a red hate bring fit thoughts for soldiers.

The mood changes.

A song is finished. Without losing a beat, as is custom, another is begun. As the solemn ballad is ended, a mocking voice sings:

> I didn't raise my boy to be a soldier

The singer smiles out of the corners of his eyes and out of the corners of his mouth. Hardly has he finished the first stanza when a roar of ironic laughter doubles up his squad, the men hardly able to compose themselves in time to join in with

> I raised him up to be my pride and joy

Laughter spreads with the singing, a strange commotion of laughs, the hearty voluminous outbursts of new men up ahead and near behind them, their first amazement at this mad choice of a marching song; and the soft dry laughter of the men who had already bellowed their surprise and are now realizing that for them, that day, that marching moment, this cheap meretricious jingle, this drivel of a song, held a strange and terrible mockery, a prophetic irony.

> Who dares to lay a musket on his shoulder
> To shoot some other mother's darling boy?
> Let nations arbitrate their future troubles,
> It's time to put the sword and gun away. . . .

In a few minutes the song has roared towards the infantry on ahead, through the Ohios and the New Yorks and the Alabams and the Iowas, and down the artillery, Reilly's Chicagos, and all the rest. It leaps from regiment to regiment, losing a few seconds in each skip, so that while the original Ohios are singing

> It's time to put the sword and gun away

the Kansans have just gotten wind of it and are beginning

> I didn't raise my boy to be a soldier
> I raised him up to be my pride and joy

and so the whole division is shaking with laughter and song

as it is marching, back to the trenches, back to the blood and mud, singing

> There'd be no war today, if mothers all would say
> I didn't raise my boy to be a soldier

*   *   *   *   *

When the Ohios finished it they were silent. There seemed to be no mood to be tricked out with a new song, and when the New Yorks and the Alabams and the Illinois and the Kansans finished their verses, they were silent too for a few seconds, listening to the sound of nails and leather on hard stone road and from the north the uninterrupted sputtering — like a man choking in the sea — no louder at this distance, but somehow filling all the universe. Now subterranean coughing — all the Titans of the earth and sky, invisible, smiting their breasts and making incoherent sounds: that was the war front to which they were marching back again. Occasionally a " jeeze " or a " christamighty " from one of the singers. Twenty-five thousand men, volunteers and conscripts, men out of colleges and men out of sewers, all going north again, marching to meet death half way, up there where that choking sputtering noise was the whole world at war — and singing a ridiculous song that only two years ago had been the sentimental rage of a whole nation.

> There'd be no war today, if mothers all would say
> I didn't raise my boy to be a soldier

What a prophetic irony this foolish song had become. They all felt it in that fleeting moment of silence. And being good soldiers they met it with laughter. Yes, that was the only way to meet irony and tragedy at the front. After their little silence they laughed again and looked at one another, each to see if the next man detected any weak emotions behind the laughter, as they kept pounding northward, towards the trenches.

*   *   *   *   *

I thought this episode was humor for the Homeric gods. I thought it the grandest thing I ever could write about the spirit of our men. Nothing during the war had so stirred me — not my first night in the trenches east of Luneville with these same Ohios — nor the day of the St. Mihiel push when we went to taunt death and found silence and sunshine — nor any lying out in the open in the rain, with gas shells exploding like duds a few feet away — nor any other encounter with victory or danger.

So the next day I did my best to draw this picture of heroic soldiers going back to the trenches singing ironically " I didn't raise my boy to be a soldier," and laughing as they marched. I thought it grand wartime stuff.

" Say, what the hell is all this?" said the army censor. " What are you trying to put over, Seldes? This is damned pacifist propaganda. . . . Yes, I know it is true, but that doesn't matter. You can't print that. . . ."

CHAPTER II

"U. S. Infantry Won the War," — Hindenburg

THE charge against us was simply: first violation of the Armistice; crossing into Germany; passing through the Great German Retreat; and interviewing Hindenburg the week the war ended. We made no defense.

General Dennis Nolan, under special orders of General Pershing, conducted our trial at Chaumont. The verdict put us into an awkward position — either resign from the Press Section, lose our army standing, and depart for home, or remain in the A. E. F. under technical arrest and refrain from writing the greatest story of our lives. Thus spoke army discipline and military press censorship.

Today we are proud of our crime, if crime it was. We can afford to forget the humiliation of arrest, the discomfiture of the trial, but we remember the thrill of that day we left Luxembourg, the sudden terror of being caught (in the midst of his marching men) by a furious Prussian colonel, and the great climax, the meeting with Hindenburg.

For it was then that the commander of the enemy, the one man in the world who could best make a historical judgment, made an admission in the honesty of tears, an admission which for political reasons he can never repeat:

"The American infantry," said Hindenburg, "won the World War in battle in the Argonne."

* * * *

First, a word on the nature of our "crime." We were all members of the Advance Section, G-2-D, G. H. Q., A. E. F.

24

In other words, in that part of the Intelligence Corps of the American army known as the Press Section. We were given the uniforms of officers without insignia of rank and entitled to the privileges of generals. We ranked with the doughboys when we were in the trenches and just below Pershing on our visit to Chaumont. We found the question of saluting and getting saluted difficult because we had refused to take the two bars of a captaincy which our British colleagues wore. But more important, we considered ourselves more free than a ranked and placed person in uniform the day the eager doughboys, still hoping for laurels, fired cannon five minutes after eleven and the Armistice hushed the thundering front.

That minute we felt ourselves civilians again. Again we felt free to use our wits in getting scoops — to think up some big stunt which would rattle the morale of our competitors and amaze the world.

" Let's cross into Germany."

Spoken as a joke — hiding a mighty desire — needing only a seconding motion to light an enthusiasm which would carry us over that yesterday's horror which was No Man's Land and that yesterday's hatred which was Enemy Land — and to a tomorrow which was grand and thrilling and perhaps laden with death.

But someone must have suspected such a plan even before it was born. We had already heard our sergeant and corporal chauffeurs whispering instructions received either from Pershing's headquarters or through the major commanding us that there must be no violation of the Armistice, that while we might drive into No Man's Land, we must never drive across the Armistice line.

" Youse guys can boss us anywhere you want to go," Sergeant

25

Jack Corper, one of the best drivers in the army, told me, "but dere's one thing you can't make us do and dat's cross over. We got superior orders, see?"

I still believe the two chauffeurs innocent, but I do not credit it altogether to our superior guile, for the spirit of adventure must have blinded their eyes too, to the many false roads and wrong turns we methodically took. They did protest at first.

"The map shows to the right—"

"The map is wrong. Take the turn to the left."

Every half hour a similar conversation.

And so we rode out of gay Luxembourg, that lovely city on a cliff where our doughboys had had the time of their lives what with being treated as a quarter million heroes and dragged by squads and companies from the open peaceful highways into the homes of happy and rich Luxembourgeoises where champagne and song lasted a full seven days.

It was still Armistice week when we started, dull and early, towards Germany. Well, it didn't take long to cross that tiny "Grand-Duchy," and as there was no longer an organized German frontier, we must have ridden into Enemy Land with no more excitement than the noise automobiles make on hard military roads.

But excitement, which was to hold us breathless for a week and more, began almost immediately. As we flew into the first German village we passed a triumphal arch, if you please, all decked out with flowers and laurel and bearing on its keystone the legend "Welcome Our Undefeated Heroes." And then we saw the flag we had never dreamed we would ever see, the red, white and black of the Kaiser's monarchy, waving in ignorant pride from many windows.

26

They say the civilians have the most hate and fear. At the front, Heaven knows, we had had our share of both. But certainly the civilians across the sea felt the war was over when the Armistice was signed while on the other hand so many at the front who had been in or watched the slaughter and the mud day by day, unchanging, unceasing, had felt there must be a catch in it somewhere, that it wasn't really true, that it didn't mean what it seemed. So when the chauffeurs of both cars put on the brakes bringing us to a crunching huddled halt, we too had forgotten the Armistice and felt civilians' hate and fear pointing at us in the snake-ends of the wind-snapping enemy banners.

The chauffeurs argued perhaps half-heartedly. Army discipline had never really existed in our outfit. Adventure lay ahead and nothing but explanations behind. " You might as well go on, we are ten miles inside Germany already," was someone's conclusive statement, and ahead we went.

In this town of Borg we found the German army in full retreat. We came up behind it noting immediately the splendid discipline of the defeated. Their lines were right and their step firm: even in facial expression there was no sign of a collapsed morale. Their uniforms and equipment seemed shoddy.

" Amerikaner — Amerikaner."

Without hatred or passion the surprised soldiers passed the word along the undulating ranks.

We rode slowly alongside, our hearts beating high.

Soon we were in the town square, a triangle between streets, where the German colonel on a horse was directing operations. He saw us at a distance and rode forward.

" Halt! " he commanded with a mean voice and uplifted hand.

We halted.

"What in thunder and lightning are you doing here?"

Our spokesman stammered an answer.

"You are interfering with our military movements — you must go back to the American line," the colonel said decisively.

"But —"

"I forbid an answer!"

At our left, meanwhile, hundreds of German soldiers with rifles on their shoulders, an occasional 77, and a frequent "goulash cannon" were thudding and clanking onward.

We all began to talk at once. The colonel became furious.

"I tell you to get out, and immediately, or I take the lot of you prisoner. You are in great danger. Your lives are at stake here. You are the enemy — the men might shoot you all — or the civilians attack you — any moment. I tell you to return —"

At this black moment there was a civilian flurry in the square from which a sailor emerged, running towards us. He had that universality of blue serge and seaworn face which make the sailors of all lands alike.

"What's the trouble here?" he asked.

We were immediately amazed by the daring of an enlisted man in the presence of high officers. But we noticed also there was something different about this sailor's uniform — a red band on his left arm. Later we read the black print on it:

"Arbeiter — und Soldaten — Rat," or Workers and Soldiers Council, or Soviet.

Seeing sympathetic ears, we poured a broken German explanation into them. We noted, too, a change in the behaviour of our swell colonel. His starch and bluster were gone. He sat on his horse, looking disgusted and arguing less vehemently than ourselves.

28

"They're in danger here," he repeated.

"Not while I'm in command in this area," replied the sailor cockily.

"They must leave at once I tell you," said the colonel.

But the colonel's antagonism reflexed the sailor's sympathy for us.

"You go and mind your own business," he ordered.

The colonel went.

"My name is Fritz Harris," the sailor beamed. "Does any one of you know my uncle in Cleveland?"

"But what does all this mean?" we asked, shaking negative heads.

"Well, I'm in control," replied the sailor, jumping on the running board and shooing away the old men and women who now dared crowd our automobiles. "We started the revolution in Kiel. On the ships. Just before the Armistice. Everything is going in good order. Don't worry. We did everything with shipshape discipline. Each sailor was assigned a city, his own city usually, and went with orders to proclaim the German revolution there. This is my home. Not a drop of blood was shed here. It was different in Trier and Frankfurt. Now, honoured gentlemen, what is it you want?"

This piece of diplomacy we left to our spokesman. He had considerable hold of the language but I still believe it was a slight error that made the rest of our adventure possible. He had tried to say we were a part of the press section which had come to see how Germany had lived during the war, what the food situation was, and all that, and sailor Fritz Harris interrupted him with:

"Ah, the American Food Commission — yah, yah, we had heard you would send us food. *Wilkommen, wilkommen.*"

(This promise of white bread had been probably our most effective propaganda. For months our aviators had dropped cards over the German lines saying every prisoner, and everyone who surrendered voluntarily, was getting two pounds of white bread a day — and many a German came to claim his portion.)

We let Fritz's mistake go unchallenged and were conducted with rejoicing to the Rathaus, where we were welcomed by the soldier and civilian Soviet of the town. At our request they telephoned to Trier asking that everything be done to insure safety for our lives and means for getting the information we wanted.

On the road out of Borg we had a great panorama of the German forces endlessly flowing eastward. Despite the seeming discipline peasants told us how they had bought artillery horses for 50 marks and exchanged a goose for a brace of rifles and an egg for a parabellum pistol. No bloodshed was reported in the countryside.

In Trier a reception committee met us and wanted to entertain us but we pressed on to Frankfurt which we reached the next day.

Up to now we had no thought of Hindenburg. Our secret ambition had been to be the first Americans in Berlin. We confided it to our host at Frankfurt, the usual *Arbeiter-und-Soldat-endrat,* who agreed to help us, but first we had to be given a banquet.

We sat in the spacious hall of the Frankfurterhof, now revolutionary headquarters, and ate as bad a meal as one can imagine, thin soup whose only distinguishing taste was salt, some goose, the only meat we found anywhere, potatoes and very soggy black bread. The wine was excellent.

Our hosts held long discourses and our spokesman replied. My own contribution was a one line speech: " Es lebe die Republik " — long live the Republic — which was an excuse for draining another green decanter of Rhine.

During prolonged arrangements for continuing our journey, one of the council said timidly:

" We would like you to see Hindenburg first."

Hindenburg!

It was almost as amazing as the Armistice itself. The latter was a bit unreal, but this was a dream-desire — to call on and interview the leader of the enemy, the second best-hated man in the world then, the general whose men were killing our men, the apotheosis of German frightfulness, the incarnation of that which six days before was all the evil in the world — such a thought was beyond our still khaki-clad minds.

" It can be arranged," said the Rat.

Two German cars were given us, so we could release the doughboys who were becoming indignantly mutinous — perhaps through ignorance of what was to come — and with tires exploding every hour and engines going wrong every three, we managed to arrive in Cassel, where Hindenburg had removed his grand headquarters from Aix-la-Chapelle.

We came to the Rathaus confident all was well. But it wasn't. Hindenburg politely refused to see us. He said he would meet no one in the uniform of the enemy.

That day and the next we spent in conferences with members of the Rat at City Hall and sulking at our hotel, where, by the way, our presence was objectionable. The owner was surly and the help mean. Our finances were low. I still have a grudge against that hotel man who gave me 60 paper marks for my reserve 20 dollar gold piece.

We decided to go to Berlin at once. We went to the Rathaus to say good-bye. Then a sergeant-major member of the council took up the telephone and insisted on speaking to Hindenburg himelf.

It was a long conversation in which our sergeant-major, an ugly, emaciated person with protruding yellow teeth, very much the "Hun" of British war cartoons, became more and more exasperated. Finally he shouted:

"This is an order to you, Excellency, not a request."

A moment of silence for Hindenburg's reaction.

"Then at three o'clock, you will send one of your cars."

He hung up the telephone and a proud smile came over his distorted face.

"At three this afternoon he will send his car."

The car came on the stroke. Our hotel keeper with almost oriental obeisances directed seven employees who grovelled us into Hindenburg's grey monogrammed limousine.

In the marble castle of Wilhelmshohe an aide-de-camp took us upstairs. A squat stoutish man in a regulation general's uniform with an additional white cloth around his head, received us.

"General Groener," he said to each, snapping his feet.

We shook hands.

"The general hasn't been wounded?" queried our spokesman.

"No," he smiled, "but I have a terrible headache."

Our spokesman interpreted. "He has a terrible headache."

"He should have," whispered the roughneck among us. "He has just lost a world war."

General Groener bowed us into the next room, marvellous, rococo, pale blue and gold and palatially uncomfortable.

32

Hindenburg arose.

He was dressed in field grey-blue. Tall, red-faced, broad-shouldered. The usual officer's decorations on the wide chest were absent. Around his neck, unbuttoned for comfort, was the small blue cross of the *Pour le merite*. His head was covered with stiff toothbrush-like white hairs, cropped to about a half-inch, and revealing, by their scarcity, a very pink scalp. But what I thought was funny, was the famous Hindenburg moustache. It looked theatrical. It looked false, and stuck on, and it certainly curved itself along the cheeks as no non-Thespian moustache has ever done.

" Die Herrschaften sprechen Deutsch, nicht wahr? " said Hindenburg in a kindly smiling voice, shaking hands for the first time since the war with men in the uniform of his enemies.

Three disclaimed speaking German so Hindenburg fixed on our spokesman, motioned us to a circle of chairs, and began:

"I will answer any military questions. I am a soldier. But I refuse to answer any political questions." He shrugged his shoulders. "I am a soldier."

We had previously discussed no questions for this interview — it was one of those cases where any word given us, on any subject, was precious.

"Is the demobilization proceeding satisfactorily — we have heard of some fighting and bloodshed." Our first question.

"Yes," he replied, "although there is some trouble when the men come to the cities, the return from the front is fully disciplined. Men and officers remain in their usual relationship. The troubles are not serious among the troops, officers and civilians, except when there is an attempt to disregard the present change in government."

"What is your position at present?"

"I have given my pledge to Mr. Ebert, who is in control of the government in Berlin, that I will stay in command until all the troops are safely returned from the front and to their home barracks. My functions then cease. I have finished my duties. I mean to retire into private life."

"Do you think the present socialist government will remain or will fall soon?"

"I cannot answer that. I am not a politician. I am a soldier."

Several questions followed. Either of minor importance or of a political nature.

"I cannot answer. I am a soldier," was the inevitable reply to the latter category.

All these minutes undoubtedly each of us was steeling himself for another question — a question we were burning to ask, and which was merely "Who won the war?" heavily muffled in diplomatic garments. We fell to debating "the next question" among ourselves, and finally someone said:

"Go ahead — ask him — you know what."

So the spokesman with considerable throat clearing and much redundancy, asked it.

When we asked "Who won the war?" we were ignorant of what home papers had said. Our American papers in France, like the Entente press, from October to November 10th reported nothing but French, British, Italian, Belgian victories. "British troops advance 20 miles," "Brussels captured," "Lille entered," "Italians cross three rivers." The three armies northwest of us had advanced many miles each day. City after city was captured by them. But what was the American army doing all this time? Merely fighting. Yes, fighting. In the Argonne. Through dense, almost impassable forests, over cliffs and hills, wading in ravines, struggling through mud thick as boiling rubber, bombing, hand-grenading, machine-gunning, bayonetting their way northward towards the jugular of the German armies, the Metz-Longuyon railroad, the one means of retreat of the enemy.

Hindenburg was shortening his lines. He was quitting northern France and Belgium. But he was holding the Argonne. Day by day the representative of our G. H. Q. had shown us the map with every enemy division and reserve force marked. Hindenburg had thirty-two reserve divisions at the beginning of our Argonne drive. When November began two or three remained. What had become of an army of German reserves?

Very few had appeared on the French or British front — almost all were thrown against us. We were doing almost all the fighting while the Allies were marching unhindered into famous cities and famous battle fields of 1914, and capturing the headlines of the world. We were losing men and taking prisoners and trenches — fighting most of the war then and getting no credit from the press because our work was not spectacular. Hindenburg and Pershing knew what we were doing. What would Hindenburg say?

"I will reply with the same frankness," said Hindenburg, faintly amused at our diplomacy. "The American infantry in the Argonne won the war."

He paused and we sat thrilled.

"I say this," continued Hindenburg, "as a soldier, and soldiers will understand me best."

"To begin with I must confess that Germany could not have won the war — that is, after 1917. We might have won on land. We might have taken Paris. But after the failure of the world food crops of 1916 the British food blockade reached its greatest effectiveness in 1917. So I must really say that the British food blockade of 1917 and the American blow in the Argonne of 1918 decided the war for the Allies.

"But without American troops against us and despite a food blockade which was undermining the civilian population of Germany and curtailing the rations in the field, we could still have had a peace without victory. The war could have ended in a sort of stalemate.

"And even if we had not had the better of the fighting in the end, as we had until July 18, 1918, we could have had an acceptable peace. We were still a great force and we had divisions in reserve always which the enemy attacks could never use up completely.

"Even the attack of July 18, which Allied generals may consider the turning point in the war, did not use up a very important part of the German army or smash all our positions. To win a war it is necessary, as you know, to place the enemy forces *hors de combat*. In such a manner of warfare which began when Japan and Russia met in the wheat fields of the Far East, you must engage and defeat hundreds of thousands, millions of men.

"In the summer of 1918 the German army was able to launch offensive after offensive — almost one a month. We had the men, the munitions and the morale, and we were not overbalanced. But the balance was broken by the American troops.

"The Argonne battle was slow and difficult. But it was strategic. It was bitter and it used up division after division. We had to hold the Metz-Longuyon roads and railroad and we had hoped to stop all American attacks until the entire army was out of northern France. We were passing through the neck of a vast bottle. But the neck was narrow. German and American divisions fought each other to a standstill in the Argonne. They met and shattered each other's strength. The Americans are splendid soldiers. But when I replaced a division it was weak in numbers and unrested, while each American division came in fresh and fit and on the offensive.

"The day came when the American command sent new divisions into the battle and when I had not even a broken division to plug up the gaps. There was nothing left to do but ask terms.

"Until the American attack our positions had been comparatively satisfactory. We had counted on holding the Argonne longer. The advantage of terrain was with us. The American troops were unseasoned. We had also counted on their impetuosity. There was great wastage in your army due to carelessness, impetuosity and the disregard of the conditions of modern warfare.

"Yet from a military point of view the Argonne battle as conceived and carried out by the American Command was the climax of the war and its deciding factor. The American attack was furious — it continued from day to day with increasing power, but when two opposing divisions had broken each other, yours was replaced with 27,000 eager for battle, ours with decimated, ill-equipped, ill-fed men suffering from contact with a gloomy and despairing civilian population.

"I do not mean to discredit your fighting forces — I repeat, without the American blow in the Argonne, we could have made a satisfactory peace at the end of a stalemate or at least held our last positions on our own frontier indefinitely — undefeated. The American attack decided the war."

A moment of silence.

"*Ach, mein armes Vaterland — mein armes Vaterland —*"
Hindenburg bowed his head and tears flooded his pale,
watery eyes. His huge bulk was shaken. He wept for his "poor
fatherland."

We sat and wondered over so much emotion in a military
leader supposedly devoid of sentiment and sentimentality.

Thus the interview terminated with a strange human spectacle and in an uncomfortable silence. A fallen Colossus. A
broken Superman. Blood and iron suddenly tears and clay.

*   *   *   *   *

There was no more to ask. Here we were with the biggest
story in the world, and even before Hindenburg was through
speaking, our thoughts were searching cable ends or messen-
gers or some new means of communication with our papers.

There came the usual anticlimax. "Where do you go from
here?" asked Hindenburg. "Ach, Berlin, so? Well, *glückliche
Reise.*"

"*Auf Wiedersehen.*" A loose handclasp. We were ushered
out by the snappy aide-de-camp.

My colleagues started for Berlin; I got up at four the next
morning to make the 5 A.M. train for Luxembourg. As I
reached the station I saw part of the real German revolution.

Mingled with the monarchist flags and drapery over the
Cassel railroad station and triumphal arches were red stream-
ers and bunting placed by the revolutionary sailors and town
Soviet. The troops coming by train knew nothing of the
Kaiser's cowardice or the change to a republic.

A regiment was detraining. As the colonel led his men from
the station into the public square he seemed lightning-struck
when he beheld the revolutionary color mingling with his
Kaiser's.

"Tear the red rags down!" he ordered his captains.

A captain in turn spoke to his men, who refused to move.

"I'll do it myself," said the captain, and grabbing a red streamer from the triumphal arch, he pulled.

Two soldiers with red arm-bands approached threateningly, and I stopped too.

"Pardon, captain," said one, "but we have had a revolution."

"Revolution, to the devil—" replied the captain, pulling.

The two soldiers raised their rifles.

The captain drew his pistol.

Click!—Crack!

At this precise moment the little experience I had had in the Luneville-Baccaret section with the Rainbow Division, pulled my habit muscles. I dropped flat.

A dozen rifles and a pair of revolvers snapped. A man fell partly on me. I turned cautiously on my left side. His face was in pain, and his hands were at his middle, and blood was flowing from his stomach. He was the captain who had pulled the red flag. The soldiers had shot him.

Men ran over us, around us. Lying flat, I had a panorama of flying feet in the semi-darkness. Shooting was spasmodic, now near, now at a distance. I wondered what I could do for the man lying over my feet. I pulled myself up. I think he died without a groan.

Bodies were writhing in the open square. One wounded man was shrieking. But the troops were gone and scared civilians were appearing from hiding places and the station.

"Too bad," they murmured, "but these officers won't believe the guards who tell them there has been a revolution— and a republic."

In three days and three nights the train meandered a hundred miles. It was crowded with German officers who mistook me for a returning prisoner of war and who were kindlier than any German civilians and who gave me their precious bad bread.

At Wasserbillig, the Luxembourg frontier, was the most welcome sight in the universe: a doughboy. He got me a car to Luxembourg. I was promptly arrested. Pershing insisted the German government return my colleagues from Berlin, and our trial at Chaumont followed.

I have seen Hindenburg since. No longer the broken old man weeping. Nor quite Hindenburg of the iron-nailed statue. But times had changed in Germany. Seven or eleven political parties were bitterly fighting for power, and the old monarchists and the old militarists were spreading the myth that the war was lost, not by Wilhelm's armies, but by the republican *Dolschstoss* — the civilian "stab in the back."

I recalled the Cassel meeting. Hindenburg shook his head in acknowledgment.

But for political reasons he can never again repeat his confession of Armistice week.

Chapter III

THE TRUTH ABOUT THE WAR AT SEA

THE man who won the one big naval battle of the world war was living quietly in a plain blue serge suit in a little house in Weimar. If his nation had been the winner he would be standing head and shoulders above Nelson now, guides would point him out and his words would be considered law by laymen who know all about land fighting and, because of their nautical ignorance, admire sea fighting the more.

There was once a time, however, when the whole world waited breathlessly for the publication of Admiral Scheer's report to the Kaiser giving away the secret of Jutland. The world then was juggled by two camps, the big ship and the little ship camps, just as it may be juggled again now that naval disarmament conferences have a habit of failing and marine armament lobbies are at work in Geneva as well as in Washington, London and Paris.

Scheer's report and Scheer's views, it was conceded, would do much to alter the course of warship construction for our generation. In London especially the cry was raised by *The Times* and *Daily Mail* for publication of the Kaiser's letter.

But the censors of the British Admiralty, who had captured one of the rare copies (probably from the admiral's room of a superdreadnaught sunk at Scapa Flow) suppressed the document. A bitter and insinuating battle was waged in the press of all the great nations. In Berlin I learned that no more than half a dozen copies of the Scheer report, of which 75 had been printed, were in existence, of which one was in Holland with the Kaiser, another in the war archives, a third in the library of the admiral himself and the others in the possession of former high officers who were duty bound never to permit publication. An appeal to patriotism added to a certain sum of money, however, gave me three hours possession of one copy of which I cabled enough to cause an international sensation, the revival of the question of who won the war at sea, and the most important answer to the question, superdreadnaughts or submarines. I realized why the British Admiralty, despite thunders in Parliament and press, had for years succeeded in suppressing the report, and would have censored it probably to this day. It proves easily the victory of Germany at sea.

Admiral Scheer discloses the remarkable opportunity the British had to surround and destroy the German fleet. In the numerous drawings, one for every five or ten minutes of the battle, he explains to the Kaiser how Jellicoe's fleet had formed a semi-circle, while the German was a horizontal line tending to bisect it. Realizing his serious situation, and hoping to save his fleet at all costs, Admiral Scheer sent out his torpedo fleets which hurled themselves on the enemy. *Then Jellicoe turned away.* Admiral Scheer said later Jellicoe probably made this capital error of the war at sea through conviction that it was the main German fleet, not a torpedo-boat fleet, which attacked. Had Jellicoe attacked the horizontal German line, picking off his enemy one by one, by concentrated fire on the spearhead, Germany's navy probably would have been destroyed and the war ended without America's participation.

The famous document describes other most dangerous situations of both fleets and concludes by informing the emperor that sea battle could not enforce peace. *He advises the strongest submarine warfare in the future,* advice which was not taken by the Kaiser for more than a year, and then too late to change the outcome of the war. Admiral Scheer also foresaw trouble with America for he added " despite submarine commanders' conscientiousness, it is impossible to avoid incidents in English waters where American interests are very strong, incidents which afterwards force us to make humiliating concessions when we are unable to go through with severity."

Scheer tells how he forced the battle throughout. He admits his own mistakes. He mistook Beatty's three " Invincibles " for the British main fleet and headed towards them, thus giving Jellicoe with the main fleet an opportunity of a flank attack. He shows that Jellicoe and Beatty instead of attacking during the night of the battle, drew in their torpedo-boats defensively, thereby losing their great opportunity, while the Germans passed through the entire British fleet and reached their base. Five Zeppelins co-operating with the ships failed to supply information although they hovered over the battle. Of the 15,000 word document, here follow the most important parts.

*   *   *   *   *

Scheer's Report to the Kaiser

" Our April 23rd enterprise against Lowestoft had the effect anticipated in our plans of operation. The enemy felt the challenge and, unwilling to accept a similar stroke without counterattack, began to move. By the middle of May 1916 I had sent all my submarines into the North Sea to take up attacking positions before the enemy's main points of support: the *Hum-*

ber, Firth of Forth, Moray Firth, Scapa Flow, when the enemy, coming out, would be forced to engage in battle under conditions favorable to us.

"Early in the afternoon of May 31 Zeppelins went reconnoitering. They did not participate in battle; they saw nothing of our own or the enemy's fleets, nor heard the sounds of battle, although Z 14 hung over the battle sea. At 6:13 in the afternoon the warship *Von der Tann* sank the British *Indefatigable.* (The *Von der Tann* was commanded by Captain Otto Groos, the German marine historian who aided me in obtaining this document, and whose notes appear from time to time.) Fire superiority was on our side until four or five ships of the *Queen Elizabeth* class arrived, when our situation became critical, therefore our Ninth torpedo flotilla was ordered by me to attack the enemy forcing them to withdraw in ten minutes. The enemy did not attempt to save the crews of its sunken destroyers.

"Our attack resulted in the enemy fire being forced to stop for some time. Now came the news of greater forces seen, whereupon I gave the order to clear ships for action. The situation of our First scout group might become critical; it was necessary for the fleet to come into close formation."

Here Scheer at length describes the fighting, showing that the British scouts turned northwest before the German main attack.

"At 7:30 the leader's impression was that the enemy had succeeded in escaping so I gave the order to take up the pursuit. The weather became less clear. Smoke sticking to the water blocked the view. I could not see our own reconnoitering forces. The fact is that when the leader of the scouts (Admiral Hipper) got the order to pursue, he had already passed by the enemy cruisers and light forces and was forced by their pressure to head northwards. Of this he was unable to inform me because both his wireless stations had been shot away.

" At 7:40, the enemy, judging the situation rightly, attacked with torpedo-boats forcing the German advance to give way towards the southwest and in the meantime the main fleet was forced to give way toward the east. The leaders recognizing the seriousness of the situation then attacked, being taken under fire by numerous battleships."

(Note: at this point a footnote by Captain Groos says that Scheer is in error in the foregoing. He states that there were only three " Invincibles " there. This error Groos goes on to say, badly influenced the next movements because the German fleet believed the " Invincibles " to be Jellicoe's main fleet. In later interviews Admiral Scheer admits this error and discusses the errors on both sides.)

" About this time Jellicoe and Beatty united their fleets. In consequence of the enduring battle the armored cruisers were forced to give way so much that I was necessarily forced to turn the line westward. And it was too early to begin the night march to get away.

" The enemy, before darkness, might have forced us to stay and have taken from us the liberty of decision, finally blocking the way to German shores. There was only one possible way to prevent this; a reckless attack giving the enemy a second blow, using torpedo-boats violently.

" The manœuvre must surprise the enemy and destroy his plans and if possible facilitate the separation at night."

(Captain Groos explains Admiral Scheer's sketch number nine which pictures the nautical term ' crossing the letter " T." ' Jellicoe and Beatty were drawn up in an enormous semi-circle at 9:17 in the evening which was the most critical moment of battle for the German fleet. Groos declares that a British attack at this moment with a converging movement would have undoubtedly met with success, but the enemy continued with caution to preserve a defensive throughout. There was no Nelson to direct. Beatty, too, was under orders now. This fact, Groos believes, explains the reason why the British Admiralty refuses the document for publication but he has declared that the British on account of the weather may not have realized their opportunity.)

"Our torpedo-boats took upon themselves the heavy fire which hitherto had been directed against the cruisers carrying the attack to within seven thousand yards against the middle of the British semi-circle composed of more than twenty dreadnaughts. Only one torpedo-boat was lost. Using the torpedo-boats as an objective my attack was realized. My line was therefore taken back to the west, manœuvring finally toward the southeast in order to avoid a semi-circling movement of the enemy who was already heading southeastward. The enemy fire ceased when we turned. The enemy must have turned away after our torpedo-boat attack. We surely expected the enemy to attack us by night with strong forces to push us to the west in order to fight again toward the dawn. The enemy furthermore had the power to do so. If it were possible to stop the enemy's encircling manœuvre and to reach the base at Hornesiff before the enemy, we would be free in our movements the next morning. The torpedo-boats sent out to attack failed to find the main fleet, and in the meanwhile our fleet engaged in short but heavy fighting and gave way and turned in scout groups. We were attacked all night from the east by light and part heavy forces."

(*Note:* Groos here explains that Jellicoe meanwhile had gone north-ward while Beatty in attacking had passed in front of the German fleet thereby enabling the German fleet to proceed toward its base.)

" On the morning of the first of June, Zeppelin 24 observed at Jammerbucht twelve superdreadnaughts and many cruisers bound southward."

Summing up his narrative on the results of the battle Scheer continues:

" The success we gained was due to leadership in the attack, the spirit of our officers and the splendid morale of the crews. The battle proved that we were guided by true views in the building of our fleet. The successful decision was due to the far-reaching heavy artillery of our ships, which artillery caused the greater part of the enemy's losses. The merits of our torpedo flotillas which permitted us to shake loose from the enemy are undiminished by the foregoing statements. Heavy superdreadnaughts remain the foundation of naval power. By August your majesty's high seas fleet will be ready for battle again, except for the *Derfflinger* and the *Seydlitz*.

" Without doubt, this most successful sea battle will not force England in this war to make peace. Our military and geographical situation, and the enemy's material superiority, are drawbacks which the fleet cannot overbalance so far as to be able to break the blockade or overpower England even if submarines are used wholly for military purposes. A victorious end of the war is conceivable at this time only by crushing England's economic life, that is, by using submarines against British commerce. I urgently advise again against using submarines moderately. Even when commanders are conscientious it is impossible to avoid accidents in British waters wherein

47

American interests are very strong, incidents which afterwards force us to make humiliating concessions when we are unable to go through with our actions with severity."

A second letter from Scheer to the Kaiser, dated July 16, discussing Jellicoe's report to the British Admiralty, is attached. It says:

" At 8 in the evening Jellicoe could not discover our position. He had chart differences with Beatty (eleven miles, according to Groos). We cannot understand why part of the British fleet was at Jammerbucht. Neither can we understand why the enemy light forces which were in touch at night could not inform Jellicoe and Beatty of our whereabouts.

" Evidently the enemy was split in three groups on the morning of June 1, the group at Jammerbucht, Beatty's group northwest of Hornsriff and Jellicoe's southwest of the Hornsriff base. This is apparently explainable by Jellicoe's losing the general leadership after the daytime battle."

*   *   *   *   *

Captain Groos' Comment on the Report

" Although outnumbered and outgunned our fleet succeeded in reaching its base and inflicting double to triple tonnage losses on the English. The battle shows Britain no longer has a Drake or Nelson." Groos emphasizes the point that at 9:17 the evening of the battle the German fleet was partly surrounded, that the British command cannot be forgiven for failure to attack then, and that Admiral Scheer cannot be praised enough for his torpedo-boat attack, " a masterful bluff which saved the German navy."

" Nelson said the most daring measures are the safest

48

measures," continues Groos, " a principle based on the uncon-
ditional feeling of victory, a feeling which was lacking in the
British Admiralty from the beginning of this war. They did not
feel certain of victory, therefore they avoided a decisive battle
and did not finish the Skagerrak fight.

" Before and after Jutland the British Admiralty better estimated the capacity of the action of the German fleet and its
own chances of victory than public opinion or the Nelsonites
estimated it. The British public became suspicious because of
the Admiralty's silence, and was tired of lies; it demanded the
whole truth as to why the German fleet was not crushed, even
if this truth endangered the British Navy's prestige. Across the
Atlantic there is developing mightily the American war and
commercial fleet, which is endangering British supremacy and
spoiling the joy over Germany's loss of her fleet. The British
motto for Jutland was: ' I came, I saw, I avoided battle.' "

Doctor Struve, member of the naval committee of the Reichstag, commented:

" When I demanded the publication of the Scheer letter in
1916 I was accused of treason. I had obtained a copy. Admiral
von Capelle accused me of obtaining it by bribery. It was Admiral von Capelle who despite Scheer's recommendation for unlimited submarine warfare, which we are certain would have
won us the war, gave the orders curtailing submarine building.
It was a crime not to concentrate on submarine construction
and this failure led to our defeat."

*   *   *   *   *

Scheer's Final Word

Admiral Scheer's report to the Kaiser was written shortly after the battle and for years he had not added to it. After the war he maintained his silence, a silence which contrasted magnificently with the loud caterwaulings of Ludendorff, the man who Germans say lost the war and who is devoting his life to shifting that blame to everyone on earth or in heaven except Baldur and Loki and Freya, the pagan gods he now worships.

After I had obtained his secret and confidential report, however, Admiral Scheer could no longer maintain his silence, especially as the entire British press and the British naval leaders were attempting to explain away Jutland. He therefore consented to receive me and add the final word to the controversy.

The great climax, it seems to me, was Scheer's telling for the first time of how the German fleet put to sea in August following the battle, how a decisive engagement with Jellicoe was sought, and how the British fleet returned to its bases when ten German submarines, acting as a screen for the main fleet, attacked it.

From that day on there was no decisive naval engagement. From that day on, thinks Admiral Scheer, all naval warfare changed, because of the submarine.

"The world's first impression of Skagerrak," said the admiral, "was that it was a German victory, but shortly afterwards Great Britain, which controlled all the avenues of propaganda, began using every means among neutrals, especially America, to change that impression, so that at the end of the war it was generally believed that Britain did not fare so badly

50

after all. But nowadays Britain claims it was a victory, because admission of defeat must hurt a navy claiming it is the largest and best in the world."

The admiral spread before him copies of many British newspapers, including the old thunderer, *The Times*. He found some old maps and brought out a box of matches which he called warships. With them he refought the whole battle while I watched.

" There is no doubt in fair minds about who won the battle," he continued, " why, look at the dissatisfaction in England itself both in 1916 and now. British naval conduct disappointed the country. The insular feeling of security, based on the all-powerful British fleet, is fast disappearing. The whole discussion as to whether the battleship or the submarine is the best weapon for the future shows disappointment with the fleet in wartime.

" At Skagerrak the Germans had 27 capital ships, the British 45. We inflicted double losses and took the offensive throughout, showing a superiority in gun fire and many other ways. On the other hand, the British failed in their attacks or in holding on when times were most favorable to them. *The Times* says: ' The first impression of the battle was that the Grand Fleet suffered a severe reverse. The effect of this impression was never wholly dissipated. The publication of all the papers will not bring this very desirable consummation.' Good! Later *The Times* speaks of the British driving the Germans ' once for all from the high seas.' This is not true. Again such statements as that made by King George in Parliament that ' the retirement of the enemy immediately after the opening engagement robbed us of an opportunity of gaining a decisive victory ' shows that the king's words were based on false information, and this fiction is kept up in a part of the British press in order to support belief in a British victory which never existed.

" Jellicoe is honest enough to *hint* at our two 16-point turns, which were really our attacks, but such hints can easily be overlooked by those unacquainted with every move of the battle. Jellicoe does not declare he did not follow the German invitation to fight, and he does not mention that he himself did not carry out any manœuvre to follow up the movements of the Germans, or to hold the Germans down to an engagement even if he felt himself justified in so doing.

" At Skagerrak we did not bring our submarines into battle as the British explain: the great forward rush of our torpedo-boats was enough to make Jellicoe turn tail.

"Later when the British propaganda machine began to make up for what the ships failed to do at sea, it exaggerated our losses, claiming we lost two of the *Koenig* class and alleging that the German fleet's return to its base was a flight, whereas we marched in complete order. And finally the British propaganda machine thought it had the conclusive argument when it stated that the Germans were driven from the *face* of the sea. The truth is we came out seeking a decision in August.

" Now this is the crux of the Skagerrak battle: from the beginning Beatty led us towards Jellicoe, which was excellent strategy. Jellicoe's maps show the fleets in concentric semi-circles. Jellicoe's footnote which *The Times* omits says ' Enemy apparently made two 16-point turns.' This footnote is all Jellicoe says of two great attacks lasting two hours, at which we went at the British lines continually. It is true we covered less distance, because we were the inner circle, but the whole point of my argument with Admiral Jellicoe, is that he speaks of two turns while I speak of two hours of continual attack by the German fleet.

"Likewise my turn from the spearhead position, which is another important part of the battle, will be understood by any naval man as a manœuvre, not a withdrawal. It was then that Jellicoe had his great opportunity. We were in a most serious position, this spearhead position, and manœuvred out of it. Of course at this point I was not attacking. I do not butt my head into a stone wall because I know I'll crack my skull. But Jellicoe by concentrating fire on my spearhead formation, by attacking with the same ferocity with which we had previously attacked, would have been successful in destroying part or whole of my fleet, and no amount of explanation can cover this paramount failure.

"It was at this turn of the battle that I used my torpedo-boats with great success. Jellicoe turned away under their attack. I manœuvred westward with excellent results. Jellicoe's encircling movement was broken. I saved the German fleet from being surrounded and drew the fleet in parallel long straight lines, obtaining equality of position with my enemy. The German turn was a manœuvre; the British failure to attack was an error.

"Again, Jellicoe failed to hold on to our flank. We were able to shake off the enemy and return to our bases during the night.

"Now comes the big question: why, being successful, I did not attack the next morning. The reason is that the fog and mist were impenetrable. There was a visibility of four miles and my battle fleet covered five miles. It was utter foolhardiness to invite the British torpedo-boats to appear suddenly from curtains of smoke and fog, pick off my line ships one by one, and disappear behind the curtains.

"*But we came out in August.* It is unjust of the *London Times* to say 'The British fleet at Jutland once for all drove the Germans from the high seas.' This statement is unjust and untrue. I put to sea on August 19 with the purpose of attacking Sunderland, infuriating the English, and forcing a naval engagement. I made one change. Instead of sending submarines to cover the British harbours, as before Skagerrak, I used them for flank protection. I also left my pre-dreadnaughts at home. My fleet consisted of twenty capital ships.

"*I steamed into the North Sea. Yes, Germany was the first to appear there after Skagerrak.* And this is what *The Times,* which declared we were driven from there, says of our exploit in a letter signed 'Flag Officer': 'Again on the nineteenth of August the commander of the Grand Fleet with superior forces for a second time was in contact with the enemy and made the remembered signal "I expect to be in action in a few moments and have every confidence of the result." Immediately afterwards he was attacked by many torpedoes. Two cruisers were sunk but no battleships came into action, and within half an hour the battle fleet was steering to its base.'

"Yes, our fleet remained in possession of the North Sea that day. The snarl of torpedoes which 'Flag Officer' describes in the midst of Jellicoe's fleet, came from our submarines. Our submarines taught the world a lesson on that day that is never to be forgotten, and it is this, that a few submarines could make England uncertain of the value of the Grand Fleet. Thus the August battle showed that the British fear of losses through submarine attacks kept them from engaging in an important battle. Skagerrak had lifted the German hopes. We had thought that a second battle would again cut down the British tonnage without our side losing any, so that eventually we would equalize the fleets, and then we were optimistic for full victory. But the August engagement showed that the British were unwilling to risk a decision at sea.

" The course of naval history was changed. Britain blockaded Germany. Germany engaged in submarine war against British commerce. Both fleets remained in their harbours. We built 360 and lost 180 submarines, a heavy sacrifice. Without history, experience or tradition we built a navy that came out victorious in the one great battle, and wrote a gallant record of heroic exploits. The Allies robbed us of our navy, but British propaganda must not rob us of our glory."

* * * * *

The Future of Naval Warfare

Having broken his years of silence, I asked Admiral Scheer, who was perhaps the best qualified naval officer then alive to pass judgment and make predictions, to discuss the future of naval warfare, naval holidays, disarmament conferences, a possible war involving America, Japan, Britain, and the question of big warships or submarines.

" I would like," replied the taut, sharp, gentle little man whom at least half the world regards as the hero of the war at sea, " I would like to see this world pass from hatred — national hatred, class hatred, religious hatred, which, it seems to me, have increased since the Armistice; from Bolshevism's dangers and from chaotic economic conditions, all of which result from the war — to an era of peace, justice and friendship. Universal disarmament would be a step towards that goal. But when nations having the biggest fleets propose that their rivals join in a suspension of ship-building, when nations agree to cease building huge superdreadnaughts but are unlimited in their submarine tonnage, when these and other naval tricks are played upon the conscience of the world, it looks to me like a swindle.

"Let us have honesty, not hypocrisy. Disarmament congresses interest me greatly. Idealism, it seems, still remains rooted in America despite the fourteen points which were sold, traded, lost or blunted at Versailles. America, I know, has a fleet whose purpose is not to attack or destroy rivals in world commerce; America has never been aggressive militarily.

"Naturally a naval holiday benefits England more than any other nation. At the end of the war England had not the money to enter a naval building race with America and she did not know what kinds of ships to build. The last is the reason that so much value was put on my report to the Kaiser because the British press said it would contain the answer to the riddle: big or little ships. England was therefore willing to make any kind of a deal to end expenditure and gain time. In five years or so she might have money again and the question of dreadnaughts or submarines might be answered. She would build again and again rule the waves.

"More important than money, it seems to me, is the question of size and kind of war-craft for the future. Skagerrak was followed by disillusion in England. Big ships, it seemed, had had their day. Capital ships decided nothing, they stayed in port. One political party gathers in a lot of naval men who say the line ship is dead; they clamour for submarines, torpedo-boats, destroyers, air-craft. The old-timers waver. I therefore read between the lines of the universal clamour for a naval holiday and disarmament which went up in England a frank confession that England lost the battle of the North Sea which ended the usefulness of its Grand Fleet.

"Japan has money to build but is also uncertain. She is an island empire, like England, and to some extent has to meet the same problems. America is a continent and does not face the most important of all naval warfare problems, the possibility of economic and food blockade. America therefore can more easily afford to disregard all naval holiday and disarmament talk and carry out whatever program it chooses.

"If I were an American I would not listen to either Britain or Japan but write a program for universal disarmament and the maintenance of peace, and neither compromise nor make temporary agreements.

"But I see no reason for America fearing a war with either Japan or England now or in the future. In such wars the action would be entirely naval, as the American land frontiers, Canadian and Mexican, are comparatively safe. Mexico is impotent; Canada would hardly fight the United States; and a Japanese landing on either American or Mexican soil is impractical, almost impossible.

"I say almost impossible, for a landing would necessitate the complete destruction of the American fleet. I have shown in the battle of Skagerrak that a fleet double in strength cannot enforce its will upon the weaker, and two months later I showed the possibility of a few submarines driving off a fleet of capital ships. Again throughout the war Germany showed that submarines and minefields made our coast safe against enemy landings.

"Now consider a Japanese war against America. Consider even the complete defeat of the American fleet by the Japanese. They come across the thousands of miles with their warships

57

and transports. They arrive off Mexico with their bunkers empty. Mexico cannot supply coal or oil because to coal a fleet requires enormous stations which Mexico has not got. Then the Japanese approach the coast and a few American submarines engage them, probably sink some of their transports, and prevent a landing."

"But these conditions do not hold for the Philippines," I said.

"Yes and no," replied the admiral. "It is my opinion that a fleet of submarines supported to some extent by forts and warships, enough at least to keep the submarine bases from being destroyed and permitting them full liberty of action, would prevent enemy landing. Otherwise they would fall an easy prey. Should the American navy decide to fight a decisive battle on the Japanese side of the Pacific it would have advantages over Japan in a series of bases, Hawaii, Guam and the Philippines, while Japan in coming to the American side would have almost no support.

"However, Japan has as a result of the war extended her naval bases into the ocean. I do not as a rule interest myself in American-Japanese politics but I do not see why America does not let Japan go westward if America wants to bar the way east. If you do not want them in California, let them go into Manchuria and ship their superfluous population there. You can do that and still arrange for keeping the China door open.

"I fear the Japanese want the Philippines badly and I should think that America ought not to prize them too highly. Japan wants to expand. Japan, like the other victor states, Britain and France, has the militant feeling reborn. Japan looks towards the Philippines. America makes them out to be of more value than they are. This exaggeration of value may lead America to compromise her honor in the defence of the Philippines so that she would have to go to war.

"I think Britain now realizes she made a mistake in permitting the Japanese to occupy the former German Pacific islands. Had these islands remained German, a conflict of interests would have been avoided for Germany would not be feared in these waters. Now these islands have become a bridge for expansion which England offered the Japanese, inviting that country to walk out, from naval station to naval station, far into the Pacific. The bridge tends to encircle Australia. The map shows the two semi-circles about Australia. Japan is astride one and this danger is realized. In other words England has driven her own daughter Australia into the hands of America whose interests in the Pacific are identical.

"From a purely strategic point of view, leaving aside sentiment and ideals as they were left aside at Versailles, I would say that America should have taken over the German Marianna islands as her share of the spoils. America would not have been accused of militarism had she done so and Japan would have been kept in a smaller radius of operations. As it has turned out to be, however, Australia comes closer to America, which is good for both.

"Another point to be considered is the use of the air arm in a war between America and either England or Japan. In our war against England our stations formed a right angle and our air-craft had to concentrate on a rather narrow strip of land so that an unfavorable wind quickly drove them from their course.

"The long straight American coast lines are good for aerial wireless co-ordinance. You can concentrate Zeppelins or heavier-than-air machines on a given point in the Pacific and direct them from a series of stations from Washington to Lower California, from Maine to Key West.

" But do not place too much hope in air-craft as a naval weapon. The ship has laid chains on the waves. We sink sometimes but we sail every day. But aviation remains at the caprice of the four winds and I see no way to chain them.

" America should defend itself by adequate railroad construction. There should be more horizontal lines, more trans-Rocky Mountain lines to protect the Pacific Coast in case of war. The east seems to have adequate railroad protection."

*   *   *   *   *

Big Ships or Submarines?

I then propounded the following question to the admiral: Should America in the future build superdreadnaughts or cheap submarines; battle-cruisers or air-craft; should it place its reliance on the old style navy or on new and improved naval invention.

" I said in my report to the Kaiser — and I must thank you again and again for publishing it to the world — that the heavy lineship remains the backbone of any navy," replied the admiral. " That was just after the battle where we had bested a British fleet more than twice our strength. Since then, in my letter replying to your request for an interview, I said that submarine development makes it possible for a nation possessing but a few of these weapons to withstand any of the world's four big navies.

" These statements are not as contradictory as they seem. From 1916 on Germany waged a great submarine campaign in which we gained great knowledge of this weapon. My final conclusion is that a fleet composed of capital ships only, or of submarines only, is not complete. Every fleet must be completed according to the geographical position of the country and according to political objectives. An island empire and a continental republic require navies composed of both types of weapons but in different proportions.

" I would not abandon the building of capital ships entirely in favor of the submersible. There should certainly be a greater concentration on submarines in the future. This new arm must be developed to its utmost for the possible destruction of enemy trade; it affords, however, a defence hitherto undreamed of.

" I do not hear much nowadays of a big program of submarine expansion in America. It seems to me that America is not paying enough attention to the extraordinary effectiveness of this new weapon. To speak hypothetically, in a war between England and America, or Japan and America, the American submarine flotillas could raise havoc with Japanese or British commerce, endangering the lives of these island nations which live on imports. But it would take a great fleet of dreadnaughts and cruisers to safeguard New York or San Francisco harbors from the British or Japanese fleets and protect the American submarine bases from being blown up.

" You see, each weapon has its uses and each nation its own coastal problems and must adopt an individual program, but if I were in the American naval service, or if my advice were asked, I should answer: ' Do not listen to persons technically ignorant; do not throw aside the big ships in favor of the submarine or aircraft, but build all three in the proportion you need for a defensive or offensive policy. And by all means build more submarines.'

"Land warfare has changed but little. We used Napoleon's tactics against Russia and Roumania, crushing them both. But the lessons of Trafalgar do not hold for Skagerrak. Submarines have changed naval warfare even if they have not killed the capital ship. The greatest lesson is this: for the nations fearing naval militarism, protection is guaranteed with a small inexpensive fleet of submarines. The submarine-owning nations are practically secure against invasion. Britain won the war but has lost the mastery of the seas. This seeming paradox is the lesson of Skagerrak. The mastery of the seas is now disputable, and any second- or third-class power having many submarines can withstand the whole navies of the first-class nations.

"Some day the world may realize the debt it owes us. In August my few submarines used as a screen caused the British navy to retire instead of fighting a decisive battle. The submarines have made big navies powerless as an offensive weapon and given the nations not having them a chance to remain safe from them, provided they build submarines."

I asked the admiral if he believed the popular theory that terrible electric man-killing inventions, or tanks, gas, airplanes, would end warfare in the future.

"No," he replied, "I cannot foresee mere terror preventing men fighting but I do foresee the submarine weapon helping to maintain peace. It will prevent wars, especially when nations possessing great fleets have to consider their impotence faced by smaller nations possessing a few submarines which would prevent decisive naval operations or coastal landings. Once Britannia ruled the waves. Now Britain passes from offensive to defensive, from arrogance to doubt of her own security. My conclusion is that the submarine gives weak nations peace, checks wars and equalizes the world powers considerably."

*   *   *   *   *

Admiral Scheer on the 5-5-3 Plan

(After reading the translation of the Kaiser's report and my interview Admiral Scheer corrected the word " desperate " with which I had described his position in the " spearhead formation " by replacing it with " serious," and kindly consented to write the following criticism of the 5-5-3 program entered into between the United States, Britain and Japan.)

" The formula 5-5-3 tends to equalize the British and American fleets, while the Japanese is left about half as strong as either. The main question is whether there is a healthy idea behind this plan. England's naval supremacy, hitherto always admitted, ceases to exist and is replaced by a balance of naval powers, so balanced that alliances between two of them make them extremely dangerous to the third, forcing the third to yield.

" There is no chance of a single nation becoming dangerous to another by attacking it: the attacked nation is always in the more favorable position. For instance, should England's fleet want to attack America, it must first cross a distance six times greater than that separating Germany from England, only to find a fleet as strong as itself, and with all the help which resources of a background can give.

" Likewise in the Pacific. Japan has no chance against the American coast but Japan does have a great chance for attacking America's vanguard, the Philippines. The loss of the

Philippines would be more a loss of prestige to America than a damage which would decide the war. To develop the Philippines into very strongly fortified positions would represent a direct threat against Japan on account of proximity. The main factor is therefore the development of submarines. With a hundred of them of 1000 tons each or fifty with 2000 each, each power would have a great chance in a commercial war against the other. The owner of the biggest commercial fleet needs commerce most and must be the main loser in a war on commerce. England therefore is in the weakest position.

" The 5-5-3 disarmament plan is the result of experience during the war which showed that the value of dreadnaughts had diminished. War on commerce is always the chief aim of naval warfare. It is based on the right to take booty, which is imposed also on neutral navigation by the right of contraband and blockade which could be increased arbitrarily according to a nation's naval strength — arbitrary measures and power always go hand in hand. England never wanted to resign the right to take booty, but her punishment for the starvation by blockade against Germany showed her vulnerable point to the world.

" It will be impossible to suppress arms such as the submarine, just as it is impossible to suppress aviation. It would be unnatural to build 45,000 ton ships which must be kept always in groups because of fear of meeting a superior number which would destroy them, when you can build twenty submarines for the same money, each capable of cruising independently, fearlessly, for weeks.

" In the future the fight for the suppression of the right to naval booty will probably grow more acute. It has gone on for years, I recall the fact that America demanded its suppression at the Paris conference in 1856. She did not succeed. At The Hague, England prevented its suppression. Should America insist on the suppression of the right to seize and capture commercial ships especially neutrals, she would end one of the greatest threats against world peace and give unimpeachable proof of America's unselfishness."

(In conclusion Admiral Scheer also sent me the following page of naval convictions and aphorisms.)

"In former wars naval predominance was the aim because the commercial war was the principal thing and will remain the most important.

"The owner of the strongest fleet had the opportunity for victory if he forced his adversary to stay in port or beat the fleet so that it could not show itself again. Thus his own trade was protected. Nowadays naval predominance cannot guarantee complete safety for the mercantile fleet by over-water fleets. The bases of U-boats must be destroyed. This is a far more difficult task than defeating a fleet on the high seas.

"Nowadays a weak fleet is able to do so much harm to the enemy, thanks to the submarine weapon, that he will not dare to take up the fight to the finish.

"If the British fleet did not take up the fight in the North Sea how much more difficult will it be for America's enemies to take up a fight across an ocean.

"The capital ship has lost power because the nation owning the best and the most is no longer able to claim naval superiority with any certainty.

"The small number of capital ships can be made up for through submersibles which cost much less, yet which can kill the war spirit of the enemy in proportion to the damage they inflict and the danger the enemy must expect.

" The submarine has changed naval warfare inasmuch as it places the attacker in the disadvantage. This should be a drawback to engaging in wars in the future. Thus the U-boat becomes a military agent urging universal peace."

Part II — Italy

Chapter I

THE TRUTH ABOUT FASCIST TERRORISM AND CENSORSHIP

*W*E *are bound by the worst censorship ever imposed. We must not write anything that might reflect on the Fascisti. We are confined to an apology for political assassination. It broke my heart not to be able to report the Matteotti case as it should be done, but it would have meant arrest and expulsion from Italy."*

To me this extract from a letter written by one of America's best-known newspapermen, one who is still resident in Rome and who is proud to call himself a friend and admirer of Mussolini, is a most illuminating protest against the situation in Italy today. It states in one paragraph the facts of censorhip, expresses the American desire to tell the truth and states the helpless tragedy of a land where an unseen terrorism rules. It is the sincere confession of one of the many American journalists who are trying to do an honest day's work despite Mussolini's orders and the fear that hangs over them. Compare this statement to the boat interviews of returning tourists, the " all's well with the world " of the men who have just floated Italian loans, and all the Fascist apologist propaganda, much of it paid for, which tells of the political and social Paradise suddenly wrought out of decaying Italy. Which is the truth?

I came to Italy with the same open mind I took to Russia; in fact having been expelled by the Bolsheviki and being under the power of that now proven myth that the Fascisti had smashed Bolshevism, I was probably more friendly to the idea of Fascismo.

I went to Italy as the representative of an American newspaper after nearly fifteen years of experience as a reporter, nine of which I had spent in Europe, writing cables almost every day and studying the collapse of old systems and countries, the birth of new. I had been forced to leave Russia because I would not submit to the Bolshevik censorship; but I felt I had a right to expect that in Rome I should find comparative journalistic freedom. This was to be a permanent assignment; it followed four professional trips to Italy from the years 1919 to 1925, during the first of which I had reported the communist uprising in Milan and Turin and had visited Fiume, where the romantic d'Annunzio had organized the black-shirted, black-fezzed Arditi who were later to form the swashbuckling leaders of the Fascist militia.

I was soon disillusioned. "You must watch yourself here; you cannot write about the Fascisti as you do about politics in defeated Germany," everyone at the Sala della Stampa Estera, the press club, warned me. "You'll be expelled if you tell everything."

"Is there a censorship?" I asked.

"There is, for the local press; you won't get much information from the papers; sometimes there is some news in the first editions, but the censor cuts it to bits. There is no official censorship over cables. We wish there were. But the foreign office watches you, delays your cables, sometimes suppresses them, sometimes alters them. It's all done secretly. And if you write anything unfavorable to Fascism you will be expelled."

Within a few weeks I received a letter from the American ambassador asking me to call. Mr. Fletcher was apologetic. He began by assuring me that he had informed Dino Grandi, the under-secretary of state, that my news dispatches were no business of the embassy. Yet he had consented to transmit to me a warning from Mussolini. Mussolini didn't like my work.

Strange how these grand dictators sitting in their Kremlins and their Palazzos always have time to look into some reporter's dispatches! But almost every one who has ever interviewed Mussolini and Trotsky or Chicherin will remember the colored pencil scanning the columns of the local or foreign papers. These great men seem to care so much for public opinion!

The ambassador and I discussed the news to which the Fascist chieftains had objected. Certainly not to any item of the grandiose plans for a world-conquering army and navy, for magnificent colonies, for Italianization of the Mediterranean, for the "battle of the wheat" to make Italy self-supporting in food; not to my reports of the fight to stabilize the lira, or of the efforts to obtain a loan from American bankers. Certainly not to any of these items which came up almost daily in the carbon files. But there was an item about the persistent troubles due to the unpunished Matteotti murder, and there was another telegram about the revolt of five political parties under the leadership of Amendola, the only strong force left to the Aventine, the Opposition.

After a long talk with the ambassador, who seemed to sympathize with the difficulties of the American reporters in giving the two sides of the Fascist case, I wrote a long letter to the foreign office. It said in part:

It would not be honest for the Paris correspondent to give only the radical-socialist viewpoint, the Berlin correspondent to give only the coalition viewpoint or the Moscow correspondent to state the successes

71

of Bolshevism and leave out the Soviet terrorism. For the same reason it is necessary for the Rome correspondent to give more than the official Fascist press viewpoint.

We are required to give the facts, to relate happenings; not viewpoints of foreign governments, but facts of interest to the American viewpoint. The American people are not satisfied with official governmental statements alone. The bankers, tourists, holders of foreign bonds, business men, the foreign-born, want the journalists to tell them the truths which the consuls and ambassadors send to the state department in confidence. Sometimes this is most difficult, especially where censorship prevails, as in Bolshevist Russia. If you permit me to speak frankly, I will say that the greatest alarm prevailed in America when the Italian censorship was announced, and even today the greatest suspicion attaches to Italian news. Even your great friend, Cortesi, the correspondent of the Associated Press, representative of a co-operative society known for its disinterestedness, objectivity and honesty, has been forced to mail his telegrams to Paris this week, and from there these news items affecting Italy's foreign relations have been disseminated throughout the world.

My duty is to my American employers, who ask a fair, unprejudiced report of facts, and I must give both sides to every question. If you would read all my telegrams for the past three months I am sure you will withdraw your charge that they are misleading and alarming. They are a recital of events as they happen. I hope I have made my position clear.

There was no immediate reply. In the next two months much happened to bolster Fascist credit abroad, but the Matteotti affair stalked like a hundred ghosts of Banquo through every Fascist ministry, every session of the chamber of deputies, and every editorial room. Fascist signs appeared: " We have 6,700 martyrs, the Opposition one." Every department of the government was furiously working to eliminate the Matteotti case from the public mind, and about once a week some important incident warranted a cable in which the assassinated deputy was mentioned.

My Italian assistant was approached by a minor official of the press bureau with the request that we refrain from naming Matteotti. "No correspondent of any nationality is mentioning this affair," the agent said, "and it will lead to unpleasantness if your paper persists."

"But the Matteotti case is the biggest news item in Italy; it involves the future of Fascism; it is the outstanding subject in politics today," I protested.

The agent shrugged his shoulders.

Then everything came to a climax.

General de Bono, chief of police at the time of the assassination, was freed from complicity in the murder of Matteotti for "lack of evidence." The courts which are under orders as absolute as the Soviet courts, were commanded not to accept as evidence the confessions of two co-accused because they had written confessions, and the confessions involved persons in highest Fascist authority.

Matteotti had detected certain Fascist leaders attempting to collect a lot of money for themselves from an American oil company which sought a concession. He accused Filippo Filipelli, editor of the *Corriere Italiano,* Mussolini's own newspaper; Cesare Rossi, head of Mussolini's foreign office press bureau and then the Duce's right hand man; and Giovanni Marinelli, treasurer of the Fascist party.

The radical elements, with Matteotti leader, led the attack on Fascismo using this oil corruption as an example. Mussolini, shaking his fist at the radical members, replied, the press reporting as follows:

Mussolini: *" In Russia are great masters!* We have only to imitate what is being done in Russia! (Noises, applause, exchange of remarks between the extreme right and left.) They are magnificent masters and *we are wrong not to imitate them in full,* for you would not now be here — you would be in jail. (Noise, applause.) *You would have had a bullet through your spine.* (Interruptions.) *But we have the courage and we will prove it.* (Applause, noises.) *We are always in time! And it will be done sooner than you think."*

Four days later Matteotti was assassinated; a chaotic week followed in which the Opposition could have destroyed Fascismo had they been willing to shed blood; calm followed the arrest of Rossi, Filipelli, Marinelli, Dumini, (called an American-born gunman at the trial), the head of the Italian Chekah, and two other Milanese terrorists. From out of jail Rossi smuggled a copy of a previous letter to Mussolini and a confession. The letter says in part:

If during the coming days you fail to furnish me proof of solidarity, not so much for the past and for my position as your collaborator and executor of our sometime illegal orders, but of your solidarity for essentially governmental reasons, I shall put into effect what I told you this morning. I deem it superfluous to warn you that if the revolting cynicism which you have displayed up to now, complicated by fear that has seized you just at the time you should dominate a situation created exclusively by you, should advise you to order free violence, while I am in jail or in the unfortunate case of my arrest, you will equally be a doomed man, and with you will be destroyed the régime. . . .

The confession says in part:

All this has happened according to the direct will or complicity of the Duce. I allude to the clubbing of Amendola (Deputy), the order given De Bono (commander general of the militia and director of police), by Mussolini, unknown to me and executed by Candelori (*Console* of

74

militia); the beating of Misuri (Deputy) carried out by Balbo (*general-issimo of the militia*) at the suggestion of Mussolini; the aggression upon Forni (candidate in the political elections of April, 1924), the order given me personally by Mussolini and carried out in agreement with Giunta (Secretary General of the Fascist Party and a Deputy); the demonstration against the villa of Nitti (ex-Premier); the recent demonstrations against the opposition parties ordered by Mussolini to be undertaken by Foschi (Secretary of the Party for the Province of Rome); the proposal advanced by Mussolini to the *Quadri-univierto* (central assembly of the Fascist Party), in order that the Honorable Ravazolo (Fascist Deputy) should be given a well-earned lesson in consequence of his insubordination; the destruction of the Catholic circles in Brianza, ordered by Mussolini to be undertaken by Maggi (Fascist Deputy) and then complacently repeated to me. I add that daily the Comm. Fasciolo (attached to Mussolini's Cabinet) had to order, at the suggestion of Mussolini, to forward to the Fascist locals the names of the subscribers of the *Voce Republicana, Avanti, Giustizia, Unita, Italia Libera, et cetera,* so that they might be dosed with castor oil and clubbed.

Filipelli confessed. His memorial says in part:

On Wednesday Rossi told me that Dumini used my machine in good faith; that the situation was grave; that Mussolini knew everything; that he and Marinelli were given orders to do what they did, after a conference with Mussolini; that it was necessary to hush up everything otherwise even Mussolini would be overthrown. I went to the police and reported (about my car). I learned that Dumini's victim was Matteotti, that the order to kill Matteotti came from the Fascist Chekah whose chief executioners were Dumini and (other names); whose deeds were known to Mussolini; that they had conferred with Mussolini on Wednesday; that Mussolini received Matteotti's passport and other papers in proof of Matteotti's death. They asked me to suppress the facts about my machine as the régime and Mussolini's head were at stake.

* * * * *

The five Opposition parties prepared a protest to the king and a document embodying both confessions. The Fascisti issued a new order that, instead of suppressing editions of the liberal newspapers daily, they would suppress them altogether after three warnings. The confessions and the Aventine document were duly sent from my office and so keyed that within three days I knew they had been suppressed by the censor. We then telegraphed our Paris office, which had received by mail carbon copies for filing, to cable them to America; and three days later Mussolini ordered my expulsion from Italy.

Again the foreign office attempted to force my deportation through the American embassy. The letter spoke of " *tendenziose ed allarmistiche* " telegrams, pleaded for " *serena, spegiudicate ed obiettive* " news, and was supplemented by Dino Grandi's remark to Ambassador Fletcher that " he (Seldes) has represented the Mussolini Government in the worst possible light and *given the views of the political opponents of the Duce.*"

This time the Palazzo Chigi appended the suppressed telegrams. No. 1 related the attempt to assassinate Amendola. The second most important figure in Italy had gone to a hotel at Montecatini for a rest cure. He left Rome secretly at night. But somehow the Rome head-quarters of the Fascist party heard of it, and the telephones rang in Fascist head-quarters throughout the Montecatini district, so that shortly after Amendola arrived at his hotel a thousand black shirts appeared, some of whom had travelled twenty miles. They demanded the surrender of the Aventine chief and, being refused, stormed the hotel, smashing down every resisting door, searching the rooms of American and European guests who had retired for the night, and threatening with death any one who might be harbouring the fleeing man.

Amendola was pursued in automobiles, overtaken, and clubbed by twenty Fascists. Many of his bones were broken and his seemingly lifeless body was left for dead in his wrecked car. (He expired three months later, and since then no man has arisen in Italy to lead the Opposition parties which have now been outlawed and crushed.)

Exhibit No. 2 began: "One hundred and seventeen members of Parliament out of the 140 comprising the five political parties of the Opposition have signed a document addressed to the people of Italy and warning the King not to ratify Mussolini's appointment of General de Bono as governor of Tripoli following his release from prison for complicity in the Matteotti murder, nor to issue an amnesty for the five arrested leaders of the Fascist party charged with murdering Deputy Matteotti."

There followed a summary of the 15,000 word document which included the Rossi and Filipelli confessions which the courts had refused to read when they freed De Bono.

Exhibit No. 3 concerned Salvemini. Gaetano Salvemini is now well known in the United States, but at the time of his arrest and trial the chief interest in his case arose through the fact that it brought to official light the afore-mentioned confessions. Salvemini was accused of printing them. He was found not guilty by a Fascist court. Several hundred Fascisti, knowing there was no evidence against the venerable professor, gathered in tens and twenties at each exit of the palace of justice in Florence, and when the professor, his attorney, and the war hero Rosetti emerged, they attacked the three, beating them with clubs and stones.

Of the three items of news which Mussolini's office sent to the American ambassador, the first never appeared in the Italian press, the second appeared three days after my cables had been published in America and Europe, and the third appeared in one edition of a liberal paper, *Il Mondo,* which was immediately suppressed.

Now, it had been either my fortune or misfortune to obtain the first two items exclusively. Regarding the third, I know that the Italian head of one of the largest American press bureaus ordered his American assistant not to write anything about the attack on Salvemini because "such little things are of no interest in America," and that this young American secretly and at night cabled a report which was published everywhere. It was quite true that despite the threat of deportation my dispatches never toned down the news, never aimed to apologize for violence or veneer with propaganda favorable to the Fascisti certain acts of which they were proud at home but which made a bad impression abroad and sometimes caused their loans to drop three points. Perhaps it was true that these items "depicted Mussolini's Government in the worst possible light." But such was the light that beat upon the throne in those days. There was no question of either the importance or the authenticity of the news. Moreover on the days when these reports of bloodshed and suppression were being sent abroad my office had also sent dispatches pleasing to those who cry out against "destructive" journalism. On the "constructive" side my file showed such items as these: "Complete recovery of Mussolini," "Economic improvement of Italy shown by minister of finance," "Italy scores success with artificial silk industry," and dozens of minor stories of Fascist triumphs in business and politics.

All of this I duly explained to the ambassador. It was not the first time this envoy had fought for the liberty of the press; the time he banged his fist on Carranza's table and demanded the release and freedom of movement of American newspapermen in Mexico City is still well remembered.

Mr. Fletcher went to the foreign office to protest against my expulsion, and the same day the American and British correspondents also went to the palace; to the ambassador it was the rights of an individual citizen, to the press representatives it was the climax of a long battle against censorship and suppression. Concerning this protest meeting the Fascist *Epoca* could not bring itself to tell the truth. It said: " *L'on Grandi ha ricevuto a Palazzo Chigi S. E. Fletcher, Ambasciatore degli Stati Uniti, ed un gruppo di corrispondenti Americani che ha intrattenuto in cordiale conversazione.*"

This " cordial conversation " was a bitter dispute lasting a long time and ending with Grandi's statement that " the foreign office would reconsider the case." The correspondents thought it was a victory. Jubilation and a banquet followed. But it was interrupted by an agent of the police who came to my apartment to tell me how much longer I might stay in Italy. The embassy was puzzled too. At the ambassador's suggestion I requested that a formal order of deportation be given me, and my office requested Secretary Kellogg to cable the Italian foreign office to safeguard life and limb. These things, however, are not important; it is important that in the four days allotted me to settle my Roman affairs I was visited by all the American newspapermen, many of the British, French and German journalists, and some Italian ones; they came with one demand, that on reaching some free country, Switzerland or

France, I publish a full report about the intolerable conditions under which the press of the world works in Italy.

* * * * *

The hundred or more representatives of the foreign press in Rome have to ask themselves every day, " Is this piece of Fascist terrorism worth mentioning? Am I to risk being thrown into the ' Queen of Heaven ' Jail or being thrown over the frontier for this small item? " And the reply is always, " This is too small. Wait for something big; another Matteotti assassination; a national uprising, something big enough to warrant the risk."

Thus we voluntarily suppressed the truth about blackshirt terrorism, waiting for a big day. Occasionally we risked a small item, and immediately there would be a call from Baron Valentino's office, and the chief of the press bureau would complain that any one who mentioned violence was an enemy of the greatest movement for the salvation of humanity the world has ever known.

Valentino spoke as an idealist. The real intimidation department was operated by Grandi, a subordinate in the department of state of which Mussolini holds the portfolio. Grandi likes to work through foreign embassies, and by this method has had considerable success in keeping the French and German journalists in line. He tried it once with the representative of *The London Times*. This correspondent, instead of going to the embassy to listen to protests from Grandi, notified his paper, which is said to have replied: " Tell British ambassador to mind his own business; we mind ours." But *The Manchester Guardian* correspondents, who are frequently asked to report the true state of elections, crime, and the budget, the movements of the liberal elements and leaders, and news generally more interesting to a liberal newspaper, are continually warned and threatened with deportation.

Hardly a day passes in which every correspondent does not learn of several happenings worth cabling if there were liberty of the press. When I was in Italy it was still possible to find in the first evening editions of the Rome papers a budget of items which were suppressed in later editions and therefore doubly interesting.

Here is a sample day:

Item: Boara. — As a result of a fight between Fascisti and Opposition, one Fascist militiaman killed; Fascist reinforcement arrived, killed two Opposition.

Item: Padua. — Fascisti staged demonstration smashing office and printing plant of the *Popolo Veneto,* Catholic newspaper opposed to the dictatorship.

Item: Rovigo. — A Fascist quarrelled with a shopkeeper. Both drew knives. The Fascist was killed. The Fascist local came in an auto truck, killed the shop keeper and his brother, and wrecked the house. General de Balbo made a speech lauding the heroism of the first Fascist killed in the knife battle.

Item: Rome. — The public prosecutor asks that the parliamentary immunity of Amendola, leader of the Opposition, be lifted so that he may be tried for criminal assault of a Fascist. Five Fascisti attacked Amendola with clubs but the Opposition leader, armed with an old umbrella, succeeded in driving the gangsters off, hitting one rather severely on the head.

Item: Milan. — Rioting in favor of the king of Italy and against Fascism was a new phase of the political situation when the sovereign came to inaugurate the cancer hospital. A large part of the industrial population engaged in a demonstration and strike. Battles between Fascisti and workingmen, many arrested. The laborers shouted "Long live the king, long live liberty" and "Down with Fascism." Leaflets were distributed calling for a return of free labor unions, free speech, free press, all the old constitutional guarantees promised by the king and suppressed by Mussolini. A banner was carried: "King Victor, restore us our former freedom."

None of these items was worth the risk of deportation. If I had had a three-year lease on a house in Rome, or a wife and children and other obligations there, I too should have waited for bigger news; having obligations only to my paper, I accordingly cabled the Milan story and it was recorded in the Roman foreign office against me and reported in the Fascist journal *Impero* as a libel on fair Fascism written by a "*grosso porco,*" a fat swine.

Much more interesting for America were the attacks on two American consuls by Fascist mobs, incidents which the government was afraid might hurt the tourist business if given wide circulation. Unusual efforts were made to suppress the news of these attacks, but the facts were revealed despite the censorship of the state department and the American embassy at Rome. This story of Fascist brutality and American docility is related in the chapter on American diplomats as censors.

And so it goes. Every newspaper representative in Italy, including perhaps the Fascist Italians still employed by American agencies and newspapers, could supplement these cases with scores just as important, many of them unknown to most of the Italian people. There was a time when non-Fascist newspapers published a small proportion of this sort of news; even the *Becco Giallo,* the satirical weekly, could hit unmolested at some acts of violence in the Fascist Utopia. But by a campaign

begun in 1923 and concluded in 1927 the government has completely suppressed the liberties of the national press, so that
today the average Italian knows nothing except what his
masters want him to know.

*   *   *   *   *

The suppression began with an edict prepared by Mussolini,
signed by the king in 1923 against his will it is said in diplomatic circles, and kept on Mussolini's desk until the danger of
a national mutiny followed the Matteotti murder in 1924. On
July 12 the edict was promulgated. It provided for warnings
(i. e., suppression) " if any newspaper or periodical by false or
misleading news causes any interference in the diplomatic action of the government in its foreign relations or hurts the
credit of the nation at home or abroad, causing undue alarm
among the people, or in any way disturbs the public peace . . .
if the newspaper or periodical by editorial articles, notes, titles,
illustrations or inserts incites to crime or to class hatred or to
disobedience of the laws of the established order or upsets
the discipline of those engaged in public service or favors the
interests of foreign states, groups, or persons as opposed to
Italian interests, or insults the nation, the king, the royal
family, the Summo Pontifex, the religion, the institutions, or
the authority of the state or of other friendly powers.

" Newspapers or other periodicals published in violation of
the preceding provisions shall be suppressed. . . ."

On January 8, 1925, a manifesto to the Aventine group was
suppressed but read at a meeting of one hundred members of
the chamber of deputies — a private meeting because their
immunity had simultaneously been abolished. (The date,
therefore, is a landmark.) The document said in part:

83

The mask of constitutionality and normality has been thrown off. The government is trampling on the fundamental laws of the state and suffocating the free voice of the press with a despotism hitherto unheard of, suppressing every right of assemblage, but mobilizing the armed forces of its party, persecuting citizens and associations while it tolerates and leaves unpunished acts of devastation and destruction against its opponents which degrade Italy in the eyes of the civilized world.

In November, 1925, the *Corriere della Sera* was suppressed. *The London Times* editorially declared that Mussolini was making Italy a suspected and incomprehensible state, like Russia, and concluded, " It will be hard in the future to understand Italy and Fascismo. The disappearance of the independent *Corriere della Sera* is a serious loss to European civilization."

On December 31, 1925, a new censorship law was passed which almost completely suppressed independent journals and herded journalists into registered police dockets. The law contained ten points, No. 10 being:

> Prefects of police are empowered to seize editions of newspapers which attack the government in the foreign policy, or which injure the national credit at home or abroad, or which alarm the people without justification.

In 1927 all non-Fascist newspapers and periodicals were abolished.

But even that was not enough.

In 1927 the directorate of the Fascist party divided all publications into two categories, those officially recognized by the party and those which did not enjoy that honor. The first category includes those newspapers " which by their origin, their activity on behalf of the Fascist cause, the political loyalty of their directors, editors and administrative staff, give secure guarantees of being worthy to be considered the true and real organs of the régime."

The second category is made up of journals *sympathetic to the régime,* and control over them will be exercised by means of the ordinary press laws in force. No non-Fascist writer may join the staff of a Fascist publication.

The perfect Fascist journalistic state has thus been achieved. The Fascisti have finally reached the same point as the Bolsheviki.

*   *   *   *   *

Occasionally some intrepid soul still publishes a pamphlet or a secret sheet listing Fascist crimes. Immediately local terror is instituted. Suspected persons are clubbed, shot; their homes are wrecked, and any printing presses found are smashed. Sometimes an editor reaches Paris, sometimes he is exiled. The Italian government admitted in January, 1927, that in addition to the thousands of persons convicted by regular courts, 942 persons tried by self-appointed Fascist courts had been exiled to the islands of Ustica, Lampedusa, Favignana, Pantellaria, horrible waterless, criminal-infested islands which constitute Italy's Siberia. Mussolini once stated that only anarchists and communists are sent there, but it is a fact discovered by an American newspaperman that Liberal and Catholic deputies, editors, moderate Socialists, professors and professional men, most of whom have written something unfavorable to Fascismo or critical of Mussolini, constitute the majority in exile.

The year 1927 heard the last death-rattle of the free press in Italy; it also marked a new campaign to spread Fascist propaganda and stop criticism abroad. Numerous Italian and Italo-

American publications are being subsidized. Their editors are given trips to Rome and permitted to shake hands with the Duce. A few big orders are placed with outstanding American concerns. Sometimes the equivalent to the French legion of honor ribbon is pinned on a leading citizen. Money and flattery and honours are lavishly given to the friends of Fascismo.

Whenever the Italian loan seems to float less easily in New York and when new loans are contemplated, important American visitors find that it is not so difficult after all to visit Mussolini. His hand-shake is cordial, his undeniable charm, his great histrionic talent, make delightful impressions. Senators, representatives, mayors, editors, big bankers and novelists, many of whom think the Duce the greatest man of this era, have all their doubts about dictatorships, all their beliefs in American democracy, delightfully transformed when they emerge radiant from the palace ready to carry the standard of Fascismo to the uttermost Main Streets of the United States. It is no mean honour to interview the Caesar and Napoleon of our own day. A few words from Mussolini, and all American traditions, the inheritances from Pilgrim forefathers, the ideals which roused an embattled nation in 1861 and 1917, and everyday opinions on political rights and personal liberties, are discarded as a cloak suddenly grown threadbare and shabby and unfit for royal company.

Some of these representative Americans come determined not to be personally conducted through the Fascist Utopia. They must see for themselves. They refuse foreign office guides and literature. They stay more than the week-end; they stay a full month, perhaps. They ask waiters and shopkeepers indiscreet questions. But they fail to see the tongue-in-cheek which accompanies the replies confirming the official Fascist statements that democracy is a failure, parliamentary government ridiculous, a free press a danger to progress, and that the Italian people owing to its economic, mental, and emotional make-up, has been made happy and prosperous through the only form of government fit for it.

This prosperity, which nobody can deny, is shown to every visitor. But it is prefaced always with the statement that Mussolini saved Italy from Bolshevism, a statement which despite repetition in every newspaper and every book by pro-Fascist apologists, is a historical untruth. I saw Bolshevism raise its red banners in Milan and Turin in 1919, and hide them early in 1920; during the rest of that year and in 1921 and 1922, until the Naples convention determined the Fascist "march on Rome," I saw parliamentary government survive, Bolshevism collapse, and Italy slowly rise to her feet without violence or terrorism.

The American visitor is shown *faits accomplis:* a balanced budget, cleaner railway trains and trains that run on time; a people becoming more and more disciplined and imperialistic; much material progress. The same American visitor, could he enter Russia with the same preconceived friendly attitude, would find exactly the same material progress. Walter Duranty, the leading American authority on Russia, told me recently that it is now possible for a stranger to tour Russia in comfort and safety, enjoying decent food and comparatively decent housing accommodations. But the Chekah terror, although invisible, still rules and still crushes the soul of the Russian people.

It is impossible for the visitor to go behind the scenes. It takes months of residence and investigation and a trained as well as an open mind, to determine the feelings of a people living in fear and to obtain the news of how dictatorship works in the country-side, far from the prying eyes of tourists. No one is better able to tell the truth about Fascism and its censorship than the American correspondents resident in Rome. I have already mentioned suppression of news by Italian Fascists or pro-Fascists representing the American press; the general attitude of the American corps, however, is not to compromise with truth, but to compromise with the powers. The men and women take circumstances into consideration. Sometimes it hurts to do so, but they must trim their sails to fit the Fascist winds if they are to remain at work in that stormy country.

The independents, those who do not conform, men and women alike, mostly American and British, some sunny day find a detective on their front door-step or at an adjoining table in the restaurant, who will take notes on every person seen, talked to; or they may receive a call from Baron Valentino, who lays before them clippings from their papers, news which never went direct from Rome by wire or wireless. Once they wondered where Valentino got the clippings; now they know that Mussolini has ordered every consul abroad to watch the press, to send clippings, and to report the attitude of every foreign newspaper, especially those in New York, Washington, and Chicago. Mussolini reads many of the clippings himself.

Nor are Italian journalists abroad safe if their views do not conform. Their property is confiscated by the state, their citizenship is revoked; they are in constant fear of being beaten up by members of the Fascist locals which are planted by Rome in whatever country they may reside, and their lives are made generally miserable so long as they continue their non-Fascist attitude. The censorship, by fair means or foul, reaches throughout Europe and extends to the United States. An example is furnished by the following case reported to Sir Eric Drummond, secretary-general of the League of Nations.

Angelo Monti and Carlo a'Prato are two Italians of high reputation, members of the International Association of Journalists Accredited to the League of Nations. Monti represented *Il Secolo* for twenty years, a'Prato was once secretary to Nitti, later to Count Sforza. He became associated with Don Sturzo, leader of the Catholic Opposition to Mussolini, and was forced to flee for his life. He is representing a Paris paper in Geneva. The two journalists complained to the association that the Swiss police, at the request of the Fascisti, have done everything to make their residence in Switzerland unbearable, their work impossible. They have been arrested, their credentials frequently questioned, their expulsion threatened. The chief of police, M. Turritini, they alleged, is a pro-Fascist who enjoys terrorizing Mussolini's enemies when they escape to Switzerland. The association has determined to defend its members before the Council of the League of Nations, the International Press Conference, and, if necessary, the League Assembly.

A part of the European press is easily controlled by Mussolini. The pre-war system of selling "zones of influence" to governments, although curtailed by rearrangement of boundaries, still prevails. A Paris newspaper, for instance, may offer its services to two governments about whose politics France is not vitally concerned, say Peru and Chile; whichever pays the price will be supported in whatever it does in its zone, even in war, perhaps.

Support can be bought outright or by indirect means. Many big organizations, the *Ente Nazionale per le Industrie Turistiche,* now known as the C.I.T., the Grandi Alberghi Association of Hotel Keepers, and various associations of hotel men and tourist agencies, are heavy advertisers in almost every part of the world. These organizations demand subservience to Fascism as part of their advertising contract. They dangle their millions of lire before business managers and withdraw their advertisements if the editors menton Fascist violence in Italy. Following my expulsion from Rome, the big hotel and tourist groups and the government railroads cancelled their advertising in my papers and wrote many letters which I have read in my office to say they would resume if unfavorable news were suppressed in the future.

Finally there is the splendid bribe of five thousand words a month free over the Transatlantic cable for all correspondents and newspapers who agree to send and print propaganda favorable to the Fascisti. When I took over the Rome bureau of my paper I found that my predecessor, an Italian-American blackshirt enthusiast, had been given this award for faithfulness to the cause, and that other American newspapers had accepted it also. At my first encounter with the censorship I was threatened with its withdrawal, and at the second it was withdrawn. Today nearly all the pro-Fascist organs in America are partly subsidized by this means.

*   *   *   *   *

But somehow Mussolini cannot prevent the American reporter from telling at least a part of the truth. With the possible exception of two Italians who place Fascismo above their duties to their American employers, the corps representing America today makes every effort to break the censorship. Its methods are many and various. The easiest is a letter to a private address in Paris or London which eventually becomes a cable with a

Swiss date-line. The second method is aptly termed the " grape-vine." It passes from one side of the wall to the other. Somebody in Rome communicates (by telephone or letter) with an agent in Lugano or Chiasso or another frontier town. The agent crosses the border — a mere city street sometimes — and tele-phones to Paris. In all cases the Rome correspondent remains protected and anonymous.

The cleverest, most effective means of obtaining the news is " relay reporting." Floyd Gibbons first introduced the system of sending a stream of men from country to country, each of whom was met by foreign office rebuffs and sneers, really meant for a predecessor, and each of whom gave lengthy ex-planations, perhaps an apology, and departed to write freely at a distance of conditions that existed. The system was tried during the Irish troubles, the Silesian plebiscite scandal, the Fiume madness, during a score of European events concerning which it was really dangerous for a man to tell something of the truth and remain on the scene. Today one New York news-paper (*The World*) has adopted the relay method with great success in Italy. Apparently three representatives of this paper were at the Matteotti trial in relays, and could, by going to Nice or Lugano, report the brutal Fascization of justice at Chieti. Readers of almost all the papers of the whole world got only a distorted, censored, almost totally untrue report of this trial which, if reported faithfully, might have undermined the Mus-solini régime and certainly would have changed the sentiment of many people towards Fascism. Only one paper (*The New York World*) was able to report the truth. The other newspa-permen simply broke their hearts and kept quiet.

But it will not be for always. An important effort is now being made through the League of Nations which, while it may not prove successful, will at least officially call the attention of both hemispheres to the terroristic censorships of several countries. Under the leadership of Sir Eric Drummond meetings of two hundred accredited representatives of the press have been held in Geneva and a program adopted. It demands, first of all, the abolition of censorship in time of peace. The report says in its preamble:

Censorship in peace-time is a fundamental obstacle to the normal exchange of international information and makes understanding between peoples more difficult.

Where censorship exists at present, the League committee asks:

1. That telegrams be censored promptly.
2. That journalists be informed of the censorship orders.
3. That journalists be informed of deletions and given an opportunity to withdraw their dispatches completely.
4. That money paid for suppressed telegrams be returned.
5. That all journalists receive equal treatment.
6. That a committee of journalists examine the case of any journalist whom a government would expel.

Russia is outside the League. Of the twenty or more League members which maintain censorships, either by blue pencil or intimidation, Italy is the only big nation which must reply to the above indictment. With the exception of Russia, Italy offers today the most flagrant example of journalistic terrorism in the civilized world.

* * * * *

American Bankers and Tourists on Fascism

About Bolshevism one general opinion exists, but about its blood brother Fascism, there are two such violently different opinions in America that it is hard to recognize them as relating to the same country or policy. Public opinion regarding Fascism is formed 1. — by the press: 2. — by the reports of eye-witnesses (tourists): 3. — by the propaganda of politicians and bankers.

It is an undisputable fact that the entire press in Italy is completely corrupted and that American reporters dare not tell the whole truth for fear of deportation. A vast system of propaganda in favor of Fascism counteracts the few unpleasant truths that do get printed. So, with the main fountain of intelligence polluted, it is already evident that only a perverted public opinion regarding Fascismo can exist.

The international bankers of course are out for money which is no crime. (Eventually they will be "shaking hands with murder" in Bolshevik Russia and liking it.) If I could violate a confidence I could dispose of the favorable opinion for Mussolini's régime created by American bankers by appending the name of the man who made the following statement. However, if the reader will name three of the biggest international bankers in America he will probably include the one in question.

This banker does not permit himself to be interviewed. When members of the American press suspected he was in Italy to arrange a loan of hundreds of millions, he consented to an informal talk. His name, as usual, was "not for publication." He said:

"No dictatorship is reliable, especially a one-man dictatorship. When Mussolini goes, chaos will follow. It will be worse than Bolshevik Russia in its worst days. This is the most dangerous country in Europe (outside Russia) for an international loan. Why, I could as easily float a ton of lead in New York harbor as an Italian loan in Wall Street. I do not dare betray the American people by asking them to risk their money here."

What happened in Wall Street in the next three months I cannot know, but we in Italy read with great surprise a statement from this same great international banker, which said in part: "Italy now has the soundest and safest government in Europe."

Several weeks passed silently. We were not surprised when this man floated the Italian loan easily on Wall Street's troubled waters.

So much for bankers. There remain therefore the hundreds of thousands of tourists who mould public opinion. They go on rubbernecking parties from ruin to ruin and proclaim: "Italy under Mussolini has found her soul: the trains run on time," "Mussolini has saved the country." "Mussolini is the greatest man in the world." And they are believed. Occasionally there are a few American consuls or plain citizens who have bloody experiences, and sometimes a radical comes back with the report: "Terrorism reigns in Italy." "Bloodshed and murder are daily." "Worse than Russia." "Revolution is near." These two extremist views, of course, are exaggerated. Italy's Chekah and Italy's reign of terror are neither as drastic or universal as Russia's; in quality and quantity Fascist terrorism has never approached Communist terrorism, but the amazing truth about Italy is that it is the only country where a beautiful serene surface is offered the visitor who may stay months and never see the hidden terror. Tourism and Terrorism in Italy are skilfully combined.

A thousand tourists and the writer spent the same night in Bologna. If the hundred Americans who slept tranquilly the eight dark hours in their good hotels want the exact date to compare it to their recorded diaries, it was April 8 of the year 1925. For tourism it was a perfect day. It was also a good day for terrorism.

There had been an encounter the day before between Fascists and anti-Fascists. The one fatality was a Fascist militiaman. Throughout the day of April 8 Fascist headquarters were humming with plans for vendetta, and at night the poorer section of Bologna was the scene of rioting in which hand-grenades were thrown into houses, stabbing and shooting occurred in twenty places and several names were recorded by whoever plays the county coroner.

Groups of blackshirts roamed the streets looking for blood. One band met a drunken man whom they jostled on the street. The drunkard stammered. An argument followed. The Fascists killed him with their clubs and left him in the street.

They picked quarrels with every man they met in the workers' section of Bologna. They didn't ask whether their victim was a Fascist or not. They clubbed everyone who didn't give them the street free, and they beat two more men to death.

Another group entered a *trattoria,* a cheap saloon, threw the chairs and tables about, and finding one wine-drinker ready to oppose them, shot him through the head. Throughout the night frequent explosions of war-made hand-grenades inside houses and alongside walls kept the quarter in terror. Citizens

95

bolted doors and shuttered windows and prayed. It was something like a Zeppelin night in London, a Gotha night in Paris, with the fun left out.

And the next morning, in the sunshine, a thousand careless tourists went looking at the cathedrals and the University of Bologna, and declared the city beautiful and peaceful, Fascism the God-sent restorer of public safety, Mussolini the saviour. (Five dead, 22 wounded, the Fascist victim revenged.)

The tourist has seen nothing, heard nothing, suspected nothing, but on arriving in Paris he has had his vanity fed when a reporter from Paris editions of American newspapers has given him a chance for free publicity when he will talk well of Fascism. For days, weeks, years this constant tourist drivel is published by sychophantic newspapers, every line of it impressing other tourists, and the whole lot making a body of propaganda which cannot help moulding public opinion. Here are samples of tourist bunkum, mostly from *The Paris Herald:*

Senator David A. Reed (Republican), Pennsylvania:

Washington: An eloquent and impassioned defence of Prime Minister Mussolini was made today by Senator Reed in which he depicted the Fascist chieftain not only as a saviour of Italy but as a benefactor of Europe, who saved the old world from the menace of Communism.

"Signor Mussolini has given Italy a particularly strong and stable government; he has restored order where once chaos ruled; he has increased the productive capacity of Italy and conferred happiness upon all classes, the high and the low, the rich and the poor," said the Pennsylvania solon.

Bishop Ernest M. Stires, of the Episcopal Diocese of Long Island:

"Only the personal unselfishness and the modesty of Signor Mussolini added to his great self-discipline and strength could give him the ascendancy over the Italian people enabling him to fan into purifying flame the vital spark inherent to the Italian race since the time of the Romans, thereby bringing about a new renaissance. Three years ago when I was in Italy and met Mussolini, Fascism seemed to be a noble experiment; from what I see now it appears to have become a fixed principle."

Colonel James H. Logan of Dillon, Reid & Co., international bankers:

ROME — Colonel James H. Logan of Dillon, Reid & Co., who has been visiting Rome, declares that he is impressed with the continued economic and financial development in Italy. According to Colonel Logan, this should be reckoned among the achievements of 'Italy's great son and leader,' Signor Mussolini.

" Every one who has been so fortunate as to visit frequently the great, charming, happy and hospitable country of Italy, as I have done, must surely receive the same impression," continued Colonel Logan.

Harold MacGrath, the " great " novelist:

" Having snatched his countrymen from out a chaotic state and injected verve, spirit and pep into their very souls, so much so that Italy is one of the most thriving nations in Europe today, Premier Benito Mussolini has proven himself to be the greatest leader of men in Europe since the days of Napoleon.

" Everywhere you go in the land of the boot, you are impressed by the sincerity of purpose, the diligent way they attack their work and the apparent happiness of all the Italians.

" When one stops to consider that Italy was on the brink of red-radicalism, revolution and tyrant Socialism and that Mussolini stepped in and with one mighty grasp of the reins brought the entire nation to its senses, one must give credit to whom it is due.

" The greatest cankers that have existed there, the Mafia, Camorra and the Black Hand are now things of the past. The great secret organizations that formerly held Italy in dreaded fear have been stripped of their mask by the premier, so that they can no longer operate.

" The strongest attribute that strikes all of those that have had the good fortune to talk with Mussolini is absolute sincerity."

S. S. McClure (In his youth a publisher for muckrakers):

" Italy is undergoing a bloodless revolution, and it is only partly completed. It is accomplishing what could not be done by parliamentary debate. In my study of governments for twenty-five years I found in Italy the first contribution to the science and theory of good government since the founding of the American Republic. The Italians have real self-government. The difference between the government of America and that of Italy is theoretical rather than actual. If three or more men quit work in Italy, they could be arrested and the attempted strike ended.

"Just how do the people of Italy feel about the new government?" Mr. McClure was asked.

"They feel," he replied, "they are the only free people in the world. They are free from caprice and oppression."

Vera Bloom, semi-journalistic daughter of no less a person than the grandiose American congressman Sol Bloom, Esq.:

"Premier Mussolini has sold to the Italians the idea that Italy is a worthwhile enterprise, and he is making them invest in it willingly. They do nine hours worth of work for eight hours pay, they curtail their use of white flour, but what does Mussolini himself do? He gets a salary of less than $1,000 a year and lives in a small bachelor apartment of a friend at Rome. He has taken his tremendous personality and impressed it upon the people in the last three years so that one sees a change that is almost miraculous and he continues to impress himself upon them.

"But even though the latter may be true, it is a great fallacy to believe that Mussolini is a two-faced actor. When he appeals to his people at a public assemblage in a dramatic manner, he is intensely sincere, just as he is intensely sincere when he is sombre in a few hours later in his office. He has a characteristic that many Italians possess — that of living fully and ardently every situation in which they find themselves placed."

Cultured men and women, humanitarians, leaders of organized labor, liberal college professors, broad-minded lawyers, liberal preachers and untrammelled writers also visit Italy and come to Paris, but I have never seen their views on Fascismo played up in the Paris editions. Balance the foregoing expressions with the following, which certainly cannot be called the expression of trashy writers, corporation attorneys, lickspittle politicians, publicity seekers, venal editors, narrow-minded reactionaries, or loan raising bankers, and wonder why these American papers never find a non-conformist opinion regarding their pet theory and dictator:

William F. Green, president of the American Federation of Labor:

" The American Federation of Labor will work with you (the anti-Fascist Alliance of North America) until we have succeeded in driving Fascism from the face of the earth. I am deeply in sympathy with the anti-Fascist movement. I should like to call it the movement of human freedom and human liberty.

" Fascism stands for repression and denial of freedom and democracy, and any movement which is seeking to deny natural expression to the human race, is an enemy to society."

Professor F. W. Taussig of Harvard:

" The Mussolini régime seems to me hateful, and full of danger for Italy and almost so for other countries. I cannot but believe that eventually it will come to a complete crash, and I hope the end will come soon."

Professor E. A. Rose, University of Wisconsin:

" Fascism is the most sinister thing that moves on the political stage today. It behooves us to look closely at the case of this beast in Italy, for in every society there are elements which yearn to stamp democracy into the dust and bring the people under the yoke of condottieri paid and supported by the rich."

Charles Nagel, former secretary of commerce and labour:

" If Italy's affairs could be confined to her own borders, well and good. But this can never be. The policy of Mussolini means repression at home and expansion abroad. Its unprovoked threats of war, without cause or excuse, are a menace to the peace of the world, in which we are directly interested. But apart from the immediate effect upon Italian conditions, the influence upon civilization generally must be deplored."

Rev. John A. Ryan, professor, Catholic University, Washington, D. C.:

" In principle, Fascism is naked political absolutism rejecting representative government and upholding government by force operated by persons who regard themselves as alone qualified to govern. Formal refutation of this theory is superfluous. As applied in Italy, Fascism has destroyed liberty of speech, of the press, of assemblage and association, and has likewise abolished local self-government and democratic representation. ' By their fruits you shall know them.' "

Louis Marshall, lawyer:

" To those who regard the liberty of the individual as a sacred right, Fascism is an abhorrent reversion to the brutality of primitive man. In essence it is despotism and tyranny. It means the overthrow of the noblest ideals of mankind achieved after centuries of struggle — free thought, free speech, a free press, the free choice by an untrammelled ballot of representatives protected in the exercise of their political functions and free from the ever-threatening menace of dictatorship, whether it be that of monarch or mob. Fascism is a new form of slavery. It may flourish for a time, but like all its prototype it is doomed to destruction."

Robert Morse Lovett, professor, University of Chicago:

" The Fascist régime is a complete repudiation of all that has been gained in the last two centuries in political democracy, and control by the people of their common interests . . . a return to the age of the despots without the enlightenment and toleration which individuals among these manifested. The danger to all Europe from such a dictatorship is evident. The crusade which President Wilson preached against governments not responsible to the will of their own people, has direct application to the dictatorship of Mussolini.

" The peace of the world rests on the mutual goodwill of free peoples. Italy is today a menace to that peace, a heavy liability to the cause for which Wilson called on his countrymen to fight. It is disheartening to find Americans who were most active in insisting that such a call should be made, now supporting with their influence and their loans a régime so hostile to all that this country assumes to represent."

Professor Holcombe of Harvard:

" Mussolini's first years do not augur well for Italy or for Europe. The most ominous symptom is his apparent disposition to increase rather than diminish his reliance upon force and violence. Long ago Machiavelli pointed out the error of that policy."

The Truth About Fascist Terrorism and Censorship

Rev. John Haynes Holmes, minister, Community Church, New York:

"Fascism is without exception the most dangerous and despicable power now existing in Europe. It is the incarnation of force which has not in this case the excuse of liberation and enlargement of life for the multitudes, as in Russia, but represents a frank reversion to old ways of tyranny and death.

"The megalomania of its leader, Mussolini, is the perfect symbol of its essential character of madness. At one stroke Fascism has robbed Italy of the glory bestowed upon her by Mazzini and his compeers, and may at any moment plunge Europe into the vast disaster of another war. While Fascism endures there can be no freedom for Italy, no security for the world. To protest against the Fascist despotism, to expose its injustice and horror, to labour for its overthrow, is a first duty to the cause of human liberty."

Felix Adler, leader, American Ethical Culture Society:

"Democracy is challenged today on two sides: by the Soviet minority which rules Russia, and by the Italian dictator, who would substitute discipline for liberty, the control of the economic forces of a nation for self-government, and dangerous imperialistic ambition as the motive for consolidating and subordinating the nation.

"The poignant challenge comes from these two directions, and with the exception of a few commendable utterances there seems to be no pronounced reaction in the United States. Have we no publicists potent enough to take up the challenge?"

It is a balance of Brains versus Babbittry, but the Babbitt tourists, who are in the same proportion in Europe as in America, have succeeded in maintaining the myth of peace, contentment, freedom, liberty in Italy — thanks to a rotten press.

I have already quoted an experience during a riot in Bologna. Take, again, the case of ten thousand tourists during an election. Of course elections in Italy always did entail some disorders, and it is certain that the Opposition to Mussolini did not hesitate to exaggerate tales of this violence, but it is also true that even if the American tourists had numbered a million that day, the election could have been held without ten of them feeling the state of terror which existed.

Rome, Milan, Florence, Naples, Venice hardly felt this terror; only the workers' sections where tourists never go, saw the disorders. But throughout the country it spread like a nightmare. The newspapermen in Rome who remained in the capital saw and felt nothing. But throughout the country-side the terror reigned and Fascism won.

Many an anti-Fascist head was split that day. In every town and village the local blackshirt organization armed with black-jacks, revolvers, knives, drove the faithful to the ballot-boxes; attacked the Opposition; they broke ballot-boxes; stuffed them; reported majorities where none existed. Castor oil was administered to protestants. It was like a state of martial law in which illegal elements enforced illegal methods to obtain an illegal end.

An English woman journalist, representative of an American newspaper, and an ardent friend of Fascism, went from Rome to Molinella because she wanted to disprove statements that terrorism existed in the country-side. She was surrounded by Fascist militia and, despite her protestations of love for the Duce and all his works, was driven from town. In a village near Mantua a young American sent by a Rome correspondent was arrested, not by the government police, but by Fascists, taken to party headquarters, cross-examined, and because he was an American he escaped a beating and a dose of castor oil. But he was driven from town. He did, however, see something of the terrorism. Blackshirts controlled the polls. Opposition voters were not permitted to cast votes. At Fascist headquarters a list of proscriptions was being checked up, absent voters were being accounted for and Opposition voters were being marked with a cross for future reprisals.

As he was escorted to the outskirts of the village and told to go to Rome, the Fascist leader gave him the following warning:

" The tourists must stay in the cities. The country is no place for them during an election."

The American tourist hears nothing, sees nothing, understands nothing. He finds the surface serene and bursts into print in *Heralds* and *Tribunes* with his discovery. If he went to Russia with an open mind, to that terroristic Russia which still shoots the Opposition down every night in the Chekah prisons, he would have to report even a sweeter Utopia of freedom and liberty under the Soviets.

Because the Soviet terror is even more secret than the Fascist; they order things better over there.

Chapter II

"The Sword," Cries Mussolini

AFTER Wilson and Lenin, Lloyd George and Trotsky, my hope was set on meeting the hero of our time, the only hundred per cent. dictator, Mussolini. But I did not want to ask him political questions. I was sick of politics and I hoped he was the same. He had given so many useless political interviews and I had written so many useless thousands of words. I wanted to know what manner of man he was and what he did out of dictatorial hours. But when I did interview Mussolini I could not print the whole story. There was censorship in Rome, there was censorship in my editorial office, and there was my fear of expulsion if I dared write one uncomplimentary word. Only in a book can the truth be told.

I first met Mussolini at the Palazzo Venezia. This noble building had been outlined in flares one midsummer night in the year when some of the formalities of freedom were still observed in Italy, for the meeting was to mark the opening of the nationalist Fascist election campaign against the Opposition.

All the minor heroes of Fascismo were there, the politicians and the warriors, talking their heads and hands off. They were in the tapestried marble hall, a thousand of them, men who had discarded the black shirt that night for the more conventional black evening clothes, and they were impatient for their chieftain, their Duce. The hall was shimmering in waves of light. There was but one dark mass, the heavy velvet curtain nearest the rostrum.

Suddenly through this black velvet curtain a white hand appears, disembodied, thrilling, like a spiritual seance. The white hand, fist flat, rises quickly, appears over the heads of the thousand heroes, so that falling silent and looking up, they immediately recognize the Roman salute, the sign of greeting of their order, and recovering from their silent surprise with a rumbling of a thousand men in movement, they acknowledge the Fascist signal.

Then, into the now whisperless super-lighted room, emerges from the black mass of curtain behind the white hand growing into an arm and then a man, the dark figure of Benito Mussolini, successor to the Caesars in Rome, founder of the third New Italy, self-styled Napoleon, and — actor extraordinary.

*   *   *   *   *

> *" Giovinezza! Giovinezza!*
> *Primavera di bellezza! "*

The thouand leaders of Fascismo sing as soldiers sang, full throated and gaily: Mussolini raises his hand again and there is silence. Then he speaks.

He began coldly, in a voice northern and unimpassioned. I had never heard an Italian orator so restrained. Then he changed, became soft and warm, added gestures, and flames in his eyes. The audience moved with him. He held them. Suddenly he lowered his voice to a heavy whisper and the silence among the listeners became more intense. The whisper sank lower and the listeners strained breathlessly to hear. Then Mussolini exploded with thunder and fire, and the mob — for it was no more than a mob now — rose to its feet and shouted. Immediately Mussolini became cold and nordic and restrained again and swept his mob into its seats, exhausted.

An actor. Actor extraordinary, with a country for a stage, a great powerful histrionic ego, swaying an audience of millions, confounding the world by his theatrical cleverness.

When I began plotting my interview I asked friends of the Duce to tell salient stories of his youth and career. Was he always acting a part? Did he give signs in his boyhood of a consuming ego? Was he a leader? A superman?

When a boy, said one who knew him, Benito led a gang which robbed orchards. He did not share in the spoils; he was content with the glory; he played the hero. At Forli, his birthplace, he distinguished himself one day when some learned professor failed to arrive for a lecture on some literary topic. Benito sprang to the platform and held discourse. One day his mother, to whom he like Napoleon says he owes everything he is or hopes to be, heard him pacing his room, shouting, gesticulating wildly.

" What is the matter — are you ill? " she cried.

" Do not worry, mother," he replied, " I will become a great man. Italy will tremble before me."

And later, as a rebel, an international Socialist, hammering at society just as his rebel father, the Forli village blacksmith, hammered horseshoes, he faced trial for anti-militarist activities. He was then the editor of *La Lotta di Classe* — The Class Struggle — which urged Italians not to enlist for the war in Tripoli. Found guilty, Mussolini addressed the court:

" If I were in your place I would sentence such a fellow as I. If you should free me you would do me a favour. If you convict me, you do me an honour."

And that was the first time that Mussolini went to jail for

his radicalism. Of a year's term he spent six months in a cell feeding his rage against bourgeois society, studying Karl Marx and other Socialist philosophers, and tightening his determination to be a leader of the people. He came back to them a martyr to the cause of Socialism. He enjoyed his martyrdom thoroughly, and, like most other modern martyrs to that cause, he exploited it fully. The mob of radicals paid homage to him. He accepted it with dignity and led the mob.

And among the stories of his more recent shows of superiority and histrionic egotism, there is one which concerns his duelling lessons. In aggression he was superb. The instructor said:

" I will now teach you retrocession."

" Why? " demanded Mussolini.

" You must learn to defend yourself when your enemy presses too hard."

" That will never be *my* strategy," replied Mussolini nobly.

*   *   *   *   *

So I studied his character in those doubtful days while I was waiting for the interview. Finally all the doors of the Palazzo Chigi opened. A blue and gold flunkey pushed apart the last barrier revealing an enormous museum-like room, gloomy, hung with dark paintings, empty but for a few chairs, a great globe on its stand, and at the farthest corner, the dictator of Italy, the most interesting man of our era.

On the right of his desk was a battery of telephones, four or five, and he was speaking through one, as all Latins speak, passionately and with illustrative motions of the free hand, which, alas, his auditor was missing. I had an interpreter with me in case my fallow French of A. E. F. days should fail, and we halted on the threshold. Mussolini rang off. Without looking up he made notes on a pad, and while his eyes were still on his pencil he cried:

" Avanti."

It was like the command of an officer.

We advanced our positions at least ten yards. (The room was enormous, fit for a museum.) He let us stand at the side of his desk, as he lets all his interviewers stand, until they become somewhat nervous, then he arose, extended a hand quickly, motioned to a chair.

" Dunque! " he exclaimed, " you have asked to see me. Ecco-mi! Here I am. . . ."

" And to ask a few questions."

" No questions," with a definitive gesture.

" But — "

" I never answer questions."

He frowned. He pouted. His eyebrows came down over his wonderfully large, expressive, fine Italian eyes. Yet he seemed to be acting again.

" No questions about politics," I hastened to explain, " but about you, your life. . . ."

" There are books — read the books."

" But I want to know the things that are not in books. I want to know neither the history nor the politics of Mussolini, but the human Mussolini, the man who plays the violin and has lion cubs for pets, the man who does not touch spirits or wine, the man who . . ."

" Because drinking is useless," he interposed at the word " wine," and suddenly he smiled and added " I have never been interviewed that way. Tiens. It would amuse me. Pro-ceed."

" You have given up alcohol? "

" Yes. There is but one explanation. Alcohol bores me. Alcohol is useless. But I am no bigot. I read with amusement and sympathy all the efforts to make or keep America dry, all the efforts to restore wine and beer. I say, let those who want it, drink. I would not infringe upon the personal liberty of any man. If the Italian people want their chianti, they shall keep it. If they feel it makes life brighter, so much the better. But as for me — water."

" And your hobby is the violin ? "

" From childhood. I must thank my sainted mother. I was a quiet lad, and I found joy in music. Now it is my refuge. People have said sometimes ironically that music sometimes brings tears to my eyes. As if it were a sign of weakness! But I am not ashamed to admit it. I play — always — now — in the midst of all the cares of state, yes, in fact, when the cares of state are heaviest. And I suppose," he added, " that my enemies, for want of something better, will say, ' Mussolini, like Nero, plays the violin when Rome burns,' but I do not care. In music I find rest! "

Now as he spoke about his hobby he became a changed man. All of his first pose, the actor's pose, was gone. Gone the frown and the scowl and the pouting lips, and his forehead cleared of the furrows, even revealing that one of them was a large scar. He not only smiled gently but a pleasant fire was kindled in his eyes. He became real and human.

" Music for me," he said, " means Italian music. I like the German's too, but Italian music, seventeen hundred to eighteen hundred, appeals to me most. My favorite composer is Vivaldi." And he added dreamily, " Music must be an experience of the heart and soul. It is the one experience that brings us into relationship with all that is divine. . . ."

At that word " Divine," I wanted to ask abruptly: " In what do you believe? " but thought such a question undiplomatic. Years before Mussolini in his Socialist speeches and writings had acknowledged himself agnostic, if not wholly atheist, but since coming into power he had engaged upon a constructive program of rapprochement with the Catholic church.

He had first of all restored the crucifix to the schools, later permitted priests to give religious instruction in them and finally raised the cross in the Coloseum, thereby atoning for an affront from Garibaldi many years ago.

Of course, the Catholic Fascisti used these facts to point the redemption of Mussolini's soul. His enemies, however, called it hypocrisy — political expediency — religious opportunism, of a match with his political opportunism. To seek the aid of the church, to make a friend of the Pope in a land where all the voters and all his own followers are Catholics, was simple strategy. Mussolini, argued the realists, had not been " converted " or " saved." In the old days when he was a radical agitator preaching the dictatorship of the proletariat and materialism *über alles,* he had cared little for God or the Devil. He was an agnostic and a fatalist.

" Are you still a fatalist? " I asked.

" I am," he replied. " All I believe in is a star of destiny. I am a fatalist in that I believe that what must happen must happen and nothing can change the destiny of any man. That is my religion in its entirety.

" I have lived according to it. I have no fear. I am not afraid of anything in this world. I am not afraid of life. I am not afraid of death.

" I believe in my star of destiny. I go up in an airplane. It falls. I am wounded. I am not afraid. I go up again. It falls.

I have no fear. I drive my car — I am a speeder you know," (with a vast smile) "and I run into the gates of a railroad crossing, lowered to let a train go by. I crash. I am seriously hurt. But my nerves are not shaken. Why? Because I have no fear, because I believe it is all so written in the star of my destiny which alone is my guide, my present and my future."

(Could he have read Napoleon's: "I have become great through the influence of my star," I wondered. Much that he had said and was to say savoured of that other Italian dictator who shook the world. Napoleon himself liked to imagine himself a reincarnation of Charlemagne or Caesar; Mussolini, it is no secret, not only believes himself the successor of Caesar and Napoleon but kin to the latter. He is in fact Napoleon — Napoleon Bonaparte stripped of his Concordat, his Constitutions, his great Napoleonic Code and the Napoleonic victories.)

Like Napoleon, Mussolini says he owes much of his religious and political views to books. Character and career, he says, were greatly influenced by what he read. He prepared himself for mastery in quiet libraries and in hall bedrooms, when he came home weary from a day's manual labor. Then it was he pondered the philosophers. Essentially Mussolini is a book-made Hero-Conqueror.

"My whole life," he told me, "has been shaped by what I read. Sorel, Machiavelli, Nietzsche, have been my friends, counsellors, instructors. To each I owe a great debt. Machiavelli I have studied from page to page. (*Cf.* Napoleon's Machiavelli and Plato.) For the conduct of public affairs, such as I perceive them, there is no better guide than Machiavelli even today. I not only study every word of his advice but I put his ideas into life.

"Nietzsche, I must admit, has influenced me more than any

man alive or dead. Those who know Nietzsche will under-stand. His ' Will to Power ' I took as a personal message. . . .''

Even at the mention of these words Mussolini clenched both fists and seemed to radiate power from his massive face.

" Sklavenmoral," he exclaimed, " the morality of slaves, that is what the world is made up of today. We are ' Human, all too Human.' Our ideas of good and evil are old and stupid — we must look ' Beyond Good and Evil ' toward ' The New Day ' when the present religions of all peoples, which are the religions of enslaved minds, will be replaced by ' The Will to Power,' the motive force of the Superman."

He showed he knew Nietzsche thoroughly, even to that ridiculous discussion which once followed the publication of one of Nietzsche's phrases, torn from its setting, and given to the world by sensational newspapers as a mad German phi-losopher's guide for the treatment of women: " Thou goest to women, do not forget thy whip."

Mussolini smiled at this and coined his own epigram:

" La fortuna è donna — bisogna prenderla e batterla." " For-tune is a woman — you must seize her and beat her." And laughing quietly, he added: " Frequently the best proof of a man's love for a woman is shown in beating her."

But this is part of his misogynistic pose. He has read that there is no place for women in the lives of philosophers and emperors, and pretending that he is both, he has let himself be influenced by such Nietzschean precepts as please him. In Rome Mussolini has a large reputation as a Don Juan. His physicians, his intimates and his political cronies love to delight even foreign correspondents with tales of Mussolini's amorous adventures and easy conquests in an idol-worshipping land. But for public interviews Mussolini prefers to paint himself kin to that Kipling hero who rises to heights and who travels the fastest because he travels alone.

This self-announced misogyny of course has only served to intrigue all the women who come near him, the nobility, the theatre, even the visiting "lady" journalists. Women who would guard their secret of any illicit love-affair with a lesser mortal, are proud to entertain social gatherings with details of the hero's love-making. When Mussolini himself is discreet they can at least describe his *garçonniere* in a little side street not far from the palace. Paul Morand writes somewhere a little interview with Miss Constance B—— whom he asked what she thought of Il Duce.

"Mussolini," replied Constance, "is the greatest man of our time. I interviewed him about two weeks ago — look! My arms are still black and blue."

Signora Rachela Mussolini is in "exile." Her husband has done handsomely by her, he has provided her and his "first series of children" and the "first of his second series" as he so delicately called his new son, with a better apartment than they ever had in days of his poverty, and does he not call to see them all once a year? On this grand occasion all the photographers are invited to be present and to make as many exposures as they wish of scenes of connubial perfection and bliss. But Signora must not visit the capital or otherwise interfere with the career of the hero.

She is a daughter of the proletariat and was a fitting companion and housewife for a struggling man. But Mussolini outgrew her when he quit waving the red shirt and put on the black, so making a virtue of his marital failure, he boasts the philosophy of Schopenhauer and Nietzsche.

Let the great man have his little jest! Brilliant or beautiful women take up a large part of Mussolini's life. Spiritual consolation at least he has found in the friendship of a marquesa, a leader of the women Fascisti, and although he professes to hate high society and the dramatic stage, he is credited with many a conquest among noble ladies and footlight stars.

But we did not linger long on the dangerous ground of sex relationship. In an impasse I asked: " What would you say was the turning point in your life . . ."

". . . from Socialist to patriot," supplemented my interpreter. To this addition Mussolini objected.

"No. That is wrong. I have always been a patriot. Even when I was a radical Socialist. Socialist and patriot are not incompatible."

"Well, from internationalist to nationalist patriot," I suggested.

"The turning point was the war," the dictator then resumed. "The war showed the world plainly, I think, the utter bankruptcy of internationalism. We had been fighting for a hollow fraud. I had fought for internationalism all my life, preached it, gone to prison for that same cause, and suddenly the war came, and I realized first that internationalism was dead, because it had never really lived, and that I had a real duty in life, and that was to my country."

I made a long pretence of writing all this down while my brain itched to ask him a question I dared not ask. I had made one such *faux pas* years ago, in 1909, when I was a cub in Pittsburgh and my city editor, being a staunch Republican hireling, had sent me to interview William Jennings Bryan and to ask him if he would run for president again. How I trembled in the presence of the Great Man, that day, in the big room in the Fort Pitt hotel. I trembled, yet I had to ask, and I did.

"Get out of here," roared the silver tongued mountain, "get out quick, you are the most impertinent cub I've ever met."

It made a good Republican story, but I have learned self-censorship since. So I did not ask whether the 400,000 francs (more or less) with which the French government subsidized the Milan newspaper of which Mussolini was the editor, had any bearing on his discovery of his patriotic duty on the side of the Allies, suddenly, in 1915. We talked about the war. Of this there is agreement among friends and enemies alike: Mussolini was a good soldier. He joined the Bersaglieri, distinguished himself in the mountain trenches, was wounded with some thirty splinters of a hand-grenade, was promoted, and at the terrible defeat of Caporetto, a name which you dare hardly whisper in Italy even today, Mussolini was seen to weep freely. This fact is much talked about. Because Mussolini, legend has it, has cried but twice in his life, the first time, also during the war, when his mother died at home, in Forli.

Mussolini recorded his experiences in his book *"Il Mio Diario de Guerra,"* a fairly honest document despite the inevitable posing which goes into all diaries.

"I am not a militarist," he said, resuming the interview.

Then I remembered a question, trite in itself, but interesting in relation to the man. Both Trotsky and Mussolini were journalists, and both had become heads of armies. Both were expert with pen and sword. One day I had asked Trotsky in the Kremlin, in Moscow, "Which do *you* think is mightier, the sword or the pen?" and Trotsky, chief then of a movement which had sprung full grown from the head of the great god Propaganda, had replied: "The Pen."

"The Sword," replied Mussolini.

"But why?"

"Because it cuts."

"Cuts?"

"Yes. Cuts. Ends things. *Finish.*" This last word in English, with both the i's pronounced like double e's, thus, "feeneesh."

"The time comes," added Mussolini, "when there must be an end to idle talk, idle writing. *Dio mio,* we have too much of it in this world. Words. Words. Words. And then, one blow — the sword — it is all over. It is decided. It is finished. What was Fascismo? Talk. For years. And then one day, the march on Rome. The sword is drawn. The old order is finished.

"Yes, I believe in action, I believe in the sword. But please explain to your readers who might think I talk militarism, that I am not a militarist. I do believe that when the limit has been reached, when it is a last necessity, as an extreme it must be the sword. That alone, not the pen, can end intolerable things. The sword is decisive. It cuts."

Home from the war, with the scars of battle, Mussolini was to learn that the rapier also cuts. He was to add new scars through duels. He had become editor of the *Popolo d'Italia,* and had made enemies of all his old Socialist friends who were refusing to recognize that a new era was opening for Italy and who were attacking him as a renegade and deserter from their cause. He fought three duels. Fencing remains a great sport with him, but it has not replaced riding or automobiling or flying. When I began questioning him about sports he was happy again. When I had mentioned music he had become human; on the subject of sports he actually became friendly.

"I love all sports," he said in a voice which embraced them.

" I want more sports for Italy. For myself, I prefer those which have danger in them. Live dangerously! I hate saturated men. Man's best qualities are brought out by the dangerous life — energy, power, pride. I fence. I fly an airplane. Look! " and he pointed to a scar across his forehead which had made an artificial furrow — " this is a reminder of the time I fell in flames. I have crashed twice. But I am an enthusiast for air-planing and I must live to see the time when the air will be black with them, when they will darken the sun and cast shadows over the peasants' fields like swift travelling rain clouds."

*   *   *   *   *

Mussolini's co-workers in the Foreign Office, the Palazzo Chigi, had told me that much as the Duce loved the open-air life, he hated the indoor social whirl. Mussolini could rule Roman society had he such ambitions. But when he put aside his wife he put aside such temptations — and saved himself from the errors of other statesmen. He was asked to join the Club de la Caccia, composed of noblemen exclusively, and did so. He came to one reception, was initiated, but rarely afterwards went there again. Idle noblemen bore him. Society bores him. The man of action prefers the simple life.

" Do you have time for the theatre? " I asked, wondering what he did with all his evenings.

" I do not care for the theatre," Mussolini replied. " It seems to me there is enough sadness in life, enough tragedy, without a repetition on the stage. As for comedy and farce, musical shows and all that, no man who has ambition and a rôle to play in this world, need waste his time on them. Tragedy is what the theatre is for — for those who need that catharsis. I do not.

Nor do I go to the café — in a land where national politics have always been made in cafés."

"So of course you do not care for the movies," I ventured.

"Ah, but I do," he hastened to reply, "that is, comedies — American comedies. I care for no other films, European or American. The attempt to create serious movies in America leaves me unmoved. They are nearly all sickly in their sentimentality, puritanical and filled with such unbelievable bunkum as to make any European burst with amazement to find such trashy naïveté still existing. But your comedies! Need I mention Carlino — Charles Chaplin? That is where the American film approaches a great art and has a value. The American comedies are among the best things we get from America and I never miss them."

We discussed American art and letters for a while, American customs and manners.

"Is it true you once planned emigrating to America?"

"Yes. When I was nineteen — a political exile working in Switzerland. I thought I would like to try my fortune in America as so many Italians did at that time. I intended to engage in my calling of that time. I was a mason. Well, I tossed a coin." He went silent, meditating, he seemed to see that coin spinning in the air, falling, sending him to America, to be swallowed, obliterated in the ranks of labor-union masons in New York.

"Youth — youth," he sighed, "a dream — a dream. I wonder — what would have become of me in America? Had I gone over as an emigrant what would I be now?"

Could I reply that I thought his talents as an actor at least could never have been lost?

*   *   *   *   *

118

I was to see Mussolini almost a score of times before my
expulsion. If this was Nietzsche's Superman I must study him
closely. So I attended every session of Parliament and watched
him from my office window in the Galleria Colonna whenever
he came out to address his followers clamouring outside the
Palazzo Chigi just opposite.

In Parliament he sat, a bored and thirsty lion, tugging
with the last chains which bound him to democratic government. He paid no attention to the speakers; sometimes when
the Communists and the Fascists quarrelled (the other five
parties had gone on strike after the murder of the Deputy
Matteotti) he showed a wan interest. Frequently black coffee
was brought him on a tray and he drank to overcome his
sleepiness.

So the debates would run endlessly.

Suddenly: —

" Basta! "

" Enough! "

With a smash of his fist Mussolini would rise to his feet
and break the flow of words. " Basta! We have had too much
talk. Now we will vote. You will now pass the resolution as I
have prepared it."

The vote would be taken — as he had prepared it.

Thus one day, with a noble gesture of a modern emanci-
pator he gave women the vote and received the applause
of the Marquesa Piccolomini and other gaily-dressed noble
ladies of Rome who had brightened the galleries. Shortly
afterwards, in accordance with the long laid program of
Fascismo, he abolished the right to vote of both men and
women.

At the Augusteo another day I heard the Duce make the

famous speech which severed him finally from all pretences of democracy and free human institutions as the rest of the world, with the exception of Russia, understands them and struggles for them. Not only did he declare democracy a failure and the Parliamentary system of government dead, but he spoke for the Terror.

"La violenza è profondamenta morale," he said, " più morale del compromesso e dello transazione." (Violence is profoundly moral, more moral than compromise and dealings.)

One of Ibsen's *Enemies of the People* might have said that. Surely it would have been applauded too in Nietzsche's Superman, and it was heartily applauded by the mob in the Augusteo which applauded every time Mussolini stopped for applause. But a few days later some Fascisti attacked a Catholic procession, and the Pope in an address to a pilgrimage from Perugino blamed this declaration for the act of violence, thus showing the gulf between theory and practice in a rather sudden way.

Superman as he undoubtedly appears to the vast majority of this world's population, Mussolini was not able then, nor is he able to this day, to explain away to the satisfaction of non-Fascists the assassination of Matteotti.

Matteotti stood in Mussolini's way, just as other men have stood in the path of Caesars and Neros, Napoleons and Robespierres. And there is the sworn testimony of former aides who have fled the country that Mussolini said "Remove that man."

Matteotti was removed. Mussolini's closest friends murdered Matteotti — and two years later confessed the whole miserable affair. It is the cruellest crime in the long criminal record of Fascismo. No one can deny that unleashed violence has marked the reign and that bloodshed was an almost daily occurrence for several years. Nor can anyone deny that the Anti-Fascists killed many enemies. Workingmen, policemen, journalists, priests, landlords, shopkeepers were slain in riots and brawls and plots. But party-planned political assassination startled Europe almost as much as Sarajevo. Giaccomo Matteotti is to Mussolini's conscience what the Duke of Enghien was to Napoleon. At St. Helena Napoleon until almost his dying day exposed his tortured soul by continual defence of the duke's assassination. Mussolini has shown no remorse. Nor has his press yet been able to disprove the Rossi and Filipelli confessions, the Aventine documents and all the evidence necessarily given abroad by refugees, of which I give extracts elsewhere.

* * * * *

Because there was nothing outwardly important about Lenin, whom I saw several times during my year in Russia and talked to twice, Mussolini remains the most impressive public personality of my eighteen newspaper years. Europe regards Mussolini as its strongest man, now that Lenin's mantle no longer covers one person but a group. Recently I had occasion to ask Dr. Alfred Adler of Vienna, founder of the school of individual psychology, to discuss Mussolini as Superman.

Dr. Adler said he considered Mussolini the product of an intense inferiority feeling acquired in childhood from a Socialist blacksmith father and a doting mother. With Mussolini it is not strong enough to be called an inferiority complex, for complexes might drive one into an insane asylum, where many of his enemies think Mussolini now belongs, but a just strong enough feeling of inferiority to compensate itself in extraordinary shows of superiority in recent years.

"Inferiority," continued Dr. Adler, " is a natural feeling. We must not be ashamed of it but must admit it and fight it. We all have it, you and I and Coolidge and Mr. Tunney, and the milkman, and of course Mussolini. In fact Mussolini, from all one learns by reading about his early life and studying his history, had a particularly hard case of inferiority feeling, consequently today his expression of superiority is so violent.

"Nations and individuals, you can study their psychology in the same manner. The present reactionary movement in many countries of Europe, the arrival and successes of dictators, and the intense nationalistic movements accompanied by so many proclamations of superiority, are particularly striking in countries either crushed during the war or generally suffering from an intense feeling of inferiority.

"Italy the nation and Mussolini the man synchronize in movement. Mussolini's father was a rebel; he wanted to reform society; he was a Socialist, a syndicalist of some sort. His mother was superior mentally to the father and the neighbouring peasantry, but too much the kind, doting mother who is responsible for so many difficult cases of inferiority feeling. The father wove rebellion into the child's inevitable sense of inferiority.

"Benito Mussolini as a child suffered the slings and arrows of various misfortunes, and as a youth found Socialist activity the one outlet for his strife with his inferiority feeling.

"I quite agree with H. G. Wells that Socialism is an expression of the inferiority feeling of the perpetually disinherited. Certainly the depressed and oppressed and suppressed of the world, the unhappy and the have-nothings, do suffer from a more intense feeling of inferiority, and certainly the strife is more severe and very often the reaction, the compensation, the arrival of the feeling of superiority, is more violent.

" The whipped, starved, unloved slum child becomes a bank robber or a gunman; his subconscious battle with his feeling of inferiority sends him shooting and robbing. The gunman sees himself a romantic hero, bold and brave, and he may even go to the scaffold with a noble song on his lips — it is all part of the same behaviour pattern, woven by suppression and cruelty and endless sufferings in the first years of life, the years of the birth and intensification of inferiority which require almost a lifetime to overcome.

" Mussolini became dictator through violence, the violence of the gunman on a national scale, and he rules through violence, stimulating a meek people to shake off the unseen, terrible chains of inferiority and become brave and successful, full of pride, respected in the society of nations, conquering and ruling and altogether superior.

" The more intense the inferiority, as I have said, the more violent the superiority. Such is the equation. Mussolini's life shouts it: so does the history of modern Italy. It accounts for all that you find in that man and that people today. It accounts for their threat to the peace of the world. It accounts for that bombardment of Corfu which astonished the world, for the defiance of other smaller, weaker nations, all the sword rattling which keeps France mobilizing troops on her side of the frontier, for the threat to England in Malta and Cyprus and Gibraltar, for the re-use of Bismarck's historic expression, usually credited to Kaiser Wilhelm, "Our future lies on the sea," which you see posted up in Rome today; for the attempt to spread Italian culture in the Austrian Tyrol as a holy crusade; and it accounts for the forcible suppression of all individualistic movements which oppose Fascism or advocate liberalism and democracy and personal liberty or in any way differ from the dictator's formula.

"Men and nations cannot bear to feel inferior. Strife for power develops. Robespierre the aristocrat, Marat the sansculotte, Mussolini the downtrodden Socialist, each sought the equation for his individual inferiority. By a turn of fate the Socialist party crushed Mussolini, where he had already found considerable compensation and power, so he sought a larger outlet for his driving force.

"After the war Europe was full of discounted gentlemen. France had been that way before her revolution. The men who grasp power in time of hesitation need not necessarily be great — their contemporaries are too small. The clever man, the orator, the organizer, wins easily when the other leaders of parties are discounted and weak. Italy needed satisfaction. It wanted the world to value her. Mussolini promised satisfaction and valuation. Napoleon came and was successful in a similar period of history.

"The behaviour pattern of persons can be studied from their relations to three things: to society, to work, to sex. The feeling of inferiority affects the man's relations to society, work, sex. But there is no 'complex,' no need to consult an expert unless a man says, 'I cannot work. I cannot love. I have no friends.' Mussolini's behaviour pattern is quite clear in two things — society and work. Of what is generally whispered regarding his 'superiority complex' in sex I cannot judge. History will have to study that too as it has studied the sex expressions of Napoleon and other conquerors.

"Mussolini as Superman? I do not think so. Mussolini as super-Italian? That is evident. Mussolini as the personification of man's battle with inferiority — that is one way history must regard him."

Chapter III

THE POPE AND FASCISM

THE Vatican holds itself aloof from the usual methods of governmental propaganda: there are no press conferences, no confidential sources, no " well-informed circles," no " semi-official authority." Therefore every correspondent knows that the subject " what the Vatican thinks " about world affairs is a dangerous one, and in place of government censorship or police censorship, you have self-censorship. Great care is exercised and very little sent about Vatican politics although it plays so great a rôle in European affairs.

Every week for months Monsignor X——, whom I will identify only as a priest who was the advisor of the Pope when the latter was Cardinal in Poland and who today occupies the same confidential position, came to my office to discuss politics with Signor Cianfarra, my Italian assistant, a cultured, broadminded liberal, a friend of Amendola and yet no narrow enemy of Fascismo. From these conversations I learned much of the relationship of Catholicism to Fascism.

I had come to Rome under the impression that the Pope was the friend of the atheist Mussolini, and that Catholics the world over shared this view. I had heard at least a hundred Americans say, " Whatever may be said against Mussolini as a dictator, we American Catholics are for him because he is the first Italian premier to be fair to our religion. He has restored the cross to the public schools and permitted the reintroduction of religious instruction in them.

These two facts are incontrovertible. Mussolini did just what they say. Italy is some 90 per cent. Catholic and it did not take a particularly Machiavellian brain to see the value of friendship with the Vatican. Mussolini always did place opportunism above his agnosticism.

Throughout the first years of his reign Mussolini exerted himself to win the church. An attempt was made to heal all the wounds Garibaldi once inflicted. Church and state were to become friends — Quirinal and Vatican were to co-operate, and the Pope was to be released from his noble prison.

In November, 1922, the Pope sent an order to all the bishops of Italy to help the new government, which then consisted of a cabinet including Liberals, Catholics and Democrats as well as Fascists. Gradually all non-Fascists were eliminated and simultaneously a policy of violence was inaugurated to crush them. When the violence increased, and the dead and wounded began to number thousands, the priests of the victims' congregations were alarmed; when the Catholic churches and institutions were attacked, the Cardinals complained to the Pope. The church, which was preaching Christ, had to denounce the crucifixion of the non-Fascist parties.

In Pisa anti-Catholic outrages had been particularly violent and persistent. The Catholic clubs and their newspaper had been attacked, the rooms and machinery wrecked, men assaulted. Cardinal Maffi, one of the intellectual leaders of the church, following the murder of Matteotti, issued a pastoral letter which deeply impressed the Pope. It was entitled " Thou shalt not kill " and in it the Fascisti are called " The Race of Cain." The Fascist government twice suppressed this pastoral letter. It begins:

"It is with feelings of surprise and sorrow and unspeakable bitterness of soul that I bring myself to the performance of a duty which I never thought would have fallen to my lot. But recently there has been crowding in upon my mind, ever closer and closer, the feeling that I ought to bring to your notice and comment upon the fifth commandment of the Decalogue: Thou shalt not kill. Considering our wide-spread and manifold education, the progress of civilization, and our vaunted brotherhood of nations and mankind, I allowed myself to be deluded into believing in a general cessation and total disappearance of crimes of blood. I thought that they could have remained only as words in the dictionaries and fading records and in the memories of veteran survivors of an age that had passed.

"Delusion. The dismal heritage of the war, the familiarity with arms and with blood, and, even before the war, the bitter and violent hatreds between classes and parties, the decadence and disappearance of the religious sentiment, to these we must attribute the fact that if there be one thing which no longer counts and is of no price or value on the market, it is life itself, our own and that of others."

and concludes:

"It is said of murderers that they boast of the number of their victims. But the word is merely on the lips, presented rather than pronounced, in a moment of confusion and excitement. Other words come in the night and ring with a different sound, causing fears to arise that are uncontrollable and sometimes even insane. O, Cain! O, Judas! O, all ye who shed the blood of your brothers, you lie when you speak of security; for we know you have it not. Nor could you have it. Do we not see you turn pale and look furtively around, as if seeking some way of escape, at a chance sound that may strike the ear, at a chance light that may strike the eye, even at the murmur of the wind, at the chirping of the birds? . . .

"War had and has its poison-gas, its liquids of destruction; but bear this well in mind: No acid, sulphuric or nitric or prussic and no sublimate is so corrosive as one drop of blood criminally shed. There is no chemical basis that will resist or neutralize it. There are no forces to control it. Armies will not hold it in check. It flows on. It corrodes. It destroys. Woe to the hand that sheds blood. Woe to the feet that trample on the corpse. O, Dynasty of Cain, carry on. But listen to this, where men fail God is to the rescue — God who gives no quarter to the culprits but incessantly pursues them, crying out judgment over them: Accursed. Accursed. Accursed in time; accursed in eternity."

After Cardinal Maffi had braved Fascist wrath by speaking out, the *Osservatore Romano,* the official organ of the Vatican, printed numerous reports of Fascist violence directed against Catholics. Where party politicians were afraid to open their mouths and where the terror-stricken press failed, the Catholics dared. One day the *Osservatore Romano* recounted:

"Unfortunately the bellicose discourses of Farinacci (Secretary of the Fascist party) coincides with a vigorous recrudescence of violence. Besides an attack on Deputy Amendola, we are informed of other similar attacks in which Catholic groups were the victims.

"In Alife, in Piedmont, a Facist parade, unprovoked, invaded the Catholic club, 'God and Fatherland,' smashing the furniture, pictures and windows. The under-prefect, upon receiving protests, expressed surprise that these facts were not known to him. This is not surprising, inasmuch as the commissary of public safety, who reported to the under-prefect, was the leader of this Fascist expedition.

"On the 21st, the club rooms of the Saint Marius club were invaded and everything smashed. The same thing happened at the Saint Domingo club, where the door was broken in and the furniture and pictures were smashed. This invasion was preceded by a number of revolver shots to intimidate the population.

"The following night, Fascist squadrons at Spezia devastated the Catholic club, Silvio Pellico, burning the furniture and also burning a crucifix, a picture of the Sacred Heart and a portrait of the Holy Father.

"When will this sad chronicle end?"

The climax of the controversy between the church and the Fascisti came, according to Monsignor X——, when Monsignor

Pizzardo, under-secretary of state for the Vatican, following the receipt of numerous telegrams by Cardinal Gaspari from Spezia and other towns relating to Fascist attacks, went to the Pope with the facts. The Pope expressed surprise at the sudden anti-Christian move on the Fascisti's part. Pizzardo said there had been numerous cases before in the past year, but he had not believed them important and he had not wanted to trouble the Pontiff, whose time was already overcrowded with the exactions imposed by the millions of Holy Year pilgrims.

" Don't keep the truth from me — I want to know all about such matters," the Pope said. Monsignor Pizzardo then explained how for a year there had been more and more cases until in the last fortnight there had been a series which were not coincidences.

The Pope already knew of the Pisa outrage and how Cardinal Maffi had branded the rioters. Moreover, the Pope had read Mussolini's speech at a recent convention of the Fascisti when violence as a moral measure was upheld in words which Mussolini had once learned from a French communist. In his discussion with Monsignor Pizzardo the Pope further learned of Signor Farinacci's fire-eating speeches in Sicily urging physical violence against the Opposition and his speech which resulted in the attack on Amendola, the leader of the Opposition.

Accordingly the Supreme Pontiff ordered the *Osservatore Romano* to write an editorial which would not be signed, meaning that the Vatican and not any individual was responsible for it. The editorial which the Pope inspired did not hesitate to blame Mussolini and his violent speeches. It mentioned the violence at Spezia, Montecatini, Alife, Florence, Signa, Parma, Sarzana, etc. The *Osservatore Romano* warned the Fascisti that the stories of their violence were creating a bad impression, especially in Catholic countries, and that they would create a worse impression unless the government did its duty and punished the guilty. Finally the inspired editorial concluded with a significant Latin phrase which may be translated, "Nothing built on violence endures."

Then on June 14, 1925, the Corpus Christi procession was attacked and broken up by blackshirts, and on the 21st, addressing the Holy Year pilgrimage from Perugia, the Pope, who rarely even remotely refers to political events, protested against Fascist attacks on Catholics and especially the Corpus Christi outrage. The Catholic newspapers used the mild heading, *" Il Papa deplora le violenze contro i Catholici,"* and stated that the Pope had declared that religious demonstrations had been from time to time disturbed, even in Italy, by acts which, he said, might be called " neither human, nor Christian and certainly not Italian." Such acts, the Pope said, had occurred in this sacred city on the occasion of a solemn festival of the church. He added that such acts should be prevented by the authorities, or, if they happened, punished in an exemplary manner.

The *Osservatore Romano,* official organ of the Vatican, gave some details of the incident to which the Pope referred. Among the victims, according to the *Osservatore,* was a certain student, Allessandro Dofano, who was assaulted by eight or nine men in the Fascist blackshirt uniform, including one in the uniform of the " musketeers," Mussolini's personal bodyguard. The police arrived in time to rescue him from the worst of the beating which the eight or nine were administering — but made no arrests. Instead, the Fascisti quietly repaired to the " Senato Café " and ordered drinks.

I have already mentioned the Catholic Party which in 1922 co-operated with Mussolini. After the Matteotti murder it joined the Opposition. Although this party is by no means a Vatican party, it is a Catholic party and numerous priests and leading Catholic politicians belonged to it until its suppression in 1927. The Fascisti carried on a bitter political war against the Populari, as the Catholic party was called, and against the *" preti politicanti,"* of politician-priests. The Vatican had discouraged the activities of the Populari and the parish priests in the early days of Fascismo. But the blackshirts had little respect for tonsured heads. One of the most serious Fascist crimes was the murder of the priest Don Minzoni of Argenta, near Ferrara, who was killed for revenge because he denounced violence. That the Mussolini government was directly blamable was indicated by letters written by Italo Balbo, a hero of the Fascist march on Rome and a pillar of Mussolini's strength. One of Balbo's letters urged making life unlivable for the Argenta element and others prepared for the escape of assassins. These letters brought about the fall of Balbo from his official position, whereupon Mussolini sent him a letter saying he had acted as " a Fascist and a gentleman."

Mussolini, in 1925, in addition to delivering the orations in favor of violence which caused the Papal organ to lay much blame on him, almost single-handed passed the anti-Masonry bill. This caused considerable disillusion in American Babbittry and probably cost the dictator more votes of sentiment than any other action, including the Matteotti murder.

The general impression prevails that Mussolini forced the bill in order to please the Catholic church. Nothing is farther from the truth. The Catholic church was considerably displeased by Mussolini's measure, which, while aimed at Freemasonry, was worded so that any lodge could be broken up and the Jesuit or Trappist orders were in the same danger as the Oriental lodge of Freemasons. Mussolini merely killed another potential source of political opposition; religious views had nothing to do with the case.

*   *   *   *   *

These are some of the cross-currents in the history of the Vatican and the Palazzo Chigi. The undertow is philosophical.

From my friends in the Vatican I learned that there have grown up two parties in the Roman Catholic Church of Italy, one favoring co-operation with Mussolini, the other bitterly demanding that the church anathematize him as Anti-Christ. It is said that the Cardinals are divided, with Cardinal Maffi the leader of the anti-Fascist group. The Pope and his cabinet, despite the famous attack on violence, while not being completely satisfied with the gains the church has made under the friendly régime, favour support for many reasons. One, and a most important one, is that Fascism is the enemy of radicalism. Although Fascism despite such a claim did not kill Bolshevism, which had committed suicide in 1920, it had stamped out its remnants, with Socialism and all sorts of radical movements, when it made a clean sweep of all its opponents. Fascism had restored national discipline and individual acquiescence to the state of things as they are. The Vatican approved.

In the church opposition there are many Jesuit leaders who are alarmed by Mussolini, his philosophy of violence, and his tremendous grip on the soul of the people. The Jesuits believe that the soul belongs to the church. They see " Mussolinism " growing up as a religion, a fanatical religion. Devotion to it surpasses Pope and king.

The Jesuits see Mussolini's new philosophy making the State warden for the human being. The State is supreme; individualism must cease; not only democracy but personal liberty must come to an end because they interfere with the powers of the Fascist Corporate State, and slavery of the worker, if necessary, must be accepted because the State and not the man must succeed.

The Jesuits see the church left out.

The era of violence against the Catholic church is passing but the conflict with the church and between church and state is entering a new phase; the battle-ground is a philosophy. The struggle has been sensed by a newspaper, *Il Piccolo,* which said one noon:

"We cannot live on good terms both with God and Duce Mussolini. Christianity and Fascism are absolute antipodes. The choice, therefore, of good Catholics of Italy is love or violence — Christ or Mussolini."

The edition was suppressed.

* * * * *

At the end of March, 1928, the French press, which is largely Catholic, surprised its readers with a repetition of the 1925 headlines: "*Le Pape contre le Facisme italien.*" All the propaganda written to prove that the Pope and Mussolini, the Vatican and the Chigi, were working hand in glove, was suddenly destroyed. When Fascism, continuing its policy of capturing the spirit as well as the body, ordered the disbanding of the Catholic Boy Scouts, because, "only the Fascist state has the right to bring up the youth of Italy," the Pope protested. The *Osservatore Romano* again elaborated the Papal views, and Mussolini again remained defiant. However, there is sure to be a big "Vatican-Mussolini Rapprochement" story in the papers some day soon.

Chapter IV

MUSSOLINI'S SIBERIA

WHENEVER there is a conference of editors and reporters in Europe it is inevitable that the question:
What is the big story to get right now? is asked. For years the
answer has been: Russia. The Bolsheviki turned the key of
censorship in the lock of terrorism, and excluded impartial
journalism for a long time. Therefore they provided a goal for
truth-seekers.

Today the answer is: Mussolini's Siberia. Ever since the Duce
took his lesson from the Czars and established exile for all
Italians who were vocal and active and non-Fascist, foreign
correspondents have known that a big and good story can be
had at any time for a little exertion, not too many dollars, and
considerable ingenuity.

For a long time I doubted my own news sense; I have been
expelled from Italy and try as I can to be objective to the Fascist
experiment I may have prejudices. It may have been a prejudice
that made me believe a secret visit to Mussolini's Siberia would
result in a sensational series of articles, almost as good as a
visit to the similar Bolshevik horror in the Arctic Sea.

But one day I heard the correspondent of a New York evening
paper assert that the Liparian Islands today hold the biggest
chance for a newspaper sensation. And another day I saw a
number of telegrams addressed to the big American news-
agencies and newspapers suggesting an assignment there. In
Paris and London I heard the leading American correspondents

say what a great chance was being missed, and whenever Rome correspondents came north they recommended that some one else — for them it was too dangerous — should do the Fascist Siberia.

But nothing seems to have come of it all. James Vincent Shean, after receiving many smuggled letters describing conditions in one of the islands (which corroborate many statements in this chapter), attempted to land at a town where a friend is imprisoned. He found that blackshirt guards had replaced government guards and the Fascist régime forbids even the natives to speak to the politicals. With the change in police has come more savage treatment. One case has caused quite a scandal recently: a Fascist guard during an argument with an unarmed political stuck a bayonet into the latter's eye and blinded him. Violence marks the island as well as the mainland régime. Mr. Shean tells me the Fascisti are efficient policemen and the cordon is now more difficult to break. He believes, however, that an American reporter, if backed with sufficient money and enthusiasm in the home office, could penetrate the prisons. But it is still obvious that American editors (1) do not think the story good enough to warrant the adventure or (2) are afraid to offend Mussolini. So far as I have been able to find out, the only statements regarding the entire system of island deportation have appeared only in *The New York World* and *The Manchester Guardian*.

The institution of "confino" is not new in Italy. Before our immigration quota law was passed an Italian criminal sometimes had the choice of confinement on one of the barren, waterless, flea-infested islands which surround Sicily, or of going to the United States. Many preferred the latter. In fact my last assignment in Italy was an investigation into the relationship between crime in America, chiefly Chicago, and the land of birth of a large number of the criminals, Italy. My Italian assistant, Camillo Cianfarra, a former member of the Italian embassy in Washington, an expert on emigration, a cultured man and a liberal thinker — (he died two weeks after my expulsion from Rome, from heart failure, as a result of being beaten up by Fascisti, apparently for the reason that he helped me obtain the documents which charged Mussolini's complicity in the Matteotti assassination) — was able to obtain very interesting information. Cianfarra showed that Sicilian judges, especially, made it a practice to suggest to members of the Mafia and other habitual murderers, cut-throats and bandits, to emigrate to the United States. There was no death penalty in Italy then. When criminals were sent to the islands there was the danger of their escape and return, and always they proved a drain on the treasury because their living expenses had to be borne by the government. The judges therefore suggested the name of a boat a week or so before the criminal was to be sentenced, and in nine cases out of ten Italy thereby rid herself of a bad citizen and the United States gained one.

Mussolini's magistrates do not offer an alternative to the political prisoner. Although America is closed, there are other lands for emigrants, but these are too dangerous for the Fascist régime, because in other lands there is freedom, of voice and press, and the exiled editor or politician could remain an active force opposed to Fascism.

The anti-Facisti say there are five or more thousands of prisoners in the islands, the Fascisti admit only one thousand, which, they add, was reduced to 700 by Mussolini's amnesty last Christmas. In addition there are probably as many in "exile" on the mainland. Almost without exception the prisoners, no matter what their number, are men of considerable worth, whose only crime has been activity in behalf of an ideal which did not fit into the Fascist paradise. They are doctors, lawyers, schoolmasters, journalists, priests, writers, college professors, members of the chamber of deputies and politicians.

In almost all cases the victims were tried by self-constituted Fascist militia courts. In the island of Lampedusa the political prisoners were domiciled with murderers and thieves, criminals so dangerous that the state could not take the risk of keeping them in mainland prisons.

In Pantelleria the politicals are allowed to buy housing and food if they have private incomes, which many have not, having either lost their means of livelihood when unable to continue their professions, or having had their property confiscated by the Fascisti.

In Ustica 350 politicals are housed by the government, from eight to twelve sharing each filthy and unsanitary room.

The curse of the islands is monotony. There is nothing to do. The criminals cannot feel the torture so much; they are not sensitive, but the intelligent politicals are, in some instances, driven actually insane, not by torture, but by the horrible monotony of unchanging existence. Some find relief by reviving the stale political quarrels of the mainland! Others exchange lessons in languages. Tyrolese patriots, who are maintaining a feeble struggle against a Versailles iniquity which deeded them without plebiscite or protest to their enemies, have brought in the German language with its soft, pleasant Austrian intonation and a new element of political discussion.

"Bolsheviks," "anarchists," "communist rascals," are the words used by Mussolini in his usual immoderate speeches whenever he refers to the island prisoners. Occasionally one or two of the political prisoners having a choice between misery, suicide, or recantation, embrace the Fascist faith, are released and received with loud " evvivas " in the camp of the new Czar.

But it seems no American newspaper, despite the frequent and urgent requests of its Paris and Berlin and Rome representatives, despite the fact that every report confirms the existence of a big and sensational story, can bring itself to spend the necessary dollars to smash the black halo of the Latter Day Saint of Italy.

Chapter V

FASCISM IN 1928

DESPITE my expulsion from Italy and blacklisting at consulates, I have been able to make an investigation of Italy in 1928, thanks largely to several American newspaper correspondents who, being unable to write the whole story of Fascismo, probably derive a vicarious pleasure from assisting those who are free.

The gains in Italy are material and evident and one would have to be not only deaf, dumb and blind, but worse, prejudiced and unfair, to disregard them. The moral values are harder to estimate. The conflict of State versus individual continues — in fact it has become so important that it is arousing more and more discussion in the church, which also is alarmed over the shackles government is attempting to fasten on the free will and spiritual autonomy of a people.

In 1928 (as in Russia) the terror by which government is maintained is less in evidence; as in Russia there is less need of force, violence — even murder — when the will of the opposition, like the will of a young child, is completely broken and a sullen, sour, impotent submissiveness takes its place. Italy like Russia has achieved peace and calm through crushing the free spirit of the intellectual, intelligent and articulate class: the mob, peasant and common worker, have never had any power nor have they today in either country.

What is left of an opposition, Russian or Italian, resides abroad and bides its time. Many doubt if there is the smallest hope for them. All they can do is write and talk. If we contrast, however, the following two statements of the leaders of Fascism and anti-Fascism, we can see that the fight has not been abandoned in Italy — as it has been largely in Russia. Mussolini said recently:

"In the creation of a new State which is authoritarian but not absolutist, hierarchical and organic — namely, open to the people in all its classes, categories and interests — lies the great revolutionary originality of Fascism, and a teaching perhaps for the whole modern world oscillating between the authority of the State and that of the individual, between the State and the anti-State. Like all other revolutions, the Fascist revolution has had a dramatic development but this in itself would not suffice to distinguish it. The reign of terror is not a revolution: it is only a necessary instrument in a determined phase of the revolution."

To which ex-Premier Nitti, one of many leaders of Italians who seek the re-establishment of human liberty, replied:

"The ignoble phenomenon of a dictatorship is a shameful blot on European civilization. Reactionary minds, which are indignant at red dictatorships, have only sympathy with 'white' dictatorships, which are equally, if not more bloodthirsty, no less brutal and unjustified by any ideal, even a false one.

"The Fascist government abolished in Italy every safeguard of the individual and every liberty. No free man can live in Italy, and an immoral law prevents Italians from going to a foreign country on pain of punishment. Italy is a prison where life has become intolerable. Everything is artificial — artificial finance — artificial exchange — artificial public economy — artificial order — artificial calm.

"Without a free parliament, a free press, a free opinion and a true democracy, there will never be peace."

* * * * *

The New Leaders in Italy

The anxious world which opposed bolshevism waited for the passing of Lenin and Trotsky to mark the collapse of that movement; likewise anti-Fascists predict that the passing of Mussolini will mark the end of his régime. The death of Lenin and the political passing of Trotsky had no more significance than accompanies the birth of an heir to a throne nowadays. The system did not change.

In Italy small changes have taken place. Mussolini has now taken to himself even the few powers he had loaned to his two strong assistants, Farinacci, secretary of the Fascist party, and Federzoni, minister of interior.

These two men once sat at his left and right hand. Farinacci, the so-called "left hand" of Mussolini, preached more and more violence; Federzoni, the "right hand" represented the old conservative royalist support, and had the backing of the army and the clergy. Both were too strong for an egotist's entourage and both have gone. There is a rumour that Farinacci was preparing to seize the dictatorship, but, while this is in the character of the man, the accusation has never been proven.

Italo Balbo is having his troubles in the air ministry. He is the same Italo Balbo who was forced to quit the command of the Fascist militia following the murder of the priest Don Minzoni of Argenta, one of the many Jesuit victims of blackshirt violence. Gentile, who for years represented the few intelligent Italians who remained Fascists, and who saw himself derided by all the writers and poets and dramatists and liberal and ethically alert minds, has quit the ministry of education.

Three new men have arrived. Dino Grandi, under-secretary for foreign affairs, is becoming a power, but a power in the shadow of Mussolini. He has had an interesting career, typical of the new generation of diplomats in the Fascist service. During one of the early revolts, when the Duce was within an inch of being crushed, Grandi smashed the uprising, and since then has been honoured by doing many of Mussolini's dirty little jobs, such as intimidation, personal terrorism of opponents, diplomatic espionage and press censorship.

He started his Fascist career in Bologna as head of the secret service commonly called after its Russian model, the Chekah. A Bologna banker, Baroncini, was his opponent. The latter edited a newspaper (*Assalta*) which discovered and exposed a 300,000,000 lire Fascist graft in the construction of the 700,000,-000 Florence-Bologna tunnel. Baroncini blamed Grandi's Chekah gang for the graft. The Fascist secret service conspired to assassinate Baroncini, obtaining, at a price, the services of a doctor to administer poison and disease germs. At the last minute, it seems, the physician remembered his calling, and confessed. *Assalta* published all this evidence.

Grandi then challenged Baroncini to a duel. The latter replied:

"Physical strength is cheap, but moral courage is rare in Italy today." He refused to meet Grandi.

Another big figure in the Fascist State was Count Volpi. He is one of the "new" Fascists, having joined the party in order to hold office. It was Volpi who stabilized the Italian lira, a process, however, which brought considerable conflict between him and Mussolini, the bankers and the government. Volpi was the accredited agent of the Banca Commerciale Italiana in the Fascist government. The bankers and the Milan-Turin metal industries bought and paid for Fascism from the day they took over the romantic d'Annunzio's flowery and shouting blackshirts, but this was the first time the owners of Fascismo ever placed one of their own men in a position to administer its finances. But now Volpi, too, has resigned because he could not agree in everything with Mussolini.

Rossoni is the third important new man. He represents labour. In the Fascist attempt to make capital and labour one class by imposing a new set of laws regarding strikes and lock-outs, wages and profits, Mussolini has chosen a man who still keeps alive the old aspiration and idealism of labour seeking a better day and a better world for itself.

With Farinacci, Federzoni, Gentile and Balbo made impotent, Mussolini, unlike the Bolshevik dictators, has amassed rather than divided power. His Grandi, Volpi and Rossoni affiliations have not affected his personal strength. Italy has become more and more a one-man show.

*   *   *   *   *

Censorship and the Press

All outgoing telegraphic dispatches are still censored but the government denies that letters are being opened. Censorship is done in the foreign office, by a secretary who calls Grandi's attention to anything suspect. The correspondent is then sent for and lectured or threatened. But not as severely as formerly. Recently a Hearst representative named Horan was on the carpet for a dispatch regarding the tribal uprising in Libya, but he was not expelled. All correspondents are lectured when their Paris or London colleagues send news unfavorable to Fascism: Grandi and Mussolini not only control the reports from Italy but try to affect the news regarding Italy sent from other countries.

The Rome bureau of the Associated Press, the largest news distributing agency in the world, is still in the hands of Commendatore Salvatore Cortesi, and the Rome bureau of *The New York Times* is still in the hands of Arnaldo Cortesi. Both these journalists claim they are not members of the Fascist party. Both are Italians, however, and their sympathies are well known. As their dispatches are public property, it is not difficult for the reader to form his own opinion of their fairness. Two Americans, Hudson Hawley and Hal Walker, have now been assigned as Commendatore Cortesi's assistants in Rome.

In the past year numerous dispatches have been suppressed. There has, however, been no scandal equalling the Matteotti case. The foreign journalists were particularly vexed by the complete suppression of cables which pictured the fraud as well as the glory of the Fifth Anniversary Celebration of Fascism. This event was featured by the secret, furtive arrival of Mussolini at Villa Gloria, and his departure in a seemingly runaway automobile, as if in flight from an assassin, and the police measures which rivalled anything in Russia in Czarist days. Only dispatches which lauded the event were passed.

Much more important is the fact that many telegrams were never written because of fear of Fascist consequences. For example:

Genoa: Anti-Fascist demonstrations, thousands of workmen paraded the streets with their pockets turned inside-out to show they had nothing.

Palermo: The new 2-lire coin systematically defaced by the populace despite threats of imprisonment, because the new national money bears the Fascist party emblem.

Savona: Anti-Fascist demonstrations and riots during trial of men accused of helping Filippo Turati leave Italy. Turati reached Corsica, then London, where he exposed the newest terrorism in Italy. The riots in favour of Turati's helpers in Savona became so important that the Fascist court had to content itself with the minimum sentence.

(Not as violent as 1922–1927 — but the same old story.)

And the Italian press? Despite its Fascist control, the Milan *Corriere della Sera* remains, as heretofore, a distinguished newspaper. Sometimes it is allowed to discuss Fascist problems academically. Recently it has brought up the subject of a left and a right Fascist party, which might give Italy the appearance of having some show of political liberty. The *Tevere* in Rome can be bright at times. The rest of the Italian press is sunk in party corruption. All the important journalists are either in prison, in exile, out of a job, or poverty stricken. The press is dominated by the example of the Duce's brother, Arnaldo Mussolini, who, lacking the brilliance of the former, fulminates daily in his own paper, threatens friendly nations, and throws dirt at his enemies.

* * * * *

Fascism and Catholicism

The latest phase of the Fascist-Catholic conflict is summed up by *The Manchester Guardian* as follows:

" Fascismo has lent itself generously to the church as an ally in the battle against ' immoral fashions,' ' pornographic publications,' ' deleterious amusements,' and so on. Indeed the pleasure life of the great cities has been reduced to a minimum. One may find this zeal praiseworthy, but the dark spirit of the Counter-Reformation is abroad; and the lip-service paid to the moralizing campaign by the younger Fascist leaders is hypocritical. Indeed the whole association of Fascism with the Catholic Church sometimes seems to have had bad effects on both. It is the reactionary elements in both which profit by the alliance, at the expense of the liberal elements."

*   *   *   *   *

The Philosophical Defence of Fascism

Actually and practically, Italy is far better off than anti-Fascists charge. Money has been stabilized; the internal public debt has been reduced from 95 billions to 85 in four years; trains leave and arrive on time (*cf.* Russia); there is a more wholesale acceptance of Fascismo than two years ago; the theory of government is, after the manner of William James, a pragmatic affair because " it works."

It has been discovered, suddenly, that Fascism is *Real Politik* as contrasted to the rest of Europe's and America's fantastic and impossible belief in life, liberty and the pursuit of happiness, democracy, parliamentary government and other such romantic, impractical illusions. Even the Bolsheviks, who have hitherto announced themselves the only realists of our age, have been put in the second row because they have not compromised so much as Fascism, nor changed horses so often in all the muddy streams of politics, but have abided strictly by the tenets of Marx and Lenin.

Fascist realism has given this not new nor brilliant thesis to the world: the state is everything, the individual nothing; efficiency and economic welfare stand above the rights of man; man exists for society, not society for man. It is therefore no longer necessary for freedom to exist as man is to become the slave of the state, and the state is to be responsible for him to

God — and Mussolini. Out of pragmatism, Fascismo hopes to create Robotism.

The Bolsheviks were the first to appeal to realist philosophy as a defence for their restriction of social liberty; the apologists for Fascismo in these more peaceful days when there seems to be absolutely no reason for non-resumption of normal parliamentarianism in Italy, are also looking for philosophic excuses. But how in 1928 is Fascist " philosophy " actually working out?

Certainly the country is feeling its nationalistic oats. Patriotism and sword-rattling have made the Italians a prouder people, a people emerging from the shadows of inferiority which were never wholly dispelled by Garibaldi. Italy is more efficient, produces more, seeks a larger place in the sun and enjoys those same blessings which a strong healthy nordic people enjoyed before the world war. The German spirit is gaining in Italy.

The Gentile school system, which aims to create a Fascist aristocracy, is working successfully so far as its athletic program is concerned. The philosopher Giovanni Gentile aimed to have the schools " brought into close contact with life in all its manifestations of force, beauty, work." As there are no intellectual leaders left in the government or party, the idealistic part of the program makes no headway and the Fascisti say: " give us time." On the other hand Mussolini, the realist, encourages the Avanguardia and the Balilla, two boys' organizations which have military training and are the hope for the continuation of military dictatorship. The Balilla boys have frequently beaten up unarmed Catholic boy scouts during processions, much to the alarm of the Pope, and in several public schools the masters have put up signs, " Balilla members must not bring their fathers' revolvers to the classrooms and must not terrorize non-Balillas."

Culture is at a low ebb. Fascism seems to have produced nothing in the seven arts. The writers have fled the country — with the exception of Pirandello who has had a theatre subsidized with Fascist money, Ferrero, the great historian, who has tried to get out of Italy time and again but is held a prisoner, and d'Annunzio, the spiritual leader of Fascismo, who has never quite reconciled himself to the régime.

Political repression has resulted in national stultification. But intelligence has not been crushed completely. It exists even among the Fascisti. They, who have preached the rebirth of nationalism, and salvation through action, efficiency, and uncomplaining labor, are at last beginning to be a bit doubtful whether or not, after all, that is all there is to human existence. Even Mussolini, who all his life has been a rebel against a society of Things as They Are, is said to be wavering in his absolutist program. He who has preached against the corruption which tyrannical power gives a man or government, may yet become a leader of liberalism.

Certainly throughout Italy a wave of unrest is passing today. That Italy which never knew liberty but which followed a Garibaldi and a d'Annunzio and a Mussolini when they preached liberty, is now experiencing a real desire for freedom. The working masses, of course, have never seen anything in Fascism except the victory of the bankers and employers; the peasantry, like all peasantry, is apathetic except when something affects the price of food; the very men who tell the tourists all is healthy and beautiful in Italy, change their tune when they find a sympathetic ear. On the Riviera and in Southern France there are about a million Italians at work. Only a few are refugees. Talk to any group or individual, unafraid of the police, and you learn of the vast unrest, the longing for freedom in the native land. The majority are not anti-Fascist; they are rather proud of the place in the world Mussolini has made for Italy; but, they argue, is it absolutely impossible for Fascismo and human liberty to go together in the making of the New Italy?

Part III — Russia

Chapter I

Censorship in Red Russia

YOU climb five flights of dirty steps in the Narcomindel building and come to the press bureau of the foreign office; you arrive with a thumping heart, a little perspiration in your hatband and your breathing a bit out of control; altogether at a physical disadvantage in bearding the Bolshevik press lions in their pens.

Customary introductions. A pause.

" You must be surprised to find *me* here," I say.

(I myself was surprised: the Soviets had vowed that my paper would not be allowed a representative but the " Hoover Treaty " had made my entry possible.)

" Why should we be surprised? " This from Gregory Weinstein.

Question for question. The subtle, suspicious, oriental manner of an interview.

We indulged in discussing arrests and expulsions of newspapermen. A fine introduction to work in Russia. They brought up Edwin Hullinger.

" I knew Hullinger for years — we both worked for the *United Press* in London," I said. " He was wild about Russia — studied the language — I know he came here as a friend. Why did you banish him? "

" Hullinger," replied Weinstein, " consorted with our enemies. He held conferences with reactionaries and counter-revolutionaries. This man interfered with our political affairs."

153

" You mean he sent a telegram to a colleague in Genoa asking him to try and get the censorship lifted through the agency of the League of Nations? "

" Yes, he sent a telegram which we had turned down. We do not know how he got it out. It was submitted and refused. He threatened to get it out. We warned him of the consequences. But he went ahead. There was nothing left for us to do — "

" Didn't you realize that the expulsion of a reputable newspaperman makes a deep and bad impression throughout the world? "

" Russia," interposed Samuel Kagan, the censor, " is used to that. We have been slandered a good deal, and can afford more."

That exhausted the subject of deportation. I asked what the press department of the Soviet Government could do in arranging interviews, obtaining statistics, transportation, safe conducts, etc.

" Russia is a free country," replied Weinstein with a grand gesture. " Go where you like. Get what you can. You are free here. We have nothing to do with your work."

" And where are telegrams submitted for censorship? "

Uneasiness. Tension.

" You just file your stuff at the post office and it will get through," replied Kagan, who was the secret censor. " If you want to use the airposts, bring your letters here and I will forward them for you."

It looked all right.

But the press corps had another story to tell. From the group representing all the agencies and important newspapers I soon learned that nothing could be sent out of Russia which was disagreeable to Soviet political policies or to communist philosophy.

"It is the only honest censorship that exists," I was told, "they will tell you frankly, when they get to know you better, that they are not censoring the facts or the truth, but the tone and attitudes of your dispatches. They ask you to be objective, but they really want you to do propaganda for them. Every dispatch must be important for their party or on a subject they care nothing about; otherwise it doesn't get by."

I soon found there were three government and Communist-party controlled newspapers, *Pravda, Izvestia* and *Economic Life,* and the official government news bureau, *Rosta,* which supply news. But even a plain translation of communist news was frequently censored because the effect abroad might not be favorable.

The *Rosta* news was at that time bought by the *United Press;* now it is the property of the *Associated Press.* By a little bribery and corruption one good Communist editor " lent " me his *Rosta* sheets for a while every night. When I presented copies of *Rosta* news to the censor later he frequently denied the truth of certain items or suppressed them for political reasons.

Every day we heard marvellous and sensational news. Some of it required investigation, some we knew to be true. But what was the use of investigation, when we could not dare to send the telegrams even if confirmed? We compromised. But, as I was to find similarly in Fascist Italy, every member of the press corps, with one or two exceptions, was preparing to end his state of compromise when the big story came for which it would be worth risking expulsion. We were a lot of camels praying for the last straw to break the back of an anomalous position. (That straw was the Catholic persecution story.)

Meanwhile, without endeavouring to find conflicts, we had our daily difficulties with the censors. Little matters, because we had not tried to write the big sensations. Here are a few samples of censorship:

During the Turko-Greek conflict, when Russia insisted on sitting beside Turkey in any question affecting outlets from the Black Sea, the following was suppressed:

" In the past weeks there have been small but dangerous rifts in the Russo-Turkish lute which may change its tune. The first is a series of persecutions of Communists in Angora for which Kemal is blamed. . . . Secondly, Russia believes that a series of agreements are being made by the Entente nations with Turkey which may persuade Kemal to drop his Russian alliance."

The words " from watching Black Sea manœuvres " were stricken out from a dispatch beginning " Trotsky returned to Moscow."

A telegram addressed to me saying that American Negroes were participating in the Comintern Congress, and asking me to get interviews, was suppressed. But while I was permitted to receive a telegram saying Marguerite Harrison had been arrested in the Far East, my reply saying that nothing was known about it in Moscow was suppressed.

When the long series of attacks on the American Relief reached their climax we were permitted to send translations of all Soviet scurrility, but the following was suppressed:

" The A. R. A. has taken no steps to obtain an apology from official Russian newspapers for alleged libellous attack but has cabled its New York and Washington offices to await advices from Hoover and Haskell. Indignation is general throughout American relief centres in Russia. A foreign office official said today: ' It is a regrettable incident — merely newspaper, not the government view — ' "

The words " regret my previous telegrams unanswered " were cut out, as were all references to possible word shortage due to censorship.

During the religious troubles the censor encouraged us to write stories of violence and sacrilege. The story of the burning of crucifixes in the public square was approved, but when a similar attack was made by the atheistic League of Communist Youth on a synagogue the following line was cut out: " Jewish patriarchs protested against non-believers who on Yom Kippur and other Hebrew holidays cut the electric wires and spoiled celebrations in synagogues."

The words " no speaker credited the American Relief organization with pulling Russia through the worst period of famine " were eliminated from a description of the Fifth Anniversary Soviet celebration.

Every mention of American Communist delegates attending the congress was suppressed because the visitors had entered Russia secretly. Of course our detectives at Riga and Terioki had a full list of them. But the censor tried to suppress the fact that such things as American delegates existed. He cut from my first dispatch: " The Americans are living in gorgeous hotels, given free theatre, ballet and opera tickets, free meals, free transportation, having a regal time. Greatest secrecy their identification."

I tried it again, a day later, when the words " Six American delegates arrived " were passed; the following was suppressed: " Each approached denies he's delegate, says merely tourist, refuses name, American names suppressed meetings. Startling contrast with boastful pride German French British who announce themselves Communist delegates."

My third attempt was a dismal failure. Instead of talking of delegates I mentioned all Americans apart from accredited newspapermen, who were in the reviewing stand: "Max Eastman editor Liberator, Claude Mackay, Mrs. Eleanor Pointz, William Lindsay, Chicagoan, Prof. Trachtenberg, New York. Mackay Negro poet had place honour besides Zinovieff although declares not delegate." Out all this went. And naturally the following was also deleted:

"American delegates complaining their position in Communist International altered; say haven't same rights privileges others, cannot participate secret meetings conferences except those unimportant or public. Explain Russian colleagues chagrined over bungling session Michigan woods which department justice raided."

In their dealings with us the censors and press politicians pleaded for a fair deal. Here is a sample of one of theirs:

A woman journalist, the wife of an American delegate to the Communist International (Miss Louise Bryant) had obtained an important interview with Trotsky relative to the disposition of the red army, and Soviet relations to other States. The Moscow press bureau, however, had no interest in publication in America; it needed publicity in London for an immediate political effect. The interview was offered to the representatve of a British paper (Mr. Henry Alsberg, *London Herald*).

This journalist's sudden jubilation, however, turned sour when he recognized the interview as belonging to a rival, and bourgeois (?) ethics made him refuse it. Imagine his surprise when three days later he received cabled congratulations from

London for his splendid Trotsky interview. The realist Bolsheviks, combining censorship and propaganda, had taken the liberty of transmitting the American correspondent's hard-gained story to the British correspondent's paper, even signing the latter's name.

But what was going on in Russia which we might have cabled had there been no censorship? There was, for example, a plot to upset the Bolshevik government.

While the non-communist world was confusing the wish for the fact, and reporting the impending collapse of the Soviets — " in six months at most," ran the predictions of 1918, 1919, 1920, 1921, 1922 and 1923 — the newspapermen in Moscow, seeing the growth of internal power, realized that the only successful third revolution could come from the army. It began with a plot and ended with a fiasco. Trotsky, then commander-in-chief, had all the ringleaders invited to his home, confronted them with their treachery, clapped his hands, and gave the score over to the Chekah agents.

There were revolts. There were serious troubles between the government and the American Relief. There were splits in the Communist party. There were, in short, news items which were tremendous in those days.

Some we smuggled out through the American Relief diplomatically immune mail pouches. Colonel Haskell had told us we could use the pouch for letters only. By putting " Dear Mr. Steele " at the head of a sheet and " very truly yours " at the tail, our news items conformed. Nevertheless stories sent out that way took two weeks or more to reach London and print; too long a time for political matters. In one of my smuggled letters I sent the following memorandum to the 35 newspapers which took my service:

You Can't Print That!

Note to Editors

With the opening of the Lausanne conference the Russian censorship has been sharpened a hundredfold. Although claiming it is merely a military censorship and exists owing to the state of affairs in Russia, it exercises the meanest sort of political censorship. Truth is not a factor taken into consideration: the standard for censorship in Russia is whether the influence of the dispatches will help or harm Russian policies. The technical methods of the Russian censor are also different from those correspondents have had to struggle with in other countries. The Russian censor does a neat copy-reading job. He eliminates adjectives he doesn't like, changes verbs, cuts phrases, and writes words in to join paragraphs. This sometimes leads to complete destruction of the facts you intended sending. It would be much better if the entire item were suppressed.

In the *Saturday Evening Post* of a few weeks ago appears an article slandering the entire foreign news service of all American papers. It alleges the foreign correspondent and especially the one in Moscow, curries favour with the officials, bends the knee to the government. The fact is that in Moscow it is a continual battle against the government officials and the censorship they exercise over us.

I suggest that all Moscow dispatches be marked "censored" and when delayed more than 10–15 hours to London also "censored and delayed in Moscow." The American correspondents in Moscow have been hurt so badly by the censorship in the past three weeks that a joint protest will be made to Chicherin when he returns. To make a protest now would be to place ourselves in the class with Hullinger and invite expulsion.

We were put under surveillance day and night. Go to the window of the crawling, rat-infested, Soviet official hotel, officially, but it seemed to me ironically, called the "Savoy," and across the street in a shadowed hallway was a Chekah agent. Leave the hotel and he followed you everywhere. Our consciences may have been clear, but our nerves were soon unravelled.

Representatives of American papers who did not carry American passports fared badly. Georges Popoff (of the Hearst Service) was imprisoned and terrorized by Chekah third degree methods and P. Michaeloff (an assistant for the *Associated Press*) was exiled to Solevetsky, that vast white wilderness of an island in the Arctic where nature and starvation and disease play the rôle of Bolshevik executioner.

Curiously enough, after our united protest and intervention by Colonel Haskell had obtained the release of Popoff, officials of the foreign office, forced to admit that they had no evidence to connect him with a White Russian plot, spread reports attacking the morals of this correspondent, and the Chekah so shattered his nerves by continual surveillance that he quit Russia, and took his revenge in a book published in Berlin exposing the Chekah inquisition.

The Chekah terrorized and deported Francis McCullagh (of *The New York Herald*) because it found he had become too deeply interested in the work to free the Roman Catholic priests. It was the trial of Budkiewicz and Zepliak which aroused the world for the first time in years over events in Russia, and when the Chekah realized it they not only suppressed our work entirely, but they even deceived the minister of justice and Chicherin himself. Lies were told them and told us. The situation became unbearable. We felt like inarticulate prisoners. This was the ultimate straw.

At the request of my paper I presented an ultimatum to Chicherin.

"You must abandon the censorship and guarantee freedom of expression otherwise our correspondent will be withdrawn and so will the correspondents of other American newspapers, so that Russia will find herself without means of communication with the outer world."

When I went to the foreign office to present my cable the officials were prepared for me. They had of course intercepted and copied the ultimatum. Chicherin was furious. " The newspaper speaks to me as if it was a government of equal power," he had said. But I was admitted with friendly smiles. My expulsion had already been agreed on. (It was a Tuesday.)

" Yes, yes, we know all about it," they said in chorus, " and by a most peculiar coincidence we find that your visa expires just today. But we are not cruel, we Bolsheviks. If you happen to miss tomorrow's train to Riga you can certainly make Saturday's."

I made Wednesday's.

Chapter II

The Red World Plot

IN Moscow, annually, the Third International conspires to grasp the bourgeois scheme of things entire, shatter it to bits, and remould it nearer to the Red desire.

It is an open and shut conspiracy; the open part is the congress, the shut part the secret meetings and the distribution of orders and money. But even in the open congress, ways and means of fomenting revolutions in Poland, Germany, China, America, are discussed and the part the Russian army is to play as an international communist army is outlined.

The same leaders who meet one day as premier and cabinet of Russia meet the following day as heads of the Communist party and on another day as chiefs of the Third International. No plot against the safety and forms of government of other nations has ever been carried on on such a vast scale and with such trumpeting and drumming. And yet we were censored for writing these apparent facts.

Lenin gave the secret away when after listening to reports of progress of the communist plot in all countries, he declared revolution was necessary somewhere adjoining Russia. He preferred Poland or Germany.

"Unless the communist movement captures other countries its whole meaning is lost, and Russia is a failure," said Lenin.

Since Lenin's death, however, the one significant change in Russia has been the nationalization of Communism. The internationalist leaders like Trotsky, Kameneff, and Zinovieff, have fallen because their plans have miscarried, and the nationalist Communists are in control. The Russian Communist party has moved away a bit from the Third International. But the latter is still meeting in Moscow and still plotting. As reporters we heard rumors only of the secret sessions, but at the open congresses there was enough evidence of Moscow's control of conspiratorial work in every land. First of all we discovered something we dared not publish, namely, that there is a legal and illegal Communist party in every land in Europe and the Americas. Both were represented at the congress.

The sessions were usually gala affairs full of red banners, mottoes, and sixteen or seventeen renditions of the " Internationale." The Bolshoi Theatre, which houses more than 5,000 people, is usually employed. The heroes sit on the stage and in the boxes; the press in the orchestra pit and the furred proletarian delegates who overwhelm your nostrils with the news that washing water is scarce in all Holy Russia, fill the orchestra and galleries.

Count Brockdorf-Rantzau was uncomfortably doing his duty as doyen of diplomacy in the Czar's loge. Chicherin, shy and self-consciously smiling in a red army uniform, was part of the stage setting. The left of the proscenium arch had a picture of Marx, the right one of Trotsky and the keystone one of Lenin. Red bunting made a triangle of the three black drawings. A huge wall motto read: " We *Vill* stand by the Soviets."

Clara Zetkin, a member of the German Reichstag, was the heroine of the congress I attended. Sweet, grey, wrinkled, plump and motherly she was still capable of verbal vitriol. Every year she had brought a promise of an impending communist overthrow in Germany and they had always believed the sweet old lady.

Katayama of Japan was lionized as a Messiah of the oriental peoples. (Afterwards the Soviets made some plain bourgeois deals with Japan which made a joke of their adoration.) He was a simple soul who let one of the big secrets of the communist plot escape when he said:

"Now that the Russian revolution is safe, the red army must be made an international army to fight everywhere to create more communist revolutions."

Zinovieff, the dictator of Petrograd, in a fairy-like voice spoke as follows:

"The chief aim of our epoch is to suppress the Socialist parties which are now the most active weapons of the bourgeoisie."

Kamineff reported on the "temporary victory of capitalism in the west." He mentioned Poincaré and Mussolini, and concluded, "The workers must hold fast to their rifles."

Schmerl of Czecho-Slovakia puffed himself up. He said practically nothing. Beer and biliousness, not oratory, was the impression of this revolutionist's speech.

Heckert, representing Germany, in a hoarse, painful voice, with German lack of tact, diplomacy, or manners, made a soap-box Lustgarten harangue, shouting and screaming: "The Social Democracy is the Judas party. She must pay for her treason with her life. She must die. *Nieder! Nieder!! Nieder!!!*"

Radek, with a little clay pipe in his mouth, bowl down, and a lot of side whiskers and some under his clean shaven chin, looking very much a Jewish Ancient Mariner, made the only brilliant oration of the congress:

"In America there is no real Communist party because Communist parties are not created by proclamation, but are tempered by civil strife.

"Some say a labor party government is a necessity, the step between Capitalism and Communism. Well, in the world's evolution between a monkey and a Soviet commissar, you must go through a labor government."

But the glory of the congress was Bordega, Bordega of Italy, who spoke his own language which no one understood, yet with an eloquence, a gesture and a passion which captured even the most ignorant peasant. He concluded an oration on the sufferings and battles of his party with these words:

> "Ferro contro ferro,
> Sangue contro sangue,
> Forza contro forza
> E terrore contro terrore!"

The vast Bolshevik audience understood the poetry and the passion, also the word terror, and it rose and cheered. Bordega stole the play!

But after the Bordegas and Heckerts and Schmerls get through poetizing and screaming and panting world revolution, the secret meetings are held and the plans made. Big questions of policy are settled. Shall the Communist party fight alone or shall it join in with bourgeois elements in labour disputes, strikes, coalition governments? For years the policy of individualism was pursued, suddenly it was reversed at a secret session and from that day on Communists have joined every pale movement of unrest, which they have tried then to turn red. The Vienna revolution was a splendid example of this plot.

John Reed, Boris Reinstein and Big Bill Haywood sold Lenin a communist revolution in America annually. With colossal naïveté the Russians accepted American promises.

"We can wait a year or two," Trotsky told the American delegation once.

On the other hand the leaders were much better informed and much more successful in the Chinese zone. After various disappointments in Europe the policy of plotting was shifted to the east. The Soviet radio to Tashkent was the busiest. The Trans-Siberian express carried money and men between China and Russia. The revolution was seen by Lenin whose last written statement contains the significant lines:

"The proletarian masses in India and China are becoming enlightened enough to wage the struggle side by side with Russia. When that happens world revolution will be successful."

The question of the uses of the red Russian army in neighbouring states is of vital concern to the peace of Europe. All evidence points to Russia's readiness to employ her forces in Poland, Germany, Roumania and other lands the moment an uprising is scheduled. Bucharin discussed the subject twice, once in an open, once in a secret session of the Third International. He went into details of co-operation. Proletarian Communists in the countries to be invaded were to be supplied with Russian arms, and a joint leadership of the troops was to be established. The German delegates said the mere knowledge that Russian troops would be sent at the very outbreak of a civil war, made its beginning much easier.

When the Revolutionary Church gave its intimidated blessings to Trotsky's soldiers it revealed the fact that the army was to fight in other countries. Archbishop Vedyensky, addressing the All-Russian Ecclesiastical Council, said: "We bless our red army whose final aim is to put an end to all armies," and the Metropolitan Antonin of the Living Church was coerced into having his council pass a resolution endorsing the Communist party and supporting the red army " as the best means of establishing world revolution."

Real evidence of the preparation to make an international instrument out of the Russian army was amply furnished by the teachers in the barracks, where I saw the signs painted everywhere: " Down with the international bourgeoisie " and " The red army is the instrument of international communism." I asked the teachers if they really intended preparing the army for furthering revolution in the neighbouring states.

" We certainly will not help the present bourgeois government of Germany," was the reply, " but once our comrades (the German Communist party) take over control in Germany, we will use the Russian army to form a union with the German communist army. We will likely go through Poland, incidentally restoring Silesia to Germany, and form a red bloc to the Rhine. Then French capitalism had better look out. After that, who knows? We will use the international army to make all Europe red, and eventually," he added laughing, " we will try to have your country join."

Generally it is expected that the new red international army will be used when any communist revolution breaks out in any nation whose frontiers adjoin Russia. The plan is to place the Russian troops on the border at such times and rely upon an international attack upon the existing government in the contiguous country, causing complete chaos and demoralization, and giving the Communists within and without an opportunity to seize power.

There is also corroborative evidence in a statement I heard Trotsky make that with the beginning of good harvests, a part of the yield would be set aside each year for feeding revolutionary elements in foreign countries at such times as they begin active revolutions. Trotsky officially stated that the United States would certainly stop its grain ships when revolutions began, whereupon Russia would immediately save the revolutions by sending " a meal to every revolutionary proletarian."

The foregoing declaration by Trotsky is also an excellent example of the kind of talk that fills the Third International. While the tone of this yearly congress is an open international plot, and while closer neighbours are more definitely discussed as coming victims, the United States comes in for its share of open and secret conspiracy. And as America grows richer and more contented, and Communism disappears, the language becomes more violent.

" The American bourgeoisie are glutted with the blood and gold of Europe." " The American bourgeoisie warmed their hands at the bonfire of European war. When the flame of revolution is lighted the American bourgeoisie will be consumed."

So Trotsky thundered. A few minutes later he had the American delegation in secret session where he denounced them for their stupidities and failures and admitted " nothing can be done to further Communism in America under the existing favorable economic circumstances."

In the secret sessions the delegates are given their orders on the treasury and the funds for propaganda abroad. Money for newspapers is apportioned and the expenses of the trip to Moscow refunded. Arrangements are made for money and propaganda via the Soviet embassies, legations, consulates, trade missions and other agencies in many lands. But the chief object of the secret sessions is to hear the report on the progress of the illegal Communist party and to give it its instructions for the next year, how to work in time of emergencies created by other parties, and how to create emergencies leading to the overthrow of established governments.

Everything that happens in America, the West Indies, Mexico, Japan, Germany, Bulgaria, Turkey — every communistic event is either under the direction of Moscow, attaches itself to Moscow eventually, or is taken in hand by Moscow's agents. Nothing communistic throughout the world is small enough to escape the interference of the Third International.

Although the tendency has been a little towards separation, the "interlocking directorate" of the Russian government, the Russian Communist party, and the Third International is almost identical. The Soviet government is continually denying it is active in propaganda in the United States, Mexico, China, wherever there is communistic enterprise. The Soviets lay the blame on the Third International which they claim is an international organization outside their control. To anyone who has seen the three communist bodies function in Moscow and who knows the philosophy believed there, such a statement is quibble and hypocrisy. The three are one. When Secretary Hughes asked the Soviet government to drop its program of world revolution and world propaganda, a Communist replied: "Why doesn't the American department of justice ask the bootleggers to carry only a line of sarsaparilla?"

Chapter III

THE TERROR IN RUSSIA CONTINUES

(Being a report written for Senator McCormick for use in a
Congressional Committee)

ADDRESSING an anniversary celebration of the troops
of the G. P. U., the Government Political Militia, which
is the old Chekah except for name, Dzerdzinsky said:

"Our enemies are now suppressed and are in the kingdom
of the shadows."

In the speech following his, I heard Kameneff say:

"Not a single measure of the Soviet government could have
been put through without the help of the Chekah. It is the
best example of communist discipline."

The Chekah (Chesvychaika), or G. P. U., is the instrument
of the red terror, organized in 1918, through which the Soviet
government, the Communist party and the Third International,
Russia's indivisible trinity, maintains itself in dictatorial power
to this very day. The years have brought a change in name,
less activity, more secrecy.

The era of wanton murder has passed, it is true; public trials
within fourteen days after arrest are now ordered by law and
in most cases given. But the terror has entered into the souls
of the Russian people.

Because of the Chekah, freedom has ceased to exist in Russia.
There is no democracy. It is not wanted. Only American apologists for the Soviets have ever pretended there was democracy in

Russia. "Democracy" says a communist axiom "is a delusion of the bourgeois mind." Justice in Russia is communist justice: the end justifies the means, and the end is Communism at all costs, including the lives of its opponents.

Freedom, liberty, justice as we know it, democracy, all the fundamental human rights for which the world has been fighting for civilized centuries, have been abolished in Russia in order that the communist experiment might be made. They have been kept suppressed by the Chekah — G. P. U.

The Chekah is the instrument of militant Communism. It is a great success. The terror is in the mind and marrow of the present generation and nothing but generations of freedom and liberty will ever root it out.

The Chekah began its existence as a revolutionary tribunal (in the manner of Robespierre's) shortly after the Bolsheviks routed the Mensheviks and obtained control in Petrograd. It then did police and spy duty much after the manner of the Czar's "Okhrana," but was considered a more liberal organization. In 1918, however, a girl revolutionary named Fanny Kaplan attempted to kill Lenin. She wounded him twice. A week later the red terror was announced officially and all the horror and bloodshed attached to the Soviet régime occurred between the end of 1918 and 1920, when Lenin announced the New Economic Policy.

According to a dispatch from Riga published in *The London Times* during the unfortunate ownership of Lord Northcliffe, the Chekah executed 1,700,000 persons. The dispatch listed the victims by profession. For example, it listed some 6,000 college professors as having been killed. As there had never been a total of 6,000 college professors in Russia, the report was evidently an exaggeration. I tried on the basis of this report to obtain an official statement from the Chekah headquarters in Moscow. After months of refusal, Peters, head of the red terror in Petrograd when it was the seat of the government, received me and gave me the following statement which I have recorded literally in my diary under date of December 9, 1922:

" We have executed some twenty or thirty thousand persons, perhaps fifty thousand. They were all spies, traitors, enemies within our ranks, a very small number in proportion to the persons of this kind then in Russia. We instituted the red terror at a time of war, when the enemy was marching upon us from without and the enemy within was preparing to help him. Scotland Yard executed spies and traitors also in war time."

The victims of the Chekah are estimated anywhere from 50,000 to 500,000, with the truth probably mid-ways. But it is not a matter of numbers. The outstanding fact today is that by their tortures, wholesale arrests and wholesale murders of liberals suspected of not favouring the Bolshevik interpretation of Communism, the Chekah has terrorized a whole generation, the people of our time.

Even today there are wholesale arrests periodically. It is notorious that before the four big holidays, the November 7th and the May 1st national days, and the opening of the Prof-intern and Comintern congresses, five thousand usually are jailed in Petrograd and Moscow. The victims are usually non-Bolshevik radicals, especially Socialists, social-revolutionaries and Mensheviks, who, incidentally, are more hated by the Bolsheviks than the capitalists, the nobility or the bourgeoisie.

In addition, there are hundreds of arrests in the cities daily. The workingman, knowing it is treason to strike, finds out that it is worth a month in jail just to complain. Then there are lists of thousands of radicals taken from the Czarist records.

All who live in Russia and who have not shown themselves Communists are therefore suspected of counter-revolution, and arrested periodically just for precaution's sake. Then there are the speculators, small bourgeois business men, vendors in the markets; in fact everyone except a true Communist party member is always in danger of arrest, and party members who are inactive are suspected.

This form of present day terrorism is legalized by the criminal code of the Soviet system. The code justifies everything. For example, here are paragraphs 57 and 62. Fifty-seven says:

" As counter-revolution is to be accounted every action directed to overthrow the régime of the Soviets which was won by the proletarian revolution, and its workers' and peasants' government based on the constitution of the Russian Socialist Federated Soviet Republic, and also actions directed to help that part of the international bourgeoisie which does not recognize the equality of the communist system coming to re-place capitalism, and which is attempting to overthrow it by means of intervention, blockade, espionage, financing of the press, etc."

Paragraph 62:

" As counter-revolution is to be accounted participation in an organ-ization acting for the purpose noted in article 57 by means of exciting the population to mass commotion, the non-payment of taxes, the unful-filment of duties or by any other means clearly detrimental to the dictatorship of the working class. . . ."

In ninety-nine cases of a hundred today the charge is " coun-ter-revolution " under the above two paragraphs of the criminal code, which, as can be seen, can be interpreted to any limit. For example, petty shopkeepers, calling upon American newspaper-men in the Soviet hotel, the Savoy, in Moscow, have in two instances been arrested and given the third degree after three days in solitary confinement. They were accused of counter-revolution inasmuch as they might have given anti-Bolshevik information to foreigners who would publish it in the foreign press, to the harm of the Bolshevik régime.

It is claimed by the present Chekah that the terror can now be maintained without inquisitional tortures. Yet it is true that the torture chambers have not been destroyed. In the Petrograd Chekah prisons rooms made of cork are used for prisoners, kept without light or air until they go half mad and make any sort of a confession, preferring death by a bullet to living in the cells.

Forcible feeding is resorted to in case of hunger strikes. " Solitary " prisoners are awakened at two o'clock in the morning for ten minutes exercise in the dark. Prisoners attempting to look through windows are fired upon and in one week recently three were shot through the head and killed in Petrograd.

Physical tortures are not necessary to drive persons insane in Chekah prisons. All survivors tell of cases of insanity. Sanitary conditions even now cannot be described either in press or public speech.

The Soviet system and the Third International are justly proud of the success of the Chekah, admitting that without this organization the régime could not have survived. The writer attended the fifth anniversary celebration of the Chekah in mid-December, 1922, in Moscow. It was the first time that any great part of the personnel of the dread organization came out into the open. Some ten thousand Chekah troops paraded. Government leaders, Third International notables and Felix Dzerdinsky, head of the Chekah, reviewed the troops and praised them.

Dzerdzinsky was then head of the Chekah commissariat and his two right-hand men were Peters and Unschlicht, the latter the personal watcher over Lenin. Other notables of the commissariat are Manzhinsky, Yagoda, Lazis, Artabakow. Dzerdzinsky was a Pole and Peters is likewise a foreigner, a Lett. This mixture of nationalities is another illustration of the fact the Soviets accept any one in any post, no matter how important, without regard to race, colour or creed so long as he is a tested Communist. (*Note:* Atheism is Communist party religious requirement in Russia, members being expelled frequently for attending church.)

The Chekah organization consists of between 100,000 and 500,000 men — it is impossible to obtain reliable figures inasmuch as one of its four departments is secret. There is first of all the armed uniformed militia which is the police system of the big cities. The organization system of the Czarist Okhrana is closely followed in the division into three departments much as the American army command has its G–1's, G–2's, etc. The Chekah organization consists of Militia, the Sekretnaya Operative Odyel for prison work, the Administrative (Third) section and the Soviet Espionage and Counter-Espionage department.

The commissariat controls all the work. Dzerdzinsky during his lifetime centralized the entire Chekah system so that its ramifications throughout Russia are directed from the headquarters in the Lubyanka on the Lubyanka Square, Moscow; the Petrograd and other branches have been shorn of most of their powers. The large Chekah organization is not necessarily composed of Communists. Like the army, it contains thousands of professional men who know only their job and do not care for whom they work. Many old Czarist spies are working now for the Bolsheviks.

The Terror in Russia Continues

Much more important is the fact that every member of the Communist party in Russia is a potential Chekist. Years ago Myasnikoff wrote in the *Isvestia* an appeal for every Communist to extend his duties to spying for the cause voluntarily, and inasmuch as the Communist party is a great secret society continually fighting enemies, it is the natural thing to find every Communist reporting suspicions to the Chekah. In fact one of the reasons for the continued terror in Russia is the fact that in hundreds of thousands of cases denunciations are made for personal reasons by voluntary Chekists.

The Chekah rule is absolute. No one was ever beyond suspicion with the possible exception of Lenin himself, and it was frequently boasted in Moscow that if Lenin asked the arrest of Trotsky it would follow without hesitation. Chekists told me in 1923 that they would exile Lenin or Trotsky if they believed either dangerous to party amity.

The main work of the Chekah is to catch the faintest whisper of Socialist or monarchist expression. The Chekah hounds the liberal Socialists, in fact all radicals who are not out-and-out Communists, more than the monarchist or bourgeois oppositions. The Chekah begins its work in the peasant villages and continues up through the very All-Russian Executive Committee itself. It suspects everyone, spares no one. In fact, it is considered a point of pride by a Communist to be arrested, tried, acquitted and restored with honour to his position in the party. There can be no severer test of membership.

In the villages the Chekah keeps the few communist officials in the saddle because in every instance they are outnumbered by non-communist peasants a hundred or more to one. The most intensive campaign of communist propaganda is waged in the villages to win farmer support, but the moment a peasant voices opposition or fails to pay taxes he comes under Chekah persecution. He may not be executed as in the old days or even tried, but his life is not worth living and his beloved land may be taken away from him.

One of the chief duties of the Chekah is to control the elections. The law in Russia says only a proletarian may vote, which almost restricts voting to Communists, yet in the peasant villages where there are less than two or three per cent. of Communists, the peasants, being called proletarians, may vote. The Chekah sees that they vote " right." When the writer visited the office of Peters he saw on this Chekah leader's desk a budget of a hundred closely typewritten sheets on the subject of banditry in the country-side and another lot of 200 sheets of political reports from Chekah agents in every hamlet in Russia. The political situation is absolutely in the grip of the Chekah system.

In the factories, mines and workshops the Chekah conducts espionage and employs *provocateurs*. Peters said proudly that American " comrades " showed them how it was done in the steel plants in Pittsburgh and in Gary and that they have improved on American methods. Chekah agents are continually forming anti-communist groups of workingmen especially in the Putiloff works in Petrograd where some 40,000 are employed and in the railroad works in Kharkoff. When the time comes the Chekah betrays the whole group, some of which are exiled or executed.

Not lacking in humour was the trick the Chekah played on the remnants of the last legal opposition in Russia, the S–R's or Social Revolutionary party. After the big trial in the summer of 1922 when most of the leaders were imprisoned, the Chekists began joining the " underground " organizations of the S–R's until they outnumbered the original membership, whereupon they called a national convention to decide to give up the party and to join the Communists. Sixty per cent. of the members attending the congress were Chekists.

The S–R party continues to exist — abroad. Its headquarters are in Berlin, and it is interesting to note that in the memorandum of its congress in April, 1922, when it set forth a list of demands, the first one dealt with the Chekah:

"We demand the union of Socialists in Europe and Russia for the purpose of clearing out first of all the horrors of the terror régime, the Chekah, with its despotism, bloodshed and filth."

On the other hand contrast the statement of Gregory Zinovieff, once head of the Third International, member of the Executive Committee, and "mayor" of Petrograd:

"The red army and the Chekah build the fame and the honour of the Communist party."

No foreign business man, diplomat or journalist is free from being shadowed by the Chekah. American and British business men frequently found their offices sealed while the Chekah went through their books and papers. In one instance to which the writer was a witness, two British steamship and iron works' representatives were arrested on leaving a *cabaret,* kept four hours in a Chekah prison, after which they received profoundest apologies for the Chekah "mistake." Arriving at their rooms in the Savoy hotel everything seemed in order but closer examination revealed that all their papers had been examined, copied, and some taken.

This is not an exceptional case. It happens in practically 100 per cent. of American and other foreign businesses in Russia.

Wanton executions, mass murders, wholesale searches are

perhaps a thing of the past in Chekah history, being replaced by imprisonment in vile pens and exile to Siberia in much the Czarist fashion. But the most important fact about the Chekah today is that by its never ceasing persecution it has smothered all liberty of expression, it has cowed the souls of the people, it has continued a reign of terror which makes Bolshevism supreme, and will not let any change or liberalizing movement come into Soviet Russia.

Chapter IV

THE NEW RED ARMY

ONCE there were mercenary troops; then a nationalist spirit came over the people of Europe which you can find dramatized by Gobineau in his "Renaissance" and Shaw in "Saint Joan"; and now, after thousands of years of fighting, including that grandest tragic farce of all, the War to End War, comes the first international army, the new red army of Soviet Russia, the only force in the world organized to fight, not for feudal lord, or a nation, but for a class of society and in every country where it can be sent expeditiously.

So far as I know no one but Sam Spewack, former *World* correspondent, and myself ever penetrated the mystery of the red army, and as we were both expelled from Russia simultanously a few days later it is obvious that this enterprise bore its punishment quickly.

Like so many of the great scoops and experiences of newspaper life, this visit to the red army was arranged by fortunate accidents. Spewack had succeeded in entering the Kremlin to see the Czar's jewels at a time when the Bolsheviks were looking for buyers. Many months afterwards we met the officer who had been detailed to guard the fabulous, impractical treasure. He told us that he had rejoined his regiment and invited us to visit him. Thus all of Trotsky's refusals and silences were overcome and one bright, brittle, May-time morning a little automobile composed of Ford, Buick and other parts took us to visit regiments comprising at least a fifth of the armed forces of the R. S. F. S. R.

We were introduced first to the " Comrade-General " who shook hands cheerfully, then to the " Comrade-Commissar," the political agent, who nodded and scowled in a superior fashion. Political officials are attached to every officer, from colonel to generalissimo; they report to the Chekah and the war department, act as spies and advisors, keep the officer in alignment wtih Bolshevism, and superintend the teaching and training of the international communist soldier.

First we went to see the " initiation " of new conscripts. They were fine, healthy, ignorant, peasant animals dressed in new clothes and frightened. At a command they bent their knees, bowed to kiss the blood-red banners, stood and swore the " red oath ":

" I, son of the working class, citizen of the Soviet Republic, accept the title of a warrior of the Workers and Peasants Army.

" In the presence of the working class of Russia and of the whole world I vow to honour this title, to learn the profession of arms conscientiously, and to protect the apple of my eye, the good of the people, from ruin and corruption.

" I swear to obey the stern revolutionary discipline and to carry out without dissent all the commands of those commanders appointed by the Workers and Peasants Republic.

" I swear to hold myself back from any step, and to hold back my comrades from any step, which could lower the worth of a citizen of the Soviet Republic and to direct all my thoughts to that great goal, the liberation of all workers.

" I swear to be ready at the first call of the Workers and Peasants Government for the defence of the Soviet Republic against all dangers and attacks from any of its enemies and in battle for the Russian Soviet Republic, for the cause of Socialism,

Soldiers taking the " Red Oath " in Kremlin Square, Moscow.

When Trotsky reviewed his new army at the fifth anniversary celebration of the November Revolution. Kamineff is in the foreground with Trotsky (saluting) behind him.

and the brotherhood of all peoples, to spare neither my efforts nor my life.

" Should I maliciously violate this, my solemn vow, so may I be rewarded by universal contempt and the stern punishment of revolutionary law."

Many of them no doubt had no idea what the words meant. The vast majority were illiterate. But reading and writing are an important part of Russian army life.

After the ceremony we entered a regimental " study room " where I heard this " Red Catechism " propounded by the communist instructor of the Fourteenth Division to two hundred men:

Q. " Why do we maintain the Red Army? "

A. " To save Russia from its enemies."

Q. " Who are Russia's enemies? "

A. " The bourgeois class throughout the world."

Q. " Where are your bourgeois enemies concentrated? "

A. " In England, France, and America."

Q. " Why must we prepare to fight our bourgeois enemies? "

A. "Because the bourgeois nations are fighting against Russia.

Q. " Why are the bourgeois nations fighting Russia? "

A. " Because they know that the proletariat class and the Red Army will establish a workers' and soldiers' government in their countries instead of the present capitalistic governments that rule them now."

At this point the regimental teacher of Communism digressed into the usual propaganda talk lasting half an hour, after which he asked the questions of the catechism again, this time picking out soldiers at random to answer them.

A few minutes later with the officers of the same division I was walking in the yard between barracks. It was slush underfoot and in the shadows there were still piles of snow covered with black grime. But spring had at last come to Russia and with spring . . .

"Devil take it," said the staff colonel, "I'd like to take a crack at somebody with this new army — Poland or Roumania — they're damned fresh and the men are just aching for action."

Half an hour later, ten miles away, two squadrons of cavalry were trotted out for a cavalry charge and mimic battle — all to please and impress two American newspapermen. And then again . . .

"If people back there," said the Comrade-General, pointing to the invisible Kremlin, "would only let us try out the men in real action. The soldiers are willing and anxious."

I visited the artillery too, and I spoke to some of the young aviators who fly the Vickers Vimy bombers and the metal Junkers over Moscow. Everywhere the same thing. They wanted to fight somebody. They were young, they were full of Bolshevik propaganda; they were neither German nor French soldiers full of memories of the horrors of modern war. They wanted war.

And that is the biggest impression the red army made on me.

In the Kremlin there had been a different opinion. Trotsky, the chief of staff schools then, Petrofsky, General Danielef, and the politicians who are not officers, were united in the idea that the time was not opportune for any war-making. One party even announced as Russia's policy: "to remain neutral, sell to both sides, and with the money build up the Russian army." At all events, it was peace talk, not war talk, that you heard in diplomatic circles and the opposite in military circles.

The thing that impressed me next to the process of communizing the army and the war talk, was the statement that the artillery commander made. I was looking at the artillery park outside the barracks and remarked on the number of guns — there were about fifty three-inch rifles and a half dozen larger pieces.

" Enough," said the general, " to blow them off the map in five minutes if they start any counter-revolution."

By " them " he meant any anti-Bolshevik elements which have not been executed, exiled or terrorized into a state of helplessness in Moscow. In Moscow some time previously I had seen some of the 80,000 armed workingmen. These men, mostly Communists, were being trained to suppress any counter-revolution even if it came from the army. And so the game went, Trotsky building up, arming, safe-guarding his army through communistic teaching; and likewise building the Chekah army, one to defeat the other, should it get out of control.

The best impression was made by the cavalry.

" What would you like to see? " asked the cavalry Comrade-General, " some hurdle jumping or a cavalry charge? "

We made the expected reply. The general smiled, rather pleased. " Let's warm up the forces first with a little jumping," and away galloped the general with his staff to join the cavalry-men.

They went through a manœuvre, dividing into two squads, riding easily down the length of the parade grounds, meeting, parting, putting on speed. Then across the field they raced toward the hurdle and over the top they went a few feet and a few seconds apart. Two red soldiers immediately raised the pole a notch and the performance was repeated.

Finally the pole was placed on top of the supports and the general alone dashed for it. He was mounted on a wonderful mare, as wild an animal as ever carried a Cossack. But when he came to the pole she balked. Stopped dead. The general was chagrined but not angry. He called her by her pet name but did not give her the spur. And quite unexpectedly the mare, standing on her hind legs, drew herself together like a crouching lion, and just leaped over the pole.

"Now the charge," ordered the general and a hundred horsemen went splashing through the mud squaring the field until they came to the far corner. Then every horseman stuck his pennoned lance forward, crouched on his horse's neck, dug his spurs into his horse's flanks and charged. It sounded like barrage fire heard miles away, a muddy roar of four hundred hoofs in the soft earth, the clanking of horses' gear and the wild shouts of the charging cavalrymen. They came at terrific speed, the little hairy Siberian ponies seeming to rush over the ground, feet hardly touching, in one mad flight that amazed the eye.

We stood midway of the six-hundred-yard charge, yet they came, passed us and were at their goal in seemingly a minute. All we saw was a streak of mixed coloured bodies, black and white and bay with an occasional lightning-like flash of flaming crimson of the pennons. What would have happened to men who stood in the way — even if they had had a machine gun in action?

The officers meanwhile ordered ranks formed again — frothing horses white at the mouths, sweat turning white on their hides, mud-caked, red nostrils distended, and their riders breathing hard and laughing jerkily.

At the infantry division barracks we went through the building from basement to bedrooms. We started with the kitchens.

Here as elsewhere everyone snapped to attention, a bit ludicrously to be sure, in their white aprons and hats, especially the chief cook, a little pot-bellied fellow who probably never did or never will go through drill.

" Comrade - commander - there - is - nothing - new - to - report - since - you - were - here - last." The cook delivered himself of the standard recipe all in a mouthful, the general smiled and shook him by the hand and democracy was restored here also.

" Would you like to taste the food ? " the general asked me.

What could I answer? I was a guest. I looked at the huge pots, at the not-too-clean dishes, and the pot-bellied cook in the dirty white apron and said I would be delighted. This made everybody happy. A huge spoonful of soup was dipped up from the twenty-gallon vat and given me in a small bowl. There was a lot of cabbage, some pieces of onion, a considerable amount of fat and some, to me, unknown ingredients in the bowl. I tasted. The soup was excellent — much better in fact than the soup served us daily in the Savoy.

" Now the kasha," said the general. The kasha is a mush made out of dark grain which is used for feeding parrots and other birds. It too was excellent. Fortunately the meat was not ready. It was the one suspicious part of the meal. I had previously seen chunks of frozen beef looking very black and somewhat green in spots. I looked on the blackboard. Here is the red soldier's daily meal.

> Bread......1½ pounds.
> Meat....... ½ pound.
> Soup....... 2 bowls.
> Kasha.
> Tea.

"Do you give them anything to drink besides tea?"

"Alcohol, you mean?" replied the officer. "No. Not even a drink of rum when in action. But beer and wine are not prohibited. The national law is observed. No spirits containing more than 20 per cent. alcohol for anyone. But we go further. We bar all alcoholic drinks in barracks or while on duty. The soldiers may drink their beer and wine elsewhere, provided they do not get drunk. No, not a drop must be carried into the barracks. Our army, in fact, drinks almost nothing and no one complains."

Here the chief cook came up with a book much like a cheap autograph album much-thumbed, dog-eared and grease-spotted.

"If you like the food, please write to that effect," he said.

I wrote "Excellent," my name, New York, and the date in English in the columns provided, and the general, looking through the back pages, showed that a few days ago the word "Excellent" had been written followed by the name Trotsky.

Well, there can be no doubt that the red army is well fed and well clothed, better, one might say, than the average Russian if in the average you include the masses of the underfed and the masses of the badly clad of the country-side. Certainly the army is much better off than the average Moscow or Petrograd workingman.

Next to the spectacle of having a regiment drilled and cavalry put on a charge for two American newspapermen, what interested me most was the communizing process of which the catechism is only a part. Every day in every way Communism was being instilled into the new red army. Take for instance such a thing as a "communist roulette wheel."

The communist catechism, you see, was school work — school work for young peasant sons of not too high a mental calibre. Undoubtedly they liked it no more than the boys in the little red schoolhouse who hear roaring above the teacher's words, the springtime flooding river, and the loud invitations to play hookey.

The communist roulette wheel is a sort of red army Montessori idea. It is played in the club-room of the barracks. There are some twenty numbers and the wheel is spun until every soldier gets one. The number entitles the recipient to a type-written piece of paper on which is printed a question:

" What is the purpose of the dictatorship of the proletariat? "

" Why must religion be abolished? "

" What is the difference between the proletarian red army of Russia and the capitalistic armies of Europe? "

" Why must capitalism be destroyed and Communism be established throughout the world? "

To these questions the soldier may write an answer. It is not obligatory. It is a game. He writes an answer. For " correct " answers — the divisional communist instructor is judge of the correctness — or for the best answer, the soldier gets a prize. The prizes as I saw them displayed in a case consisted of pieces of soap, cheap razors, brushes, packages of biscuits and other useful things.

Again, a few minutes later, in a barracks across the square, we came upon a girl teaching a group of peasant boy soldiers the rudiments of reading, writing and arithmetic. But instead of the stuff that goes into little children's heads throughout the world, " I am a man," " I see a cat," " This is a dog," the communist girl teacher was calmly writing:

" The red army is the instrument of the masses for conquering the world." " Death to the Middle Class Governments," " Down with the enemies of the Third International."

Everywhere, everywhere, the communist idea pumped into the heads of the communist army.

No wonder that asking an interpreter to read some of the soldier contributions to the bulletin board which also served them as a regimental newspaper, I found the soldiers expressing themselves in an echo of their communist instructors:

" Death to the bourgeoisie."

" Down with capitalism."

" Down with priests and the church."

" Religion is narcotic for the masses."

" Long live the Third International."

These things I actually saw scrawled, painted, printed, in every barracks. Every barracks was decorated with pictures of Marx, Lenin, Trotsky, and scores of examples of the soldiers' art. These examples in oil, water-colours and pencil are sometimes neutral subjects, rather exaggerated swallows singing over green fields, sometimes horrible cartoons of manlike monsters eating human beings, their fangs dripping blood. And these monsters are labelled either " Capitalism " or " The Greek Church."

Evidence of the anti-religious teaching campaign was to be seen on all the walls of the clubs and sleeping-quarters. I asked whether the army officially conducted an atheistic movement. The officers said that was a private matter but the League of Communist Youth had the right to preach anti-religion in the club-rooms.

In the club-rooms, general and private are of equal rank. Democracy in the relations of commanders and followers provides that the soldier must salute his officer only when on service or addressed. In the club-room there are no salutes known nor is any official deference shown a general. My visit to the differ-

ent branches gave me the feeling that there was a considerable amount of friendliness as well as democracy in the army.
This is encouraged. As the number of Czarist officers diminishes
every day and the number of workingmen officers risen from
the ranks increases, this democracy naturally increases. How it
will effect discipline is hard to say. From the look of things
there is discipline in the barracks. Certainly orders are obeyed
with considerable snap. In the manœuvres and on parade not
only is there discipline but an increase in precision noticeable
even to eyes which remain civilian (despite seeing the American
army through all its campaigns in France).

There is nothing mysterious about the red army. In accordance with the habits of European nations, however, the strictest
secrecy is now being maintained about modern equipment,
chemical warfare, and the aviation section.

*   *   *   *   *

Officially Russia announces today an army of less than 600,000.
But in addition there is the G. P. U. army, the picked troops
of the secret service, numbering between 100,000 and 500,000.
In Moscow there are now about 100,000 armed communist
workmen; in Russia the total of communist irregulars, half-
trained yet most reliable of all, is another 250,000. With the
veterans of the world war Russia has a force of two to three
million men.

Russia needs heavy cannon, airplanes, tanks, gas, all the
machinery of modern warfare. I have seen at least a hundred
military airplanes and twenty British tanks being repaired in
the vast railroad shops in Kharkoff. The officer there claimed
there were a hundred in service. But there can be no question
of the Soviet's lack of materials, and on this lack are based the

Allied reports that Russia could not fight a modern war successfully.

Food, clothing and propaganda have made the army loyal. Trotsky's personality and his knowledge of military strategy were an important factor for years. Although he has spent most of his life as a red agitator and writer, he has always been a student of military strategy, has written a book on Napoleon's manœuvres and has been given credit for building the keenest morale and using the keenest military strategy in the numerous campaigns in which Russia defeated her enemies in the civil wars.

The Russian leaders, who know the historic course of the French revolution very well, and who see history repeating itself in many ways, have planned to avoid that chapter which Carlyle heads " a whiff of grape-shot." It was a whiff of grape-shot which put an end to the years of indecision and opened the way for the strong man, Napoleon, to seize the country and change the tenor of the revolution. Russia has been determined never to let Trotsky do likewise.

In 1925 the communist element in the red army was about ten per cent. or 100,000 men in the then official army. It was Trotsky's plan to make the army and navy 100 per cent. communist. Much headway has already been made with the officers. So late as the Russo-Polish war the system was to retain an efficient Czarist officer in joint command of every unit with a communist zealot who watched but who probably knew nothing of war-making. There is still a large group of old-time officers in the red army but most of them are either professional soldiers who are not unwilling to fight for Bolshevism or the communist converts. A notable case was General Budyenny, the famous Cossack cavalry leader, who was popular, a Communist, and later a member of the All-Russian Congress præsidium. The total communist force in the red army in 1928 was estimated at 27 per cent.

All the new officers are proletarians, men risen from the ranks. "An officer," Trotsky once announced officially, "is a comrade who knows more than an enlisted man." According to Trotsky the friendliest relations must prevail between officers and men not on duty but the strictest discipline while on duty. Recently the staff of a regiment was court-martialed for getting drunk in the presence of the enlisted men. Trotsky published the minutes of the court-martial throughout the army and press.

Although Trotsky claimed that the men and officers were all of one "class," the recruits are almost all peasant sons, the officers almost all industrial workers.

Almost every unit in the army and navy is "adopted" by some social organization. Thus the League of Communist Youth is the "owner" of the navy, a sort of godfather which looks after the comfort and well-being of the sailors, hears their complaints, supplies extra food, clothing, reading-matter and propaganda. Each big factory adopts a regiment, the All-Russian Congress Executive Committee adopts a division, etc. Another interesting fact is that Trotsky formed an all-communist division of some 10,000 men distinguishable by their blue helmets with red stars. Trotsky undoubtedly is a military genius. He was in due time exiled to Siberia.

Chapter V

How Methodism Tried to Capture the Church Of Russia — And How a Bishop Got His Pockets Picked

BISHOP Blake came to Moscow with his eyes open. So, at least, read his declaration the day he set out from Paris, and he repeated it flamboyantly to the newspapermen in Riga, then to us in Russia.

It was during the vast religious upheaval that this ardent and apparently sincere leader of American Methodism had the practical vision of capturing the whole old Orthodox Church and its one hundred and thirty-odd million blind followers, somewhat muddled by Bolshevism and groping for a new Moses. The Blake vision was as grandiose as a crusade and much more likely of fulfilment.

Russia had never had a real reformation. Church and state had worked as one, and just as corruption and terrorism spread under Czarist dictatorship, so had corruption and decay penetrated the monasteries and churches of Holy Russia. If ever a people were rotten-ripe for a reformation it was Russia in the first year of Bolshevism.

The Soviets had succeeded in replacing the Czarist terror with their own terror by 1923. They had exterminated the ruling nobility and crushed bourgeois opposition completely. But they had one enemy left, the greatest of all, the ignorant, fanatical, priest-ridden peasant church congregation.

While the American Methodist Church was surveying the

land in hope of one of the greatest Protestant victories of all
history, the Bolshevik politicians were not idle. They were
working with all their means, unhampered by what they termed
bourgeois morals and bourgeois ethics. With recklessness and
unshakable determination they set about to destroy the power
of organized religion.

The Consomols, or League of Communist Youth, and other
anti-religion groups were encouraged for an atheistic campaign
the like of which the world has not seen since the French Revolution, and the principle of " boring from within," which the
Third International had advocated for political parties and labor
unions in foreign countries, was practiced in the Orthodox
Church itself.

Quick to see the first signs of dissaffection among the honest
and sincere priests who were disgusted with the old church and
who wanted to cleanse Christianity in Russia, the Soviets came
to the support of the group led by Archbishop Vedyensky.
Through him the Soviets organized the Living Church and
at one stroke split off a large part of the Orthodox Church,
thus diminishing greatly the hitherto united power of its last
enemies.

With this knowledge the American press corps in Moscow
called upon Bishop Blake the day he arrived. There followed a
very strange interview. We had come for a story: we devoted
two hours to telling things and to answering questions posed
by the churchman and his aides. It was apparent to us that
either the bishop did not know of the grand Soviet plot which
was the real spiritual father of the Living Church, or he did
not care about it. His zeal for conquest seemed to blind him
to these details.

" Our Mission is one of Christian courtesy and goodwill to

a great Church and a great people," he said. " If by any word or action we can give courage and support to Russian Christianity, we shall count it a great opportunity and an honour to be permitted —— " and more in the line of Mr. Babbitt.

The kindly old soul, it seemed to all of us, knew nothing of the oriental depth of Soviet intrigue. We proceeded to enlighten the Methodist Mission and to warn them. We left them naïvely incredulous. Oh, they had their eyes open all right, but they had seen nothing.

Then came the great first congress of the Living Church.

Archbishop Vedyensky had been a handsome priest in the days of the Czar in Petrograd. He had education, charm and an unmistakable sincerity. Women had adored him. He had preached to royalty, nobility and wealth. Despite such close association, or perhaps because of it, Vedyensky had begun to express radical opinions — that is, radical for those Czarist days, because he preached Essene Christianity, humility and self-sacrifice, " do unto others," the curse of riches, the necessity of pure and holy living.

Under the Bolsheviks, Vedyensky saw the old corrupt church become more and more impotent and atheism grow. He proposed church reform and may have been amazed by the speed of communist acceptance. At any rate, the opportunity of his life had come to him.

At the very first meeting of the " All-Russian Ecclesiastical Council " Vedyensky presided. He was clad in a long black robe, flowing from head to floor, giving him an unearthly tallness, and his face would have been worth a fortune to any artist looking for models for the Christ. He alone had no beard; his forehead was high, his lips moist and his eyes flaming. He spoke softly but with a terrible intensity and when he raised his fine face and long delicate fingers in supplication, as he prayed to heaven, he seemed magically enhaloed. It was no great strain of the imagination, watching Vedyensky, to see nineteen hundred years back, the amazement on the faces of the Galilean fishermen clustered round the delicate, long-robed, beardless young Jesus.

"Bolshevism fulfils the mission of Christ," Vedyensky was preaching. "Verily the Communists proclaim themselves plain materialists who have no time for spiritual affairs, even unbelievers in anything but proletarian dictatorship. But their leaders, but Lenin, walks in the ways of Christ. In many countries of this world there is a pretence of Christianity, but capitalism not Christ is worshipped, Rockefeller not Christ rules."

He then presented the congressional resolution which begins: "Capitalism is one of the seven deadly sins. The Soviet government is the only government fighting capitalism," and concludes with:

"The Ecclesiastical Council condemns the counter-revolutionary acts of the Patriarch Tikhon and his followers. The Ecclesiastical Council lifts the anathema put on the Soviets by Tikhon and denounces Tikhon as a traitor to the Church and to Christianity. The Ecclesiastical Council abolishes the Patriarchate."

"Oh, I am ashamed of the old church," cried Vedyensky when he had finished reading. "The old church was a pigsty. And Tikhon was a member of the Black Hundreds. Tikhon opposed the order to help the women and little children, victims of starvation; Tikhon caused bloodshed by resisting the Soviet government. Tikhon was an anti-Christ."

Then the Council voted to unfrock Tikhon and to leave him plain citizen Andray Belavin; the man second only to the Czar in power was cast out as a traitor to Christ and an eleventh day which shook the world was recorded. We were all duly impressed. Bishop Blake was duly impressed.

But the newspapermen were not taken in. Although we could not trust our interpreters, because they censored as they talked, and despite the fact we could not send the truth by wire or mail, we made an effort to get it. There were some men we could trust. Bishops who voted "anti" told us that the resolution casting out Tikhon, lifting the anathema on all things red, and sending the church's greetings to Lenin and the Soviet army, had not been passed unanimously. There had been violent protest, and the opposition had been denied the right to speak. Of the 308 delegates a score had refused to vote until threatened with having their names given to the Chekah. Delegates, priests and bishops told us that the hall had been crowded with Chekah agents who noted all dissenters for future persecution. But that was not all. Later we were informed by participants that whereas many of the 308 delegates, representing 308 church districts, were honest followers of the new church, the majority had been chosen by Chekah intimidation and terror in their home towns. The whole congress had been a fraud. Seventy or more per cent. of the delegates had been chosen by fraud. The Chekah had controlled the church congress from the first meetings of the congregations in peasant villages to the final passage of the resolution unfrocking Tikhon.

Bishop Blake did not believe us.

He had been the only foreign churchman present, thanks also to Soviet intrigue, and he had delivered himself of a little speech, bringing the greetings of American Methodism to the Russian Reformation. His reception had been so cordial that he could see progress for his vast vision. So he preferred to believe the reports of the Rev. L. O. Hartmann of Boston, one-time editor of *Zion's Herald,* and now associate councillor and interpreter.

Some days later we had more news for Bishop Blake. Even before the " red clergy " had whitewashed the Soviets, a trade had been made by which Tikhon's life had been saved. The price had been the surrender of the Living Church to Bolshevism. This was the contract:

" *For the Bolshevists:* 1. — The church lifts the anathema which Tikhon pronounced against the Soviets.

" 2. — The church unfrocks Tikhon, lifts his immunity from trial and virtually surrenders him friendless to Bolshevist justice.

" 3. — The church blesses the Soviet régime and accepts the Communist program and its Marxian philosophy, excepting the clause against religion.

" 4. — The Church blesses the red army.

" *For the church:* 1. — Metropolitan Antonin, the arch-enemy of Tikhon, becomes head of the Russian church.

" 2. — The priest Vedyensky of Petrograd becomes archbishop.

" 3. — The anti-Tikhon group of reformists obtains the best church properties.

" 4. — The ' red ' clergy will receive the proper support and favour of the Soviet government, the army, the Chekah in every town in Russia.

" 5. — Tikhon turned plain citizen will be tried but his life will be spared."

Naturally the Soviet censorship would permit no word of this business to reach the outer world. How the board of bishops of the Methodist Episcopal Church, meeting in Darkest Kansas, heard of affairs in Moscow I do not know: perhaps they had not heard the facts but were merely acting from a native distrust of everything Bolshevik. But they took action immediately. So one day I brought the Methodist representative a telegram which read:

"*Board bishops Methodist Episcopal church resolutioned recall delegation Russia — refuses accept responsibility remarks purported Blake conclave at which Tikhon unfrocked.*

"*Resolution declares church neither supports nor defends Soviets as Blake alleged and assured council.*

"*Reported here Blake in address said church couldn't stand aside but must follow revolutionary upheavals and accept every movement towards greater brotherhood. First time history, bishop is reported to have said that a great nation is dedicating itself to go forward on behalf masses humanity and church couldn't anathematize such movement —*"

The last time I saw Bishop Blake in Russia we had a long argument about the actions of the Soviets. I concluded with:

"If everything is right there would be no censorship. They maintain a censorship to hide their terrorism."

"But," contended the bishop, "I saw a dispatch of yours in the paper in which you described the anti-religious campaign — even the crowds burning crucifixes and shouting 'down with the church.' Now if the censor lets you pass such a terrible item, you certainly cannot complain of Soviet censorship."

Bishop Babbitt!

A few days later I was expelled from Russia. The Methodist Mission was moving also. I went to the American Relief Administration building to say good-bye. I also settled my financial matters in the auditing office.

Suddenly a nervous, troubled little lady burst into the room and demanded aid from Colonel Haskell.

" We are in a lot of trouble — we've lost everything — money, watches, letters of credit and our return tickets — You must help us."

" Whom? " asked one of the Relief men.

" Bishop Blake and his party — I am Mrs. Hartmann, the wife of the Rev. Dr. Hartmann."

" But how did this all happen? "

" They were at the last session of the church congress and they had their pockets picked — and the Bishop's watch gone too — "

* * * * *

And so ended a vision. The Living Church of Russia faltered along; the atheistic campaign crashed through its own weight of stupidity, Tikhon's life was saved as per arrangement and the American Methodist Church continued to gain converts — in China or Africa.

And the Chekah no doubt eventually won the gold watch.

* * * * *

Chapter VI

CARMAGNOLE CHRISTMAS

HAD Mr. Carlyle been alive and devised means for breaking censorship, he could have spared his amazing imagination for a chapter by merely photographing Carmagnole in Moscow. For history waited just a hundred and thirty years to repeat in Russia scenes from the French Revolution. Once again girls dressed in the vestments of priests danced the Carmagnole and images and ideas which men had worshipped, held sacred, and had been willing to defend with their lives, were burned or spat upon or flung into the snows.

In the Red Square a group of students from Sverdloff University inaugurated the Bolshevik Anti-Religious Campaign. Laughing boys and girls, red-cheeked and good-natured, bobbed hair alike for both sexes, poorly clad, they began with a travesty of a Greek Catholic ritual service, mocking the phrases and rhyming them with Marxian epigrams.

A crowd gathered and grew.

When the players interpolated the newest street slang into the prayers there was laughter. Girls became shrill and hilarious. On the outskirts of the mob a pious peasant crossed himself and muttered a curse.

There appeared a travesty of an ancient Hebrew rabbi, jestingly chanting the psalms with exaggerated Jewish gestures and many a wink. He wore a praying cloth around his fat stomach and dozens of phylacteries in strange places.

Merriment reigned.

202

There appeared a long, lean, wily Oriental who turned somersaults with marvellous abandon. He was labelled Mohammed. With him were several students dressed as Greek Catholic priests. Some were praying, juggling prayer-books and vodka bottles, others would catch a bottle in mid-air and pretend to drink the alcohol. The juggling was excellent.

Applause.

There appeared a procession of boys and girls, men and women, the children of pious folk carrying paper and wood effigies of all the leaders of this world's religions, Jesus and Moses, Buddha and Confucius, Mohammed, Osiris, Archangel Gabriel, Saint George, Abraham and the Virgin Mary. In groups of hundreds and two hundreds they came to the Red Square from every direction. One group passed the Shrine of the Iberian Virgin, the most sacred in all Russia. The local priests had doubly padlocked the little blue building and disappeared to pray discreetly for divine aid. But braver souls, lay souls, had come to guard the doors. A woman in jewels and sables, a peasant in a greasy sheepskin, a beggar wearing ten or more cast-off coats so badly torn that his body was visible in spots where the holes in all ten coincided. Twenty in all, the rest nondescript in appearance but fanatic of eye.

Jeers. Exchange of curses and filth. But no violence.

The faithful crossed themselves. Those who jeered crossed themselves mockingly and shouted their laughter. The faithful thereupon fell upon their knees, first one then everyone in a mass movement, and there in the dirty snow, in the intense mid-winter frost, under a morbid sun, they prayed for their shrine while company after company of marchers filed by them, mocking, laughing, jeering, spitting and heaping sarcastic and ironic benedictions upon the prostrated.

Five thousand students and at least ten thousand onlookers had now filled a large part of the Red Square. The audience itself was inarticulate. Only an occasional individual had the courage to protest, applaud or show his disgust by word or gesture. The student leaders were gay and as alert as cheer leaders of a Harvard-Yale game. They kept their groups in line, found them their locations and prepared the final ceremony.

In the centre of the Red Square the snow had been cleared, and a hill of debris collected. Soon it was alight. When the flames were high and reflecting on the red Kremlin walls and the madly coloured onion and pineapple domes of the Vasilly Church, the students began to sing. They marched round and round the fire, singing first the " Internationale," then an anti-religious song to the tune of a famous hymn. Then the " Internationale " again, and as they crowded, fought their way to the fire, shouting and laughing, they threw, one group after another, the various images they had brought from the schools and universities, into the common flames.

A shout of glee, a roaring wave upon wave of joyful wordless sound greeted the appearance of a figure labelled Jehovah. It was that of the burlesque stage Jew, wearing praying cloths, a huge six-pointed star on his chest, and phylacteries on forehead and arm. Into the fire it went. Another figure labelled " God Almighty " was pushed through. It was an enormous straw dummy, bulbously red-eyed, heavily bewhiskered, much like the drunken type of Russian peasant, but carrying two gold-bags in one hand and the Greek cross in the other. Into the fire it went while the round waves of wild enthusiasm sped to the outer edges of the throng. Twenty times ribald posters called " God Creating Man," mostly scenes of drunkenness and Rabelaisian horse-play, came to the fire. Finally came a procession of coffins on each of which a communist student was perched dispensing mock benedictions. Everywhere showers of labels like confetti at a carnival. The labels were printed "Religion is Opium for the People."

Just as the climax of marching and burning passed, the oratory began.

"Our demonstration is not anti-church but anti-religious," declared one student.

"We are here to break the chains which have enslaved the Russian peasants to the church," said another.

And a third stood on a coffin and shouted:

"Your priests have told you that we would be stricken dead by a thunderbolt from Heaven if we did this. But no thunderbolt has come. See. I defy God to send down a thunderbolt! But none comes."

No thunderbolt came. The laughter and shouting continued until the last embers ceased to glow and the weird shadows of the fire had mingled in the universal semi-darkness. The onlookers and the actors began to depart. Last to go were the twenty men and women guarding the shrine of the Iberian Virgin, the most sacred in all Russia.

* * * * *

Carmagnole Easter

From "forty times forty" churches, the pale-blue domed churches and the gold domed churches, the fantastic church of Vasilly and the beautiful marble Cathedral of the Holy Saviour on the River Moskva, the thousands upon thousands of bells tolled brazenly, announcing the Resurrection.

205

Over the whole capital the air vibrated with the clangour. The clangour was a challenge. This day the Soviets had permitted celebration in all the churches, despite the anti-religious campaign, and those who pulled the cords were firing their reply.

It was midnight. Inside Tikhon's church there was no room to kneel, so thickly were the devout pressed. Outside the church the League of Communist Youth had gathered for a religious demonstration.

" Boom! boom! clang! boom! clang! boom! " went the bells.

" Down with the Church," shouted the boys and girls, shaking their fists at the bell towers.

" Boom! boom! " clashed the bells.

" Down with the Church."

" Down with the Priests."

" Down with Religion."

" Down with God," sang the communist youth in chorus.

Bearded Antonin, bishop of the new " Living Church," was preaching. Just outside the door was the newest movement in Soviet Russia, aiming at the destruction of all religion. Bishop Antonin was silent about it. Further away there was the split in the great Greek Church. Bishop Antonin ignored it. Not a word did he say of all the religious and anti-religious agitation which was filling the hearts and minds of the people in once Holy Russia. He spoke of man and his sins and how they would be washed clean in the Blood of the Lamb. He pleaded for clean lives in heart and body. At the conclusion he raised his hands to the golden ikon, the colourful painting of a haloed Christ, and in a voice full of pain exclaimed:

" Father, forgive them, for they know not what they do."

For a moment there was intense silence, then a groan, faint, gathering volume like a thunder, burst against the walls of the marble church and spent itself in the high vaulted ceiling. There was silence again.

The thousands were wedged shoulder to shoulder in a heavy crushing sweaty mass. Sables saved from the revolution by hook or by crook, chiefly the latter, and rags filled with lice — aristocrats and beggars and cripples. Some held candles, flickering dismally in such a huge space, spattering their ·neighbours' clothes with grease. The once clean, cold, sweet-smelling church had in a few hours become hot, fetid, stinking with human odors so that many reeled as if drunk and fainting. But there was no room to faint nor even to kneel.

The singing began. The slow unlyrical booming of the bells was followed by an old Gregorian chant. The beautiful belcanto voices smote the hearts of the worshippers. Tears flowed. An hour went by. Still the Gregorian chant continued, and as the singing reached a higher pitch a strong religious emotion overcame all within.

Without, there was revelry.

Mounted on a small portable platform on the top step of the church itself, a communist youth was haranguing the thousands of university students.

"We have destroyed the Czars of earth: now we destroy the Czars of heaven," he shouted.

"Down with Religion. Down with God," they replied.

An "American comrade" was introduced, evidently a Russian who had spent some time in a Pittsburgh steel mill.

"Comrades," he cried, "I am glad to be back in a land where we have succeeded in destroying the superstitious church which has enslaved mankind from tribal days. The church is the instrument of the capitalistic exploiters, nothing else, and religion is the opium of the people. How wonderful it is that we in Russia have obtained our freedom from religious tyranny. Over in America millions upon millions believe all this damned nonsense of priests and rabbis — "

"Down with Priests and Rabbis," assented the mob.

From the domes of the Cathedral of the Holy Saviour fire-crackers were exploding, apparently an old Russian custom. Mocking approval from the mob. Green and gold and silver lights circled over the marble domes. The communist boys and girls built a bonfire. They marched round it and sang. They held hands and danced, kicking their feet at the fire as they circled in faster and faster time, speeding it up with their singing:

"Down with the Church
Down with the Priests
Down with Religion
Down with God."

The doors of the cathedral were flung open. The worshippers, filled with religious ecstacy, came from the mysterious candle-lit and song-filled vault out into the cool, blue, starry, Moscow night. Behind them the voices were still chanting:

"Glory to God in the Highest."

The dancing children of Moscow replied wih the "Internationale."

"Arise ye victims of starvation
Arise ye wretched of the earth."

"Peace on Earth, good-will to men," came from the interior of the cathedral.

" Down with God," cried a crazy-eyed girl, and acting on her suggestion a thousand joined hands, encircling their bonfire and the cathedral and all the departing worshippers in one vast circle which moved slowly round the vast edifice, keeping time with dancing feet and nodding heads to their own mad anti-religious songs, while the devout looked on amazed and silent.

Chapter VII

THE CATHOLIC TRIALS IN MOSCOW

THE cry of horror and indignation throughout the world which followed our first reports of the anti-religious campaign and the trial of the Roman Catholic Clergy in Moscow, led to such bitterness against the Soviets, so many " official representations," so many threats against their régime and such a universal attack on their sovereignty that they, with the naïveté and vindictiveness and brutality of schoolboys, murdered one churchman and imprisoned others. The severest censorship since the terror of 1918 was then enforced.

When the trials began the Soviet leaders knew exactly what course they would take, their purpose, and the result. It was all arranged beforehand to pass a death penalty, to use the verdict for a further suppression of church power in Russia, and to pardon the victims in due time.

" The representatives of the Roman Catholic Church in Russia," said the prosecutor, Krylenko, " have been proven agents of foreign governments. They have expressed friendship for Poland during our war with Poland. We do not want to stir up hatred but we must uproot all organized religions which oppose us.

" We ask the death penalty for four men.

" We should ask death for all but we are not *over*-thirsty for blood. When necessary we can be merciless."

Krylenko had been head of the Extraordinary Commission, the dread tribunal of the red terror which the Chekah in-

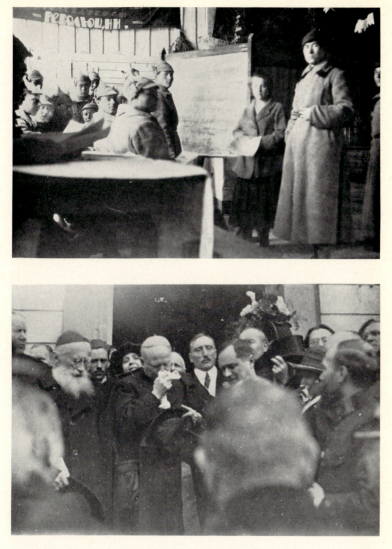

Teaching Communist propaganda in the Red Army School for illiterate Soldiers in Moscow.

Archbishop Zepliak, tried for treason in Moscow, at his homecoming in Warsaw.

stituted after the attempt on the life of Lenin by a radical young woman who had confused Bolshevism with Liberty and Freedom and in her disillusion had taken a revolver and wounded the chief enemy of her dreams. Krylenko had sent tens of thousands to their death. A relentless man. But at the Catholic trials, as public prosecutor, he seemed merely a soft, inspired fanatic, somewhat aware of his nice voice.

It was an enormous hall and it stunk almost as heavily as the cloak-rooms of the Opera House. Old Harvard men who remember the reek of perspiration in the aristocratic timbers of Hemenway Gymnasium and can imagine it intensified a hundredfold, will understand the horror a bathed person would have in going to either the grand ballet or a Soviet convention or this famous trial. The mob sat there in sheepskin coats, Persian lamb fezzes and ragged clothes, which had not been washed or cleaned for a long time. It ate garlicky food. Breath and body reeked of primitive humanity.

Electric lights none too brightly lit the oblong hall. A bare path divided the audience in two equal smells. Up and down the divide soldiers in brown or red-brown uniforms with scarlet frogs in place of hessians, giving them a pyjama effect, paraded with rifles in hand. Chekah agents, in uniform and in secret mufti, stared and noted. At the upper end of the room sat the accused and the Soviet officials, the priests unmoved, the Soviet judges in everyday garb without the least distinction from the laity.

Our attention was focussed on Archbishop Zepliak, a Pole, almost bald with a fringe of grey hair protruding from his small cap, in the conventional cassock and with a sympathetic pink face. Next to him sat Monsignor Budkiewicz whose fate stirred the world. They were a group of ten or eleven on trial.

There were no fireworks at the beginning. It was quiet and conventional. The accused pleaded they had acted within the canonical law of Russia; the prosecution denied the law and charged them as it would charge laymen, with treason. It was testified that Cardinal Roop before leaving Russia in 1919 had signed agreements with the Bolshevik régime whereby communist control of church property was recognized and placed in the collective hands of the congregations, instead of the control of priests.

When Archbishop Zepliak came to be head of the church it was forbidden for the clergy to sign more agreements and in Petrograd the signed agreements were repudiated by the priests, so that the government had retaliated by closing the churches.

Zepliak pleaded that the treaties were invalid because they infringed canonical rules, that the property belonged to the church, not to the congregations, and that it could be released only by the consent of the Pope; therefore the Soviet order to seize church treasures was resisted. As for giving aid and comfort to the enemy, Poland, during the Russo-Polish war, the priests denied all treasonable activities.

Krylenko replied with the production of a mass of evidence the authenticity of which it was beyond our power to judge. I think we all felt that the prosecution was unjust, that the evidence was insufficient, and that it was all a piece of theatricality in the existing anti-religious campaign. No one who was sane or sober believed the death sentence, which we knew in advance would be asked for and probably granted, would ever be carried out.

On Saturday, March 31, 1923, the Polish Minister, M. Knoll, the head of the British delegation, Mr. Hodgson, and Father

Edmund Walsh, the American priest in charge of the Papal famine relief work, visited Chicherin who assured them that he would do all he could to prevent the penalty. Mr. Hodgson and Father Walsh told me that afternoon that they were certain that Zepliak and Budkiewicz would be pardoned.

" Are you sure they are alive? " we asked.

" The Narcomindel (Mr. Chicherin's foreign office) assured me that they were," replied the British diplomatic representative.

On Sunday, April 1, 1923, my interpreter who knew the minister of justice well, telephoned him from my room and after being told that the priests were alive and well, received some ambiguous reply about a pardon.

On April 5, 1923, the official Soviet organ, *Pravda,* carried the following miscellaneous paragraph:

" On March 31 the death sentence imposed on the counter-revolutionary, Budkiewicz, was carried out."

It was confirmed that the execution took place in the dark morning hours, on the day Chicherin had promised to help save the priest's life, and the day *before* the Minister of Justice had continued to assure us he was still among the living.

I am convinced the Minister of Foreign Affairs and the Minister of Justice had not lied to us. They did not know what was happening. Once again the dread Chekah had snapped its fingers at the entire government.

Efforts of the representatives of the American press to report the Catholic trials had resulted in almost daily battles with the censor in the foreign office. It was partly due to this affair that of the eight American reporters four were deported or departed in protest. Before I was deported I was able to obtain from a minor official of the Chekah, whose name I cannot mention because he gave me many tips and would be shot if this were known, the real explanation of the execution of Budkiewicz.

"Russia's most touchy point is her sovereignty," said this terrorist. "She is isolated, unrecognized, treated like a fallen daughter by the smug capitalist nations. Russia's Achilles' heel is her pride.

"Who is responsible for the death of Budkiewicz? The blood of Budkiewicz is on the hands of the Archbishop of Canterbury, General Sikorski in Poland, and the Polish Premier. They led the world attack on us. The All-Russian Executive Committee had had the reprieves all ready. Then the clamour began. The world, led by the Archbishop of Canterbury and the Polish politician did not plead for mercy; it threatened. The Poles rattled the sword as usual. The rest of the world treated us like a nation in uncivilized Africa. Our right to judge according to our own laws was denied by other nations. This was mixing in our internal affairs.

"Russia was treated as an inferior nation, and the execution of the Catholic leader was the psychological reaction."

Somehow, shortly afterwards, the Soviet religious prosecutions fell off, and eventually they were abandoned. The arrival of Archbishop Zepliak in Warsaw, which I also witnessed, surpassed a national holiday.

Chapter VIII

LENIN

LENIN himself was not stronger than the censorship and the Chekah.

Many people trembled when the name of the dictator was mentioned. But in dirty little offices sat little grey bureaucrats who changed Lenin's speeches when they feared he had spoken too dangerously, and in other dirty little offices sat military political police officials who bragged that they would arrest the man if he acted too dangerously.

When we said to the censors, " Lenin himself said this," they laughed. When it served their purposes they added or deleted, and sometimes they suppressed Lenin entirely. When it pleased them they arranged interviews, but for years they did their best to keep the " capitalist " journalists out of Lenin's sight. We heard him, however, at all the big congresses.

He spoke with a thick, throaty, wet voice. He was in very good humour, always smiling, his face never was hard. All his pictures are hard but he was always twinkling with laughter. Eyes bright, crowsfeet, a real, unserious face. He had a clever motion of the hand by which he could emphasize a point and yet steal a look at the time on his wrist watch. Frequently he pointed with both index fingers, upwards, shoulder high, like the conventional picture of a Chinese dancer.

When he announced the occupation of Vladivostok and added imperialistically, " We will never give up a single conquest we have won," he seemed surprised by the sudden burst of nationalistic applause which followed. Frequently he dropped his voice, stuck both hands into his coat pocket, threw back his head, and said something ironic. Sometimes he spoke from the left side of his mouth.

In the loge on the left stood Unschlicht, a dark agent of the Chekah, surveying the house. Always in the shadow. A man of shadows. In the Kremlin, in the Red Square, in the Bolshoi Theatre, wherever Lenin went, the dull, grey, one-day-unshaven face of Unschlicht of the Chekah, was there, somewhat hidden. Little cruel eyes, furtive, quick, dangerous, nervous, forever watching, forever suspicious.

But the mob was always stricken with hero-worship. It cried, " Long live the Saviour of Russia, long live the protector of the poor," when Lenin arrived. Then he spoke.

" We have come to the doors of Utopia," said Lenin without emphasis, without the theatrical effect of Mussolini who knows a good line when he utters it. Lenin continued simply. " Utopia no longer remains in the dreams of mankind, for we have brought it to earth. Not today nor tomorrow nor in a year shall we enter it, but Utopia is now within sight of the people of our time."

It was his first speech to the common people in many months. They sat transfixed. If he were as bombastic as Napoleon or Mussolini you could doubt his sincerity, but he spoke so plainly and with a full heart. Three days earlier he had addressed the delegates to the Third International, a selected gathering of leaders of Communism, orators, debaters, parliamentarians in various lands, a supercilious lot. In neither speech was there any sentimentality, but to these last he could argue world politics.

" We have made stupid mistakes," he said, and a little shudder ran through the delegates. Communists never make mistakes. They are Marx's chosen people and can do no wrong. No revolutionary ever admits mistakes. Lenin was the great exception. But even he offered excuses.

"We have made stupid mistakes. No one knows better than I. Because Russia is backward, because we have had no outside help, because we are bureaucracy-ridden.

"Enemies will say Lenin himself admits stupidities and mistakes. I say our mistakes consist of saying two times two are five, while the undoubted stupidity of the Entente and the Second International consists of saying twice two equals a wax candle — or the Versailles Treaty."

The first time I heard and saw Lenin was the day of his first public appearance after his long illness during which his death had been reported to a satisfied world several times. It was in the throne room of the Czars, in the Kremlin, full of tables, chairs and benches. The magnificent windows, the gilt and brocaded walls, and the painted ceiling alone reminded one of ancient splendours. A huge red sounding board had been placed on the stage; behind it, carelessly out of joint, stood the Romanoff throne, no longer an object of curiosity.

Krylenko was speaking. This man who had led the illegal red terror which had claimed thousands of lives, now advocated a change in the code of laws — more laws. The three hundred listeners composed the All-Russian Central Executive Committee. They came from all parts of Russia and they were all cold. They sat in their fur coats and fur hats on which a greasy sweat had gathered, and they illustrated how terribly human beings can smell. They buzzed and yawned.

All at once there was a stir at the door. Two soldier guards stiffened. They have been told to await some one important and to be careful of passes today. They do not know why but they know their duty.

A little man in a plain black coat, hat in hand, approached them. They did not recognize him and demanded the red card. He fumbled in his pocket and presented it. He looked more the small sleek business man than a communist leader. The soldiers with peasant difficulty made out the name, one read and nudged the other, who read also, and their dumb faces opened in astonishment. The little man passed.

Krylenko was speaking drearily about more laws. The little man came into the room, passed our press table, and I noticed he was walking on his toes. Lenin tip-toeing so as not to interrupt the speaker. Not until he got to the first two steps of the platform, softly, did the congress recognize him, and there was an uproar. Everyone rose. There were a few shouts. By actual count it was an ovation of 35 seconds. While Lenin, who hadn't paused to acknowledge the applause, is still shaking hands with the men on the platform, Krylenko resumed his speech. He had the good sense to cut it short.

Another twenty seconds of applause greeted Lenin as he advanced to the speaker's pulpit. He had discarded his coat. He was dressed in a cheap grey semi-military uniform, a civilian transplanted into ill-fitting army-issue clothes. They were grey-black but the crease in the trousers was already giving because there is too much shoddy in the wool. The tunic, which is high like the American doughboy's, was open at the neck revealing a flannel shirt and a bright blue necktie, loosely tied. His eyes were not half as oriental as the photographs have made him, because he has full eyebrows, not merely stubs at the nose, which the pictures emphasize.

He glanced at the audience in the high arched room, cathe-

218

dral-like but for the plain windows through which the sun comes in garishly. He looked behind him, at the wall where there is a masonic sign, the Eye of God, which has beheld a dynasty of Czars. Outside the palace are the Kremlin walls, snow-lined, battlements and buttresses, towers with royal pennants in iron, the permanency of the Romanoffs in iron mockery. Beneath, the River Moskva, slow and muddy, drab and lazy, partly frozen, reflecting the gold and azure and red Kremlin in a mighty, tarnished way. Khaki-clad soldiers move in line like centipedes, their coats long to the ground, sweeping the snow along with no sign of individual feet, the effect of mass and machinery, with white human faces in ugly brown helmets, with bright red stars.

" Tavarashi — Comrades," Lenin began.

It was a historic moment for Russia, but no histrionics. He had to tell them of a victory on land and a victory by diplomacy. He reported on foreign and domestic affairs. He never hesitated to acknowledge defeats and failures. But he was always optimistic. My disillusion was profound. I wondered how this man, who has so little magnetism, had come to the fore in a radical environment where spell-binding oratory, silver-tongued climaxes, soap-box repartee, have been the road to success. Only once did he aim to produce a laugh, and even that had his touch of irony. " We have pruned and pruned our bureaucracy," he said, " and after four years we have taken a census of our government staff and we have an increase of 12,000."

He concluded and the congress took a recess. Everyone went into another room, one of the most regal — I shall never forget a delegate trying to pick diamonds out of the cross and crown emblem set in each of the doors. Lenin, Kalinin, Zinovieff, Kamineff and Chekah agents jostled the delegates, the newspaper correspondents, the peasants in their sweaty sheepskin coats and hats, all in good humour, crowding, elbowing, shouting, while the inevitable Soviet photographer tried to organize a historic picture.

Finally it was taken, and we American correspondents crowded around him. "Do you speak Russian?" he asked in Russian. "No, English," we said. "I speak her, ze English language — not zo verry good," replied Lenin and his pronunciation was confirmation. He could reply in German.

"I occupy a large portion of my time with American affairs," he said. "I am reading Pettigrew's 'Plutocratic Democracy' which an American friend sent me. It is a great book. I am interested in everything Senator Borah does and says. I watch all events regarding Japanese-American relations. I am interested in the American elections." Then he smiled again and added:

"Your American newspapers frequently report me dead. Let them fool themselves. Don't take away the last hope of a dying bourgeoisie."

We tried to ask all the political questions we could think of, but he was nervous and parried.

"How do you like Moscow? Not quite like New York?" He laughs quietly as if ashamed of his Babbittry.

The artist of a New York newspaper made quick sketches because Lenin was fidgeting to be free. Lenin gave the artist another moment.

"The world says Lenin is a great man," said the artist in his thankfulness.

"I am not a great man, just look at me?" Lenin replied with a gesture deprecating his size and emphasizing his simplicity.

On another occasion he showed the same stubborn prejudices which characterize all the revolutionary leaders.

" When is the war between Japan and America coming? " he asked. He was assured there would be no war because there are no causes for war. " But there must be war," he insisted, " because capitalist countries cannot exist without wars."

But he could return to his broad ironic views. To the Briton of the press corps he said:

" As you know, we in Russia have only one party, and we have to wear ourselves out without a relieving shift."

Is this hypocrisy? There were other parties once, notably the Mensheviks, also radical and communistic, but the Bolsheviks have driven them to Berlin and Paris and Siberia, slaughtered members by the thousand and finally annihilated the movement. But Lenin took the curse off this hypocrisy when he added:

" I think we shall begin a two party system like the British or American — a left and a right party — two Bolshevik parties of course." He laughed.

While Trotsky and all the small orators in Russia were snapping at America, Lenin, who was wise and who had a sense of humour, saw the futility of a radical movement in the prosperous United States.

" You might as well shoot peas at the rock of Gibraltar as to arm the counter-revolutionaries against us," he said, " and in America it is the same: do you think the weak handful of Communists we have there can upset the American form of government by talking much and by making futile little plots? "

Lenin was big enough to see the humour of many little radical episodes. He was fond of telling the story of some labour troubles at the time when he was a refugee in London. He was already known as a Socialist leader then and many times shop committees brought him their troubles. Once, he said, there was a plan for a strike in some works and a delegation came with many complaints, about which they were not definite and could not agree. Finally, in desperation, he asked them for a clear, final statement.

" ' All we want,' " he said the chairman told him, " ' is world revolution and better toilets! ' "

He realized keenly his weakness as an orator, and feeling his lack of power over certain classes of listeners who were bored by fine thinking and quick clear reasoning, he would say twice or three times in his discourse: " I assure you I am not telling you lies."

Frequently he would speak in foreign languages. His many years' exile in Switzerland had made him conversant with French and German, but he was not sure of himself. He would approach the speaker's table nervously, draw papers from his pocket, put his hands to his head as if parting hairs which were not there, and after waiting patiently for noise to subside, would begin in German. Words would fail him. He would then whisper the Russian word to a nearby friend who returned the correct teutonic, quietly, which Lenin would quickly grasp and turn it with force upon his audience. It was an actor being prompted intelligently.

Although militant Communism or the reign of terror was the direct result of an attempt on Lenin's life, he tried to stop it. He was never told the truth about the extent or viciousness of the Chekah system. Lenin hated bloodshed.

When Bela Kun was defeated in Hungary and came to Moscow he was received as a hero. Lenin, who knew masses better than individuals made the mistake of sending Kun to pacify the Crimea after an uprising. In accordance with Lenin's suggestion an amnesty was published among the "White Army" officers and leaders. They were asked three times to register and Lenin's name was pledged for their personal safety. Thirty thousand are said to have registered. Then Bela Kun, in accordance with instructions which the Chekah sent out without Lenin's knowledge, erected forests of scaffolds and hanged all of the thirty thousand he could find. Lenin heard of this atrocity. When Kun returned to Moscow Lenin refused to take his hand or listen to explanations of military necessity. He did not want Bela Kun around. The Hungarian ex-dictator, however, was in favour with the Chekah, and could not be cast aside. But he remained in disfavour with Lenin so long as Lenin lived, and most of that time in far away places. (Of course the censor never let us mention the Kun incidents.)

When they addressed him as "Comrade" Ilyitch the word had real meaning: for other leaders it was ridiculous, a word too often profaned. Lenin had the greatness and the human, all-too-human sympathy to be a comrade to all, the group of fellow dictators and the peasants who loved him. In battle with his enemies he was uncompromising and without pity.

He hated power, knowing its corruption.

His political wisdom was great; he understood mob psychology thoroughly but was a little weak in his grasp of individual psychology; he never made a mistake in dealing with the masses but he frequently did in choosing men to share power.

As an orator he was my greatest disappointment. Not understanding a word he said, I waited for his dramatic effects. There were none. Socrates sitting in the house of Cephalus and arguing on the floor was not less theatrical than Lenin addressing the peasant delegates to the Third International. He had no warmth. He was coldly intellectual. He was more effective with his fellow theorists.

His private life was the exact antithesis of Mussolini's. While his enemies blamed his sickness on youthful excesses, not a proof of them was ever produced; on the other hand his family life was exemplary. His moral purity, in another age and condition, could have been a claim to sainthood. He had no mistresses, no secret sex life.

Long before the Soviets changed the name of Petrograd to Leningrad, the peasants of his old home town showed their love for him by substituting his name for the village of Kukushkino. Lenin was so pleased when the boys he played with sent him this remarkable letter, that he put it into his diary:

"Dear Comrade Wladmir," they wrote, "do you remember the horses in the woods we watched together at night? It was 45 years ago. We have now rid our village of the landlords who for fifteen years camped on our necks. Then came catastrophe — famine. The cattle died. Our property was gone; our houses were falling to pieces. The famine wiped out everything.

"We cannot send you a present. We have paid the grain levy and two civil taxes. Two sorrows have befallen us. We have no horses and we have no school in our village. We know the Soviet government is giving horses on credit and we ask you as late co-villager to approach the government for credit horses. Without this we are workers without hands; we have land and nothing to work it with. We think it also necessary to inform you that we have asked the Tartar republic to organize a school for professions and literacy and to be named after your mother Mary Alexandrovno. In conclusion we ask you to save your health because you are the only one for us in all Russia. When the school is built we ask you to come over to us as a guest in order that we may reminisce over old days.

Lenin

"Henceforth village Kukushkino is named after you, Comrade Lenin, and now, until we meet again, with brotherly greetings,

The community of the Village Lenin.
(late Kukushkino.)"

Now Lenin is dead and worshipped by the peasants. Some never knew him but as another Czar who supplemented the goodness of that Alexander who freed the serfs, by apportioning the soil. A myth is growing throughout Russia and a legend. He was divine, of immaculate birth, and he did not die but ascended into heaven, where he sits by the side of the Trinity as special intercessor for poor Russian peasants. This making of a red god pleases all good atheistic Bolsheviks.

When I think of the red god's appearance I see always that cheap shoddy suit he wore. I see the neat crease in the cotton trousers holding on like wool. In a year I saw Lenin many times and always in the same clothes. First up from his sick bed the clothes were new. That was in the Fall. But September's creased trousers became April's baggy rags. They had held out bravely, as the man within had done. But finally they flapped hobolike as if acknowledging the surrender of all pretence to bourgeois respectability. Shortly afterwards Lenin died.

Chapter IX

CHECKING UP ON CHICHERIN

BEFORE going into Russia I helped cover the Genoa conference, "*il pui grande conferenza del historia dell' mondo.*" It being the first time the Bolsheviks had come out of the land of communist mystery to participate in bourgeois affairs, their every movement was important and eagerly reported. A touch of human interest caused a laugh around the world: the six big Soviet leaders had left Russia wearing proletarian clothes; as they entered Germany they cast off overalls and put on conventional suits, and the day of the king's reception they rushed out and bought boiled shirts, high silk hats and swallow-tails. It was a journalistic climax equalled only by the secret Russo-German treaty.

The Bolsheviks were in the open at last and no hunting restrictions. Continental European journalists, most of whom are party politicians, applauded or yelled derision at the daily Rakowsky-Chicherin press conferences: "You blood-stained murderers, when are you going to honour the Russian bonds I bought," a French journalist once shouted and broke up a meeting. The Americans and Britons contented themselves with taking notes in silence.

One day I received a series of questions to submit to Chicherin. They were a bit hecklish. He refused to answer them.

Day after day the questions appeared in print with a request for Russia to explain. Finally Chicherin called me to his rooms in Santa Margherita and gave me written answers. I took them with me when I went to Russia later, and checked them up. Here is the interview:

* * * * *

Question — When will the Soviet government establish free elections, freedom of speech and of the press, and freedom of travel?

Chicherin — Elections to the Soviets are quite free. All working sections of the community take part in elections. The intellectuals, being, as a rule, employed in the offices of the government or of the local Soviets or by industrial concerns, take part in elections of officials and representatives for the local Soviets.

No restrictions are placed on freedom of speech but, naturally, those are liable to punishment who preach revolt against the government. No government could act otherwise.

Freedom of travel is not subject to any other limitations than those created by limited transport facilities. However, regular passenger traffic was resumed some time ago.

As there does not exist in Russia a preventive censorship of the press, newspapers hostile to the government can, without check, attack it and preach revolt.

The Russian government, in consequence, will be able to admit full freedom of the press only after the conspiracies of counter-revolutionaries, which are still organized from abroad, have ceased.

Question — In what manner is the present government more democratic than the old régime?

Chicherin — The local Soviets, being direct representatives of the working masses, are following closely the policy of the government and constantly express their assent or dissent in revolutions. At the periodical All-Russian congress of the Soviets they can directly give effect to their opinions.

The trade unions participate directly in state affairs. Local administration is in the hands of local Soviets, not in the hands of officials of the central government. A considerable number of workers and peasants occupy high positions in the administration and in the army.

Question — In what particulars more communistic?

Chicherin — Property in land is completely abolished. But property in industries does not exist either and they are either worked by the nation or else property in them is replaced by long-lease concessions.

Question — Does the Soviet government consider that it is holding property seized from Americans for the American proletariat or for the Russian proletariat?

Chicherin — The Russian government does not hold any property seized from Americans. Foreigners have been subjected to laws of nationalization, seeing that legislation applies to everybody. When one economic system takes the place of another economic system there can be no oasis for foreigners.

Question — How many people have been put to death by order of the secret tribunals?

Chicherin — No secret tribunals exist in Russia. The number of those executed by the extraordinary tribunals has been officially published.

Question — If the Soviet government should obtain control of any other country or countries, would it establish in them secret tribunals of this kind?

Chicherin — Nor does the Soviet government intend to establish secret tribunals in other countries. The Russian government has not the least intention of obtaining control of other countries.

*   *   *   *   *

Tavarish Chicherin is not a liar. When he says " The Russian government has not the least intention of obtaining control of other countries " it can pass as a legal statement which no one need question. But what do you find in studying Soviet Russia? This: the seven or nine men who are the Soviet government and who have " not the least intention of obtaining control of other countries," meet again as the seven or nine men in control of the Russian Communist party or the seven or nine men in control of the Third International, and at these meetings all the intentions and all the work are aimed at only one thing, the Russian communist control of other countries.

M. Chicherin is not a liar. He says " Elections to the Soviets are quite free." Investigation reveals that no one but proletarians are allowed to vote, and their votes are either Bolshevik or so-called non-partisan. The rest of Russia has been deprived of the vote; this makes the election to the Soviets free.

M. Chicherin is not a liar. When he says freedom of speech and press are free he gives the impression that there is little or no restraint. But an investigation shows that only Soviet newspapers are allowed, and speech is confined to discussion of communist policy. Any word, written or printed, which is anti-Bolshevik means imprisonment or death.

M. Chicherin is not a liar. He is a diplomat, the foreign minister of a very large country, a successful revolutionary, a man of culture, and a master of euphemism, evasion, ambiguity, and equivocation. But you have to go to Moscow to check him up.

Chapter X

" Food Iz a Veppon! "

BEFORE the American Relief Administration was allowed to enter Russia and save five millions from death, a " treaty " had to be signed with the Soviet politicians. During the two years of activities in which $66,300,000 were spent, as many as 11,000,000 persons fed a day, 35,000 relief stations maintained and 15,000 hospitals to down the plague, the American relief heads and workers had to fight the Bolsheviks. If at any time the newspapermen had broken the communist censorship, disregarded the wishes of Colonel Haskell, and forgotten their humanitarian feelings, they could have told such truths about the Soviet sabotage that the American government, yielding to press opinion, undoubtedly would have stopped the work and many million more graves along the Volga would have been dug.

It seems almost incredible, now, that we had to beg the Bolsheviks for permission to rescue their dying people. Our representatives could not understand the resistance at first. Litvinoff, head of the Russian delegation, was proposing limitations. The A. R. A. had talked as only Americans can talk: speed, efficiency, power, quantity, brains, success. We would send men by the thousand, food by the millions of pounds — .

" No you von't," said Litvinoff.

" But — why? " stammered the American negotiator, " we do not come to fight Russia, we come to feed — "

" Yes," smiled Litvinoff, " but food iz a veppon."

* * * * *

"Food Iz a Veppon!"

How important a weapon food could be we found out very soon. Colonel Haskell had stipulated that the press must come in with him, so the Bolsheviks, who previously had permitted only journalists favourable to their system, with bad grace allowed us, "bourgeois" reporters, "agents of capitalistic sheets," to come to Moscow. But they set Chekah agents on us immediately.

The A. R. A. had committed itself to feed 1,000,000 children until the end of 1922. But by August of that year it was giving meals to 10,429,599 men, women, and children, a number five times as great as the Commissary department fed in France, and almost twice as great as the Hoover missions had ever fed at one time in France, Belgium, Central and Eastern Europe. In numbers, mileage, tonnage and area the job was the greatest in the history of the world, civil or military.

In return all we got from the Bolsheviks were sneers, insults and sabotage. These began with the arrival of the first relief workers and helped drive the Americans out of Russia the moment the famine was broken. No sooner had the men reported to their stations when they began complaining that the communist officials everywhere were trying to interfere with their work. In several cases Haskell's agents were forced to put the food trains through to their destination at the point of revolvers. Fist fights were numerous. There was bad blood between the opposing forces throughout the years.

Investigation after investigation was made. One fact, paramount, was discovered. The Bolsheviks were trying to feed Communist party members and let the rest die. They were also anxious to take the credit and the glory; they lied to their starving mobs and deprecated the part America was playing. But always and everywhere they strove to divert the food from

231

the masses, which were being fed, irrespective of politics or religion, to their own political followers.

Time after time Colonel Haskell threatened to withdraw from Russia. One day I mentioned this possibility to a foreign office official.

" Let him withdraw," was the reply.

" Then millions will die," I said.

" What of it," replied the Bolshevik. " The world war cost 16,000,000 lives; what if another five or ten millions die. Communism will survive."

" But you will have a revolution."

" Never," he replied, " haven't you learned yet that starving people never revolt. It is the half-starved, the discontented man who grumbles and eventually fights. But the famine-stricken man has given up. He hasn't the guts to revolt. Let the A. R. A. withdraw. We don't care."

(What would have happened if we could have printed that?)

In Odessa a relief worker was robbed of his official papers; every week others complained that they had been searched on trains; hundreds reported lack of co-operation from Soviet officials. During the fifth anniversary of the Bolshevik Revolution celebration in Petrograd, the Soviet insisted that the man in charge of the A. R. A. building hoist a red flag. When this was refused the Bolsheviks decorated the building so that it appeared that the Americans were joining in the festivities. Mr. Warren tore the red decorations down and a dispute followed lasting for weeks.

Then the Soviets attacked the Americans in their party press. They had tried to form Haskell's Russian employees into a communist union but had failed. Now they tried to organize a general strike among them. That the relief work would be interrupted and thousands more die, did not worry the Bolsheviks: it was the principle of the thing!

Of course I used the diplomatic pouch of the A. R. A. to smuggle letters containing censored and suppressed news out to Riga and London. But one day I began to suspect that the route was barred. I went to see C. J. Quinn, Haskell's assistant. Quinn admitted that the mail bags, which according to the Litvinoff-Brown " treaty " were considered immune, and which were shipped sealed with lead and string, had been opened by Chekah agents *en route*.

" Moreover," he said, opening a drawer of his desk and exhibiting photographs, envelopes and statements, " we have absolute knowledge that Chekah agents have taken letters out of our offices here and in Riga, copied them and replaced them." He said every waste basket in the Moscow office had its contents taken to Chekah headquarters every night.

" Yes, and they have done a thousand other dirty tricks on us."

The communist organ *Pravda* said one day:

" Why is America charitable? Why is she sending us food? Because the American farmers have so much grain they are burning it up — and besides, they get trade information out of Russia."

Everywhere the charge was made that the entire Hoover organization was in Russia for the sole purpose of getting trade and military secrets.

A booklet was circulated widely which discussed famine relief. It listed the agencies as follows:

FRIENDLY: Quakers; 265,000 children.

NEUTRAL: Nansen Mission; 138,000 children.

OPEN POLITICAL ENEMIES: A. R. A.; 5,000,000 persons.

The booklet said: "Under cover of charity the bourgeois relief agencies are systematically preparing for the coming of concession seekers; they are boring a canal for the exploitation of Russia by world capitalism. Hoover . . . has spread a complete net over Russia."

The climax of the Bolshevik attack followed an unfortunate incident. Although Colonel Haskell employed men of honour, one of them indulged in a little smuggling. It may have involved a thousand dollars or two. Immediately the corrupt communist press opened a slanderous barrage on the entire relief mission. "' How they help " was the sarcastic headline in *Isvestia* which declared Americans " were plundering as they go. This is how they help the famished; this is how the representatives of civilized America in barbarous Russia behave; this is how rich America uses poor Russia."

For eighteen months the representatives of the American newspapers had refrained from printing anything about the opposition of the Soviets; now we came in a body to call on Colonel Haskell to discuss the possible effect which the publication of the truth would have on America's continuing generosity.

"If the government and the Hoover fund moneys are withdrawn, will it mean another 5,000,000 dead? " we asked Haskell.

We were told that the worst of the famine was over. It was this which no doubt accounted for the boldness of the Bolshevik press attack.

"Have you informed Lenin how difficult relief work is becoming? " I asked Haskell.

"Yes," Haskell replied, "Lenin blames the antagonism on

minor officials, on the bureaucracy which he hates but cannot change."

Haskell had found Lenin plain, frank, sincere and thankful. He was amazed by the lack of egotism in the dictator and impressed by the honesty of Lenin's gratitude. Later he was to take specific complaints to Kamineff and Radek, from whom he also got assurances of change and co-operation.

But the battle continued to the end.

One day a report came in from Riga that showed how times had changed. At the Riga docks a big American ship was disgorging wheat into Russian freight cars of the A. R. A., while nearby a dirty little Soviet tramp grain steamer, out of Russia, was being unloaded by hand. While millions were still hungering, while American charity wheat was still coming in, the Bolsheviks were beginning to sell theirs abroad.

The famine was broken. Bolshevism was saved. The two things went together because there was no possibility of separating them. The Soviet government survived, thanks to the American people feeding its millions during the worst period of the régime. Only professional Communists believe it could have come through the crisis and still maintain its power. Gradually the American Relief Administration withdrew from Russia. As it left the frontiers it could hear the insults which continued to be directed at it from Moscow.

In all history there is probably no parallel case of such wholesale national biting of the hand which fed them.

All the non-communist employees of the A. R. A. were eventually arrested by the Chekah.

Most of the American press representatives were then expelled. Friendly relations with Russia were never established.

Veritably, "food iz a veppon."

Chapter XI

A DAMN BAD ACCENT

THE Bolshevik censors, who were also foreign office officials, advised us bourgeois journalists to mingle with the new communist proletariat and bureaucracy and report the valor and enthusiasm for the new régime. But the story which follows, and which illustrates better than statistics a phase of the life of Moscow, could not be sent through the censored government posts.

It begins in 1910, when a stranger came into my newspaper office with an offer of $5 each for articles dealing with labour. He said he was a labour leader of Swedo-Russo-German parentage, and that he intended publishing a weekly, and needed editorial assistance. As I have no interest in having him executed in Moscow today I will not name the periodical and will call him "Stan Stangaard."

In 1910 I was a reporter on Alexander Pollock Moore's *Pittsburgh Leader* then, at $16. a week — or it might have been at $14.; at any rate it was the lowest wage paid in Pittsburgh — and $5 extra was that "little more, and how much it is" of a sentimental Browning. So I went to work for Stan secretly.

We hired a small office in a big building and painted the weekly's name in much gold leaf on the frosted door. Our furniture was good and impressive. We had a good printer too. But Stan made no effort to employ advertising men and I wondered how he meant to survive.

For several weeks I wrote two or three articles for the weekly paper, praising the heroism of miners underground and riveters up in the air. I pointed out all that was noble in common day jobs and said that all that America was or hoped to be, it owed to the workingman. But Stan never allowed me to write specifically or to discuss wages. "We might do that later," he said in that Swedo-Russo-Germano-American of his.

His ways were mysterious. He seemed to have a lot of money and to enjoy playing the rôle of editor, although he could not write or speak ten words grammatically in any known language. I soon realized he was playing a game, and when he knew I knew, he took me into his confidence.

At the end of two months Stan had spent a lot of money and had nothing to show for it except a few copies of his magazine. We used to run off only two hundred copies and 195 of these we mailed to the presidents, treasurers and directors of coal and iron companies. We had no subscription roll. It was the free list that had given me my first suspicion.

One Saturday the printer sent a man to say he wouldn't get the issue out unless money was forthcoming immediately and that same day Stan had a lot of expensive apologies for not paying me my $10. He assured me cheerily that all would be well next week, but it was evident he was at the end of his shoe-strings.

On the following Thursday, however, the crisis in our affairs turned our way. Stan came into the office and produced a check signed by the president of one of the largest Pittsburgh coal companies, a name known throughout America. "Disz brakes dee eice," said Stan, and the ice broke all round us as on a hot day off Newfoundland. Stan got lots of checks, cashed them, sent the money somewhere, paid his debts and suddenly suspended publication. It seems there was now no longer a reason for pointing out the heroism of miners underground or riveters up in the air. Stan took me to a restaurant and bought a good dinner with lots of cheap wine. When he had had at least a quart himself, he beamed and bragged.

It was then I learned that the last town he had worked was Youngstown, Ohio, and the next would be Bethlehem, Pennsylvania. He made me an offer of $25. a week for which he expected me to become an accomplice.

"No," I said, "I can't do it." I was an idealist then. I believed all the world's ills could be cured by an honest press. I told him I didn't mind writing articles for him because what I wrote I believed in, but I could not become a partner in his business.

"Voddemadder die bizniss?" asked Stan. "Tamn goot bizness. Die kohlmeiners dey get exploit, no? Yes. Den I go make exploit die mens who exploit. In Rossia we have a national hero, Stenka Resen, you know vod he done?"

"Yes — a sort of riparian Robin Hood."

"Hoot? Vodt?" said Stan, "he voz one tamn fine feller vodt die hold coundry sink aboudt heem — big hero. Sum tay anodder kind Stenka Resen — beeger — come and mek revolution. Shure. Lizzen Chorch, I'm a goot man, I am."

"So am I, Stan, and I would not prostitute Fair Journalism for your filthy $25. or ten times that amount." (One could speak like that in 1910.) I'd rather starve than debauch my principles. You may think you are doing a noble work — I don't mean to criticize your methods — but Journalism to me is the noblest work of man. (At that time I was rewriting 3-line items about housemaids who fell down stairs and broke a leg, and minor bicycle accidents. Murders and divorces were to be my next noble calling two years later.)

So I lectured Stan and turned down his seductions, but I couldn't help having a sneaking admiration for the adventurer and the easy way which he had cleaned up some $50,000.

" How do you do it, Stan? " I asked him.

" Vall, I just go ride into de headman of die company und tell heem I'm a beeg labour leader, and I show heem my paaper wod I print by die week und I tells I need die sooport, vaal, five tousand or even one tousand I take it und I give von advertizemen' page und nize editoriall. Und dey bay."

" But why do they believe you are a labour man? Why do they fall so easy? " I asked. " What in the world have *you* got? "

" One tamn bat aczent," replied Stan Stangaard.

*   *   *   *   *

In 1916 in the list of dead on the channel steamer *Sussex,* torpedoed by the Germans, I read the name of Stan Stangaard, a Swedo-Russo-Germano-American citizen said to be going to Russia to enlist in the Czar's armies.

*   *   *   *   *

In May, 1923, under the presidency of Karachan, the Soviets opened a Far East Chamber of Commerce, the meeting in the foreign office being attended by many notable commissars and sub-commissars.

Out of curiosity several of us went to see the gathering of the yellow and brown men who are under Russia's domination. As a study in faces it was a reward.

Walking along the gaily lit corridor I noticed a strangely familiar face. The moment the picture of Pittsburgh came back, I knew whom this man resembled. "There, but for the fact he is dead seven years, goes Stan Stangaard of Pittsburgh," I said to a friend.

Whereupon the stranger turned around and said in his unmistakable voice:

"Hullo Chorch!"

"Hullo Stan," I replied.

"Don't call me Stan," he whispered, looking around furtively and dragging me away from my colleague. "Come here. Mine name iz now Piotr Piotrovitch." (Again I use a false name.) "Don'd forged. Mine addrezz Boulevard Dmitrovka 23/4/3 — vich means houz nummer 23, floor fordt, door tree. Come. I giff you goot dinner. Best in Moscow. Remember die dinner I giff you in Pittsabourg? Bedder!"

I went to Stan's house the next night. He had a young and beautiful Russian wife, all black hair and red lips and blossoming like a tulip. More remarkable still was his having four or five rooms, and still more remarkable were the furnishings.

To begin with the Bolsheviki had communized dwelling space more efficiently than they had done anything else in Moscow. Every cubic inch within walls and under roof, had been listed and distributed. A big room would be given to a family. A ball-room for instance would be marked off like claims in California during the gold rush, and families would camp in their allotted space. Privacy was abolished by Bolshevism when housing became the problem of the day.

Now Stangaard was a big commissar and stood high in Bolshevik circles. But that did not mean he was entitled to any special favors; in fact the party demanded that officials and leaders be strict Puritans, get no more than their allotted few cubic feet of room per person, eat rationed food and live in penury. Those caught grafting or squandering were arrested, kicked out of the party, frequently sent to Siberia, sometimes executed.

Stangaard's home was hung with tapestries and fine oriental rugs. Silver and black enamel stood on mantlepieces. Inlaid furniture, expensive but bad oil-paintings, much too many dust-collecting bric-a-brac, over-impressive tables and chairs, garish objects of many genres filled all Stangaard's rooms. Bad but costly.

Caviar is not a rich man's nor a general's dish in Moscow, costing only 85 cents a pound in those days. With it Mrs. Stangaard served smoked salmon, sturgeon, sardines, anchovies, ham, cold eggs, three or four salads and another dozen things as *hors d'oeuvres* plus vodka which was then much more a crime than our post-Volstead cocktails. And the other eight or nine courses were as gorgeous. Red and white wine. Before the coffee a glass of champagne in real Bourbon style.

It was one of the three best meals of my lifetime and Russia then was just emerging from a famine.

Stangaard offered me imported cigars and took me to see the treasures in the other rooms. In a cupboard he pointed to some clothes — nice European suits which he kept but never wore because they would arouse suspicion and betray him.

I expressed my astonishment over everything. He knew I knew all the Soviet laws about governmental corruption, even to that law which once abolished capital punishment for murder but proclaimed it for grafting.

"Oh, there are ways of getting along even here in Communist Russia," said Stan in German.

"But what have you got that works with the Bolos here?"
I asked in English.

A broad smile came over his broad face.

"One tamn bat aczent," replied the Swedo-Russo-Germano-American.

Chapter XII

The Moral Regeneration of Russia

SHE was known to all as "*The Morossova*"; some called her Santa Maria: the daughter of the Morossov who had made millions in textiles and had subsidized the great Art Theatre of Moscow. She was rich, beautiful, cultured, democratic.

The night she spoke to me of "the moral regeneration of Russia under the Bolsheviks," she was my hostess at her father's theatre. They were playing Eugene Onegin, an opera based on a novel by Pushkin.

"The duel scene is quite famous," she said, "Pushkin himself was a good duellist and lost his life in such a combat. Onegin is the personification of the blasé youth of old Petrograd, incapable of a true emotion, careless of his relations with women, full of a desire to conquer those whom other men desire. Tatiani is moody, gloomy, living the life of the gloomy, moody characters she finds in pre-revolutionary Russian novels which she reads and believes . . . were we ever like that . . . ?

"You see, that was the old Russia. . . .

"In the old Russia there was too much wealth for too few persons, too much debauchery, too much disgust with life, too much listlessness, too much seeking after new sensations, too much trying to find something to make life less boring, more worth living. . . .

"In the new Russia there is the struggle to get a piece of bread, true, but it keeps all Russia active, active, awake, alive. It is a battle for life . . . and in time of battle one does not get moody or degenerate, one does not commit suicide out of boredom, out of disgust with life — the result of reading a morbid novel . . . no, one girds himself to the attack. The mind clears . . . the body exerts all its strength . . . moral inspiration comes for victory. . . .

"That is the new Russia.

"Once there was too much time to kill . . . leisure perverted life. Now there is a tremendous energy, seeking not artistic or noble expression as yet, but the daily bitter black bread. For love and for friendship and for social intercourse, for the amenities of civilized existence, for poetry and art there is today less time and less passion. But that too will come in time. Thank God we have broken with the old Russia. This is the day of moral regeneration."

* * * * *

I put all this down in my note-book, thinking to use it some day when I wrote the pros and cons of Bolshevism. With such expressions I would refute the charge that I met only the opposition and heard only anti-Bolshevik propaganda during my year in Russia.

Could there be a better case than that of Marie Morossova? The daughter of the beloved libertarian Prince Kropotkin was in London, in Paris, in Berlin, working with the anti-Soviet forces and the Tolstoy family had disowned the revolution. Gorki had written gloriously of the flaming heart of Lenin but he hated the bloodshed and terror of the new régime. But here was a daughter of the old régime acclimated and spiritually enthusiastic under the new order. She would be my proof of impartiality.

But one day Santa Maria was missing. And when a person

is "missing" in Moscow, there is but one place to search, and that is the Lubyanka, the main prison and headquarters of the Chekah, and its slaughter-house.

She was charged with visiting the British mission headquarters and with being too friendly with foreigners. All that is counter-revolutionary. For days and nights she was tortured in the Chekah prison. When we saw her again, it was in a sanitarium. She had gone mad.

So if you want to hear about the regeneration of Russia under the Bolsheviks, you will have to read elsewhere.

(Naturally the censor suppressed all telegrams dealing with this case. It was a matter of purely local concern, they said.)

Part IV — Arabia

Chapter I

The Truth About France and the Eastern War

TO break the censorship and print some truths about the French in Syria, the new revolt in the desert, the attack on the Christian Lebanon, the Foreign Legion, and daily additions to an unfortunate situation, was an expensive but rather easy adventure. But to tell the deeper truth about French "Imperialism," the causes of the war and the part General Sarrail played, requires a statement on religious intrigue. This subject is taboo in American newspapers. I believe this to be the first and only account of all that happened from the time Sarrail first attacked the powers of the church and the feudal system to the ultimate military victory and diplomatic compromise of his successors in Syria.

It is necessary, first of all, to know that Syria with its population of 2,800,000 is a land of 29 religions and that murder for religious reasons was and is practised there enthusiastically, joyously, and in a wholesale way frequently. It is also necessary to know that Sarrail who came as General and Governor of Syria, was a fanatical anti-clerical. He is also accused of being an atheist, a freemason and a Socialist, sometimes all three.

Tragedy was therefore inevitable. You have the man, the antagonistic mass, and the conflict of wills.

All his life General Sarrail had been at war with the clerical forces in France and in the French army. When the anti-clericals were on top, Sarrail won promotion and recognition; when

249

a clerical premier came to power Sarrail was neatly shoved under.

Other Catholic and Protestant generals in France did not suffer or rejoice in the same way; most of them made their faith a subject between their God and themselves; Sarrail was a fighting sectarian.

Sarrail saved Verdun. Frenchmen admit him to be one of the great heroes of the war. A man of amazing military intelligence and unbounded initiative, he kept the eastern gate from the great onslaught of Germany and by magnificent disobedience, which may prove amazing to future historians, he won the great battle.

But for political reasons Sarrail was relegated to Salonika. No worse post could be found for a French commander. He was chief of British troops there and faced the undecided and well intimidated Greeks. Despite insufficient men and materials, despite an almost evident antagonistic spirit in French G. H. Q., despite sabotage and resistance by the British, he won success after success and prepared the great coup against the weak spot of the enemy. But he never got the laurels. He was recalled just before the attack.

Herriot, of the Radical Socialists, sent Sarrail to Syria. It was the reward given one anti-clerical by another. And immediately the French clerical press, which had printed not a word when rebellion broke out under the governorship of General Weygand, began exaggerating the troubles under ;Sarrail and screaming for his recall.

Why?

Because from the moment he arrived in Beirut General Sarrail saw two things clearly; he saw the domination of the churches and the domination of the feudal lords. He saw the population of the country bow to the Orthodox, Maronite, Roman, Mohammedan, Sunnite, Shiyite and other churches instead of to the Power of the State, and he saw misery, serfdom, virtual slavery upon which emirs and pashas waxed bulbous in well-stocked harems.

And so his socialistic, anti-clerical soul revolted and he said, "I'll change all that, and at once, too."

He tried in three months to upset the customs, traditions, beliefs, forms, taboos, usages, sacred prerogatives and impositions of two thousand years.

He reaped a rebellion.

When Sarrail came to Syria advisors said to him, "You can't rule these people with kindness. They understand only force. Terror and bribery are the means of taming the desert. Give the city Syrians posts of honour in the government: let there be graft! But the wild tribes cannot be treated like Europeans. They are famous for biting the hand which feeds them."

Sarrail was obstinate. He heard from his intelligence officers how Colonel Lawrence bought loyalty — at least temporary loyalty, with gold pieces, but the French were opposed to handing out money and Sarrail had the peculiar humanitarian view that the savages would be satisfied with schools and hospitals and good roads instead of Turkish pounds.

Again, they said to him, "Use force at the least show of resistance." But he wouldn't. They showed him how the British were ruling Mesopotamia, across the way, with lots of airplanes and few men, because they had taught vagrant tribes and town Arabs the terror of bombs dropped from the air. (This was before the premiership of Ramsay Macdonald when Socialism and sentimentality won out for a brief spell and notes instead of bombs were dropped on recalcitrant villages.) Sarrail was sure he would win Arabs and Bedouins by acts of friendship and generosity. Above all else, he determined to be absolutely fair in settling the differences between Christian and non-Christian, village and village, tribe and tribe.

(So for every air bomb he failed to use when it was time, and as the British do, he had to import a hundred shells, and for every gold piece he failed to give in bribery and corruption, as the British did, he had to spend a hundred or a thousand gold pieces on military supplies and men.)

Of course he made some terrible mistakes, being both aged and fanatical. He refused, for instance, to visit the head of the Roman Church, or the Chief Rabbi, or the Orthodox Archbishop of the Cadi or the Chief Mufti. He was willing to receive them, but he did not step out of his way in their direction. And there was no question of his attending mass with the Jesuits as Generals Weygand and Gouraud had done. He found the Jesuit order strongly entrenched in magnificent buildings largely subventioned by the French government and all he said was, " They think they are the centre of government." In his personal newspaper he ordered printed:

" The purpose of the mandate for Syria which was confided to France, is not to favor principally the Roman Church but to place above all religions the well-being of the Syrian people, and to take care to give to the Mohammedans who are in the majority, continual proofs of the friendship of France.

" But it seems that in Syria it is impossible for the Governor to act independently of the Jesuits. The latter ask only one thing, and that is to be the masters. The first duty of a French patriot given the honour of governing Syria is not to place himself in the hands of any religious sect."

Sarrail sent a man to ask questions. He stopped people in the streets and such was the dialogue:

" Are you a Syrian? "

" No, I am a Maronite."

" And you? "

" I am a Greek Orthodox."

" And is the third man a Syrian? "

" No. I am a Sunnite."

" What is a Sunnite? "

" A branch of the Mohammedan faith; we hate the Shiyites."

" And the fourth? "

" Melakite."

" And the last man there? "

" Greek Catholic."

" Like your friend number two? "

" No — no. He is Greek Orthodox; I am Greek Catholic."

" Are there no Syrians among you? "

" I am Arab."

" I am Libanase."

" I am Alouite."

And so it went on, there were nothing but religious sects and tribal groups in Syria.

Then Sarrail began to study the economic condition. He was shocked. He found such poverty as the western world rarely sees nowadays. He found men so poor and miserable they would commit murder for five piastres. He found the emirs and pashas living in idle luxury while serfdom flourished. The Arabs in the desert and the thousands of homeless in the cities knew only three things; sleep, eat when possible, pillage when possible. A large mass semi-starved. And with hunger he found cruelty. He heard tales of horror. Life was held too cheap. In war, he was told, the Druses tore out the hearts of their enemies and ate them.

Sarrail was a kindly old man despite his religious fanaticism: he was sentimental enough to stop public hangings and amazed to find the natives had hanged a French soldier; he determined to free the serfs and was surprised to find them not only ungrateful, but taking up arms against him at the order of their old masters; so far as his insult to the 29 religious cults was concerned, he suffered no disillusion because he knew what to expect.

He found that by merely enforcing existing laws he could end slavery and eventually crush the feudal lordship of emirs and pashas. He changed officers at Soueida, the capital of the Druse tribe, until he had one, very unpopular with the natives, but one who understood Sarrail's ideals of civilization.

The law was enforced. A close relative of the pasha of the Druses, himself a prince, arrested and found guilty of a common crime, was treated as a common criminal, and given the conventional sentence, to break stones on the highroad outside his feudal village.

Therefore the serfs he wanted to free arose and rebelled for their insulted ruler.

*   *   *   *   *

When Henri de Jouvenal succeeded Sarrail as high commissioner, " Christian " Lebanon chose a government, and this is how it was announced:

Maronite Christian: Auguste Adeb Pasha: premier.
Sunnite (Mohammedan): Negeb Bey Kabbané: justice.
Maronite: Bechara Effendi Khoury: interior.
Melachite: Mr. Joseph Aftemos: public works.

Orthodox Catholic: Mr. Negib Amrouni: education.

Shiyite (Mohammedan): Aluj Nostral Bey: agriculture.

Druse (Semi-Pagan): Dr. Selim Talbouk: public health.

and in the Senate, composed of sixteen men, there were also six religions announced, the Greek Orthodox being included, the Melachite being omitted, Mr. Ayoub Tabet named as representing " the minorities."

They also tried to make peace in certain sectors where neither Mohammedans, Christians, nor Druses had committed more than desultory murder. I know of no better light on the character of the people of the Orient than this peace treaty of the Wadi Ajam zone, signed, sealed and delivered this 25th day of September, 1925.

There were 111 delegates to the Versailles of the desert. They met at Beitima, which flew the banner of neutrality, being Mohammedan. There was no house big enough for the congress, so it met in the open in a garden which was part of an oasis.

The treaty was for sixty-one days, as is the custom of the tribes. The terms were:

(1) A certain sum shall be fixed by the contracting parties, this sum to be known as the price of blood.

(2) A commission of neutral Mohammedans chosen from the villages of Beitima shall count the number murdered during the time of this treaty, on both sides.

(3) If the number of murdered is greater among one of the contracting parties, the other party must pay the price of blood multiplied by the difference in the number killed.

(4) The Druses restore the flocks taken from the Christians and pay for those which have disappeared.

(5) The Druses and Christians are to be disarmed by a commission of mukhtars (sheiks) of Caza.

For the town of Kallat Yandal: Christians: Youssef Saad, Elias Semaan, Nicolas bou Akl, Michael Elias Kousseiri. Druses: Assaad Mejli.

For the town of Hiné: Christians: Moussa Dabe, Sabeh Abou Diebe, Gerios Mossalem.

For the town of Arna: Druses: Mhamad Kassem Kaboul; Fares Kaboul, Saleh Ahmeddine.

For the town of Kherbey: Druse: Fares Taleh.

* * * * *

When I tried to write the story of the war of religions in the Christian Lebanon I found not only French censorship but actual perversion of my cables.

The French had been trying to prevent the tribal Druse rebellion and the Nationalist Syrian uprising from becoming involved in religion because once the holy war had been announced they would be helpless despite their human and material military superiority.

They had two most important truths to conceal: the formation of the Christian Volunteer Army of the Lebanon and the Mohammedan support of the Druses in the massacre of Kaukaba. When I reported the latter fact French officials deliberately changed my cables and calling me to headquarters explained that this was a military necessity. Moreover when they found that I had sent a courier to Cairo with duplicates of my censored dispatches, they issued a statement to the Arab press which said that I had admitted that no Mohammedans participated in the massacre, and asked me not to deny their lie. Realizing the importance of averting more religious massacres, I conformed.

The religious war commenced with a surprise attack, the

```
A V I S
▸+▸+▸+▸+▸+▸

        La présente carte de presse est
délivrée sous réserve que les fausses
nouvelles ou les reportages tendancieux
pourront donner lieu non seulement à
l'arrêt des télégrammes mais encore au
retrait de la carte de presse elle-
même ./.
```

The " Avis " is a warning from the French army against sending false or tendancious news, but actually intimidation of the correspondents suggesting that only French victories were to be reported.

Druses, who deny they are pagans although they acknowledge neither Jehovah, Christ nor Allah, and their Mohammedan recruits from Damascus burst out of Syria and marched secretly upon the Lebanon villages where American dollars and American missionaries had spread a veneer of American civilization.

The Druses and Mohammedans entered the town peacefully; their leader, the Druse Hamsy Dervish, came in a Ford car to the home of the Christian Sheik, Khaleel Khoury Rizk, and said:

"Do not be frightened. Our errand is one of peace."

Sheik Khaleel ordered coffee, cigarettes and fruit served, and Hamsy Dervish ate, drank and smoked. Now it is the first unwritten law of the Orient that a man must respect the safety of his guest, and the guest must respect the safety of his host, and to eat and drink in another man's house is the pledge of safety.

So Sheik Khaleel believed. "But after he had eaten and drunk," said the Sheik to me a week later, "Hamsy Dervish, being neither Christian, Mohammedan nor Jew, but a vile pagan, went to my roof-tree and made a signal to his followers. Immediately afterwards Druses arrived demanding rifles, money and food as our ransom. We protested. Then shooting began in the village.

"I saw one Christian killed, then three Christians killed, and, with my few followers, I fled to the hills and we fired until our ammunition was gone. My niece and I were stopped on our flight to Sidon by other Druses who cried: 'Hands up, Christian dogs,' and took our rings, watches and money."

The sheik's brother, the Reverend Joseph Rizk, rifle in hand defended his church.

"We fought to the end," he said. "A handful, we covered the flight of 200 unarmed civilians, after forty Christians had been killed, and many more wounded, and the town pillaged and set on fire.

"I saw the Druses enter my church, shoot down the holy cross, defile the holy vessels, pillage the ecclesiastical garments. My one regret is that I did not remain fighting in the church and die there, rifle in hand."

Following the massacre of Kaukaba two thousand men, under the leadership of Patras bey Karam and Joseph Karam, descendants of Joseph Karam, the national hero of Lebanon, organized the Christian Volunteer Army, which fought valiantly to save the Christian villages but became a complex problem to the French because their very existence began to stir up a religious war on a large scale.

The blame for arming the Christians was placed on the Lebanon government, not the French command; the volunteers engaged in battle and took Kaukaba. The Druses and Mohammedans attacked, took Kaukaba, then entered Djedeide Merjayoun, known as the "American Capital" of the Christian Lebanon.

"If the National Gendarmarie had remained with us we would have saved the capital," Patras bey Karam told me the next day. "But they fled when they heard the enemy's strength was 3000. We killed 300 of them. But of our thousand many had never had a rifle in their hands before; there was no discipline, no self-reliance. Soon our forces dwindled away, it was every man for himself. I'm old but hard. At least a thousand enemy bullets went by me; when I fired I killed my man each time. We saved most of the civilians, including the twenty 'American' families."

The town of Nabataya became the Volunteer Army's head-quarters. Here Joseph Karam, a picturesque youth with a strong face, a fez, khaki shirt, two bandoliers crossing his chest, two automatic revolvers at his hips, and a rifle with a Christ on the Cross carved on the stock, was holding the road to Djedeide which was full of refugees, walking, riding jackasses, crowding in Fords from which vast masses of bed-clothes protruded and bed-sheets flapped in the wind like the sails of a wrecked schooner. The refugees were paying as much as $50. for a seat in a Ford, $25. for a foothold, and there were many other good Christians who were glad to profiteer on those fleeing for their lives. Children bound tightly to jackasses were screaming and their mothers walked and wept.

The French sent troops by land and sea. Ancient Sidon saw dirty, smelly, smoky, little destroyers where once French Knights had landed glistening in armour from square-sailed, many-oared, red Venetian galleys. Crusade and Christian massacre were no new thing in this terrible part of the world. In the memory of man, in 1860, in the very same towns which were later to see severe fighting, there had been massacres of Christians — and as late as 1920 religious war had led to wholesale murders there. Now the French were sending black Senegalese troops in greenish-brown uniforms, fezzed, their bellies bound in red flannel to ward off dysentery, to the ruins of the strong-hold called Beaufort, which Saint Louis himself had built and which overtops Djedeide. Six centuries of religious bloodshed looked down upon them.

The activities of the Christian army and the victories of the Druse-Mohammedan invasion, which echoed eloquently in the desert when fifty camels laden with loot appeared, made the danger of religious war acute, and Beirut was not beyond danger. Consul-General Paul Knabenshue, as fine a man as ever filled a diplomatic post intelligently and efficiently, had previously told all American missionaries to stick to the seaports. He now asked American war craft for Beirut. I wrote the following dispatch:

"Bulletin in view of the situation, the destroyers Lamson and Coghlan, commanded by Captain Fairfield, came to Beirut at 9 this morning stop marvellous effect population both American and native stop everybody is certain of the calming effect American war craft in harbour will produce stop practically all Americans are at Beirut with exception Consul Keeley and family still in Damascus."

Knabenshue had asked to see all reports on the arrival of the destroyers. He had realized the danger and had requested the state department to announce the visit as a mere formality, because he did not wish to excite the already panicky Beirut population nor to insult the French by showing them he did not think their protection adequate.

I showed Knabenshue my telegram and he asked leave to censor it. He cut out most of it, sending only:

"Bulletin in view of the situation the American destroyers Lamson and Coghlan, commanded by Captain Fairfield, came Beirut at nine this morning stopping a few days on tour Mediterranean ports."

This was censorship to which I could not object. Knabenshue was in a particularly nervous diplomatic position and I was glad to help him. Imagine his position when two days later the state department gave out the information to Washington correspondents that the American destroyers had been sent "by the request of Consul-General Knabenshue at Beirut who considered the situation there as very serious and who wanted the ships to stand by in case it was necessary to embark all American nationals."

The French poured troops into Nabataya, moved them to Kleat, occupied Djedeide without a battle and prepared to fight for Hasbaya. They assembled the Mohammedan sheiks, who are the wise elders of the village, not young bloods full of passion and romance as the fiction writers would have you believe, and who can be distinguished by the length of their beards upon which you can usually see the memories of yesterday's breakfasts and last week's dinners, egg yellow and mutton suet and filth of undeterminable origin. They told these sheiks just how far the shells from the destroyers in the harbours of ancient Tyr and Phoenician Sidon could carry and they received the humble submission of all towns within gun range.

But the wily Druses and their Mohammedan recruits, quitting Hasbaya, attacked Rashaya, necessitating another split in the French forces, another march on foot, another dash of a Ford convoy bulging with soldiery.

Here on the Bekaa plain, known as the field of Armageddon to the natives, I saw the magnificent spectacle of an army deploying for attack.

In fact my big car passed through the French lines and proceeded to a hilltop overlooking Rashaya where a French garrison was fighting for its life. Occasionally shrapnel exploded in mid-air; there was the stutter of machine-gun fire and the explosion of hand-grenades; in the silences the cuckoo sang blithely in its alien nest.

Standing by the roadside, between the advancing French army 5,000 strong, and the Druses surrounding the town, 3,000 strong, I saw the refugees streaming into the Bekaa plain. They came in Fords shouting:

" They're killing; they're looting; they murdered my mother; fly with us or you will be killed," they cried as their Fords slowed down then sped away.

I rode towards the battle. Soon I was able to see the Druse horsemen attacking. The citadel of Rashaya is historic. In 1860 the Druses had massacred 265 Christians in the town, and when peace had been won by the French, the thankful Christians bought and restored the Crusaders' citadel and prepared it for just what I was witnessing that day.

Suddenly I saw myself surrounded by Druses. Five of them came up with rifles in hand and spoke in Arabic to George my Syrian interpreter. They asked information about the French who were marching and wanted to know why we had come. George had but to use the magic word " English " to make them friendly. They let us go. But as we sped back we found the road had been blocked with telegraph poles and wires. It took us a long time to get through but although we saw armed Druses in the distance, sighting us through rifles, none fired.

The next day I was on the plain again, this time behind the French army, and saw Captain Landriot of the Foreign Legion charge the Druses in the citadel and defeat them while the column under Colonel Lobez routed the enemy without. Rashaya was relieved. The French set fire to the neighbouring towns from which Druses were firing rifles.

I entered Rashaya to find the results of concentrated slaughter. In the courtyard of the citadel lay hundreds of Druses and hundreds of Druse horses, heads and limbs and entrails mixed, a scene of red and purple horror unparalleled.

The next day eight burning Druse villages sent up signals like American Indian flares, signals of victory and the progress of modern arms. Mount Hermon with its snow-white head was wreathed in smoke. When I tried to enter Rashaya again the officers told me my pass was not valid despite General Sarrail's signature. But it didn't matter much. The war between Christians and Druses was over.

*   *   *   *   *

And so France saved the Christian Lebanon but got no thanks.

She built schools and roads. She found epidemics and conquered them. Trachoma and syphilis infested the country; new hospitals were built. Religious orders and schools were aided. Law and order were enforced. Billions of francs were spent. " Imperialism " was at work.

What did France take out of Syria? Nothing. It is an almost barren land, spotted with beautiful oases, containing the most imposing ruin in the world, Baalbek, the lovely Bekaa plain, historic monuments, some goats, but no cotton plantations, no vast mineral wealth, no agriculture, no oil, no hope of oil. At most Syria has a trade value as a port of entry to Iraq and India.

Militarism, exploitation, imperialism? All I found was intense disgust with the mandate on the part of the French while the natives who cried for freedom and independence feared that the enemy religious cult would fight them unless a foreign power spent its money there maintaining order.

" What we want," the whole nation seemed to shout at me, " is the Syrian mandate in American hands."

" Because," one strangely honest native confided to me, " if we have Italy or France they'll try to milk us and we have no milk; if Britain gets the mandate we will try to milk each other; but if America comes we could milk her with both hands."

Impoverished Syria, birth-place of almost all the religions of the world which teach brotherly love, home of a score of peoples practising brotherly murder, is still a political pawn, General Sarrail, whom even the liberal press of America, *The New Republic* and *The Nation,* assailed bitterly, has disappeared from public life; and whenever the political winds require it the phrase " Imperialist France " will be blown through the length and breadth of England, Germany or Italy, or perhaps America.

Sarrail was a tragic failure. His successors had no intention of fighting the dominating religions and took the hint from British diplomacy in the East; they created political posts, gave away honours, spent a little money where it brought the most loyalty. Church and Feudalism continue to rule, conscious of victory over another would-be destroyer of things as they are and always have been. The people of Syria are still willing to have rich America take over the troubled mandate. Milk and honey have disappeared from the Holy Land. But milk and honey could be imported.

*   *   *   *   *

Pan-Arabian Plot and Abd-el-Kadr

One of the reasons the Nationalists in Damascus sent me a threat of disembowelment was my discovery of documents revealing a Pan-Arabian plot. These documents, I can now say, were shown me by an American consular official who was rather sympathetic to the Syrian cause, and who sent the originals to the state department where they are probably on file today. I had cause for much secret amusement for many months when I heard Syrian notables complaining about me to this consular official, who merely looked sympathetic but dared not admit the documents were really his.

They were a series of proclamations and letters exchanged between Moslem organizations throughout the Mohammedan world plotting — and why shouldn't they plot — freedom from the British, French and Italian yoke in Asia and Africa.

The bombardment of Damascus was used by Arab propagandists for spreading the grandest lies in post-war history. Islam was aroused. Headquarters in Cairo were particularly active. Victories by Abd-el-Krim were still being reported. Then was the time for all good Moslems to come to the aid of their brethren.

The Party of the People which had been led by the exiled patriot, Dr. Shabander, was dispersed and impotent, but some of its members had gone to Egypt and obtained money and moral support. The first document is signed " Committee for the Liberation of Syria " and opens with the statement that the successive French governing generals, Gouraud, Weygand and Sarrail were " a group of assassins." It continues:

" The hour for the liberation of North Africa and Arabia from the foreign yoke, from French, English and Italian oppression is near at hand. From Tangiers and the Near East to Shanghai and the Far East the Mohammedan people will soon attack the oppressors. Syrian brethren, follow the example of the Riffians and Turks and Chinese! Drive out the foreign nations which enslave us! Aid the Druse revolt! Fraternize with the French soldiers of the Army of the Orient, most of whom are Moslems, and win them over to our cause! "

The second document, signed " Central Committee for the

Liberation of North Africa," and listing branches in all Mediterranean countries, begins by congratulating the Damascenes for their revolutionary attempt and continues:

" The patience of Araby is exhausted. The fires of revolution are blazing. You have acted like brave men. Help the Riffian brethren. Make the Mohammedan soldiers desert the French. Death is preferable to the foreign yoke. Arabians! never sheathe the sword until you have won independence! "

The patriots accused me of being a French agent and for months would not listen to my protestations of neutrality. For months I challenged them to state their side of the dispute, promising I would print any statement they made. Finally this challenge was accepted. Arrangements were made for me to meet the leaders. I was to be taken to the house of a prince; I was not to ask questions about where the house was or to try to identify any person present. To this I agreed.

Now it was notorious that Al Bakry, and other Syrian leaders who were fighting the French, made a habit of coming into Damascus at night through the orange groves. They slept, ate and drank well while 5,000 French looked for them in the desert and oases. It was that kind of a war.

We traversed the oldest streets of the oldest city in the world, rode through narrow alleys where our open carriage frequently would bump innocent bystanders against the walls on both sides, and where flat oriental unleavened bread was offered for sale lying in heaps on the uncovered cobblestones, swarming with flies which could not be scared away by curses or motions, and spattered with camel dung, which Arabs would wipe off after spitting a little on the bread. We rode around and around until my sense of direction was completely gone, and finally came to a veritable palace, not quite up to the Thousand and One Nights in splendour, but lovely by contrast to the filth and mud and dung of all the Orient.

There was a rustling of silks as the women of the harem were quickly driven behind their screens, and several pashas, emirs and assorted beys rose to meet me, saluting me by touching their breasts and fezzes, as if to say in that oriental exaggeration which means nothing at all, " My heart and my head are at your disposal."

They remained wary and suspicious. One of them wore a splendid oriental costume which I recognized as Algerian and I took him to be the Emir Abd-el-Kadr although I asked no questions. He was spokesman. There were two interpreters who apparently interpreted nothing but gave their own views so that most of the afternoon was lost in a dispute among my dozen hosts.

They began by listing their grievances: the atrocities committed by the Armenians; the failure to treat a mandate as a mandate instead of as a colony; the loss of Syrian independence which Wilson had promised them indirectly. Finally one and all came to the same conclusion: " We cannot trust the French. Every French governor has betrayed us; why shall we believe in de Jouvenal's peace terms? "

They proposed plebescites and League of Nation investigating committees. They proposed a system of government like that of Britain in Mesopotamia.

" Then you do not want complete independence, and the European powers driven out? " I asked.

" No. Not now," one replied, " because there would be chaos. The fatal trouble in Syria is not nationalism but religion. Murder and massacre, between Christians and non-Christians, which has been our history for 600 years, would be repeated if the mandate were given up."

This caused a hubbub. Some attacked the mandate system; some were for full independence; one for America to hold the mandate; one for Britain; three wanted Syria divided into four parts, each governed separately; one had another plan. . . .

I did my best to write a dispatch giving the rebel point of view. The French censor promptly suppressed it.

* * * * *

Revolt in the Desert

Strangely, quickly out of the rolling Arabian desert wastes, appears the ruin of Palmyra, "a rose red city half as old as time." Here Queen Zenobia had found water, and so built an empire. Here, today, there is a French outpost and the head-quarters of the Camel Corps, as brave and picturesque a fighting unit as ever graced ancient or modern armies.

I had come out of Bagdad trembling with cold and burning wet with the fires of malaria. For two days I had ridden in a French convoy through the northern part of the Arabian desert, hoping to make Damascus on the third morning. The sun was setting as we rode through the avenue of kingly tombs into the midst of the Græco-Roman ruins of the purple and gold capital. It grew cold quickly as if the desert sand, in anger at the sun's daily attack, was driving out the heat with amazing celerity.

The one small building, a compound called a hotel, was crowded. Travellers, consuls, oil and tobacco men and young American Methodist missionaries, each without exception accompanied by a wife and at least one howling child, had filled every available bed and covered space. Our promised rest was gone. " Why didn't your caravan pull out this morning? " we asked.

" Because Damascus is being bombarded — fighting everywhere — revolt in the desert," they replied.

All my journalistic blood boiled. I ran out among the broken Greek pillars and the futile barbed wire, found the leader of our convoy and asked him when were we to start for Damascus.

" Probably in a week — if all goes well."

" But I must go there at once."

The Frenchman merely shrugged.

A hundred yards away was the French military headquarters. The commander was a very agreeable man. " We will do our best to make you comfortable," he said, " though food is scarce and you may have to stay a week."

I insisted on going at once. " But no car must leave Palmyra," he answered. " I'll buy a car," I said. " Even then," he replied, " I couldn't return you your passport or let you go. I have orders by radio to keep all civilians here."

Military orders. Stalemate.

Three Englishmen gave me blankets and we went to sleep amidst the ruins of the temple of Jupiter, watching the Arabian moon, vast as a conflagration, burn up the few Palmyran palms and blaze a path through the grandest galaxy of stars man has ever seen. The rest was silence.

It was broken at five in the morning by the clarion of reveille and the roaring of a motor, as out of the east a Cadillac car, leaving a dust serpent miles behind, swept into our ruins. A sand covered person emerged and asked for water. He explained himself as Murdoch, driver for the rival British transdesert line, answering an emergency call for another car. He had driven all night and was prepared to go on after two hours sleep.

I told him of the embargo. He went to the French headquarters and returned with the information that he was considered neither military nor civilian, that the French assumed no responsibility for him, and that he would start as per his schedule. I asked him to take me along. He agreed, provided the French gave permission. But he would break no French laws.

At seven o'clock he tuned up.

"I'll give you anything you ask — a hundred — two hundred — five — if you'll take me," I said.

"Not without a passport in order," he replied.

So I went to the French headquarters. The black sentry saluted as he salutes every white man, and said nothing. I knocked and got no answer. I entered a room. No one was present. I knocked on another door and got no answer. I entered. There, spread on a table were two dozen assorted passports and all the trimmings of civilian bureaucracy. I found my passport. No sound anywhere. Without stopping for breath I seized two rubber stamps and plastered them on the blue sheets. I slipped the passport into my pocket and walked in dignified manner by the sentry, answered his salute, and ran to Murdoch's car. In a few minutes only the tops of broken temples were sinking into the vale of Palmyra.

The desert was hard and the going good. We rode twenty miles in as many minutes, laughing and joking at the French fears of an uprising. The trail was bordered with camel thorn giving a dusty green to the desert which rose and sank in vast sweeps towards the horizon sometimes jagged by aged, grey, bare hilltops.

Emerging from one thin valley we ran into a tribe of Arab warriors mounted on camels and splendid with banners.

Out of the dust and the clamour of yells — Arabic yells blood-curdling enough to frighten an Apache Indian — came rifle shots. Bullets kicked up desert dust in funny little spatters, no more than heavy raindrops sometimes make on tired city pavements. The Arab tribe rode to the attack.

Of the great Arabian desert which stretches from the Yemen and Has el Had north to the Taurus mountains and the Turkish frontier very little is shifting sand. There are hills and valleys all devoid of vegetation and in the north are wadies which fill with water during the month of rain. Almost all that 600-mile stretch between Damascus and Persia is bleak and barren but hard, and a large part is covered by that mean clumpy growth known as camel thorn.

Into this Murdoch flew at a speed of 60 miles. We bumped along, losing velocity, tearing up thorn and getting it caught in the wheels and radiator. We flew, without aim or goal, off the trail and into the desert.

The Bedouins wheeled around. Mounted on war camels which are faster than race horses for short distances, and unhampered by thorn, they came after us at a great pace. But Murdoch would not turn back. As he accelerated the car he directed it at right angles to the road, keeping his eye always on a spot just beyond the attackers. Bullets continued to fall short of us. But if our engine failed our lives were worthless; Bedouins never stop to ask for passports.

Riding the bumps into the desert, Murdoch succeeded in getting the Arabs to follow him far from the road; suddenly he wheeled, as if to ride at them, then headed at a wide angle back to the road. The Arabs wheeled also. The three hundred of them and our car dashed on converging lines, back to the main trail. They had the inside track and less to cover; we had a Cadillac. As we came closer they began firing more heavily, but they were either bad shots or the ships of the desert had made their aim seasick; they hit the car in no vital spot and we made the road. As our wheels bit clear hard ground again the car leaped with joy and we left the Bedouins to be swallowed up by their own dust and the horizon.

An hour later we came to the end of what had once been a railroad line. Allenby or the Turks had torn up rails and cross-ties but the stones remained. Over this we rode at the rate of ten miles an hour, while Damascus was being bombarded, the biggest story in the world with no one to report it.

Every five or ten miles there would be a break in the metal road. Nothing but boulders and ditches through which men had difficulty in climbing. Murdoch got over them too, but one by one the leaves in his left front spring dropped off. This he remedied by placing all sorts of levers and monkey-wrenches in the open space and tying them with rope, piano wire and a chain.

And so we made Homs and Tripoli at night.

From Tripoli the road leads perilously over hill and precipice, along the waves of the Mediterranean to Beirut. Despite a missing spring we made good time until we came to the outskirts of Beirut when an Arab asleep on a jackass came across the middle of the road. To save killing the valuable jackass Murdoch was forced to run his car into the Mediterranean. It sank into a mixture of stone and quicksand and we worked for three hours raising it on pieces of log and cobbles. And still the bombardment of Damascus continued.

At dawn Fords, each carrying from seven to ten Arabs, began

collecting around our sunken car. For another hour we tried every means, and finally, when we had seventy Arabs around, we were able to pull the car out on to the road. By an irony our Cadillac crashed through the Ford of the first seven Arabs who had stopped to help us. So we paid.

We rode into Beirut, changed cars, got on the Damascus road, came into town before noon, and when I got to the American consulate I found James Keeley, his wife and their baby standing on the roof, watching the cannon of Fort Gouraud hurling three-inch shells into the bazaar section.

The bombardment of Damascus lasted just long enough to have one journalistic eyewitness.

*　　*　　*　　*　　*

Day and night the shells had passed over the consul's house, falling into the seething city. At night the bursting shells set fountains of flame spurting brightly in the starry darkness; in the strong sunlight they had turned to whirlpools of dust and debris. The guns exploded with terrifying regularity and the crash of the shells in the adobe city came as a louder echo.

In the European section there was no panic. In the native section Arab women were risking their lives to save another pillow. From Keeley's roof could be seen the long line of wallowing donkeys and laden men, a black stream flowing fitfully out of the burning zone, emptying in the Merje Square or breaking up again into all the inlets of the Christian and rich Mohammedan quarter.

Regularly the shells clattered and crashed, followed by deep rumblings of mud and timbered houses, which had leaped in the air, and collapsed into the shell holes. Once a shell fell short, into the bath-house which looked like a mosque; another

273

time a stately minaret lost its head. Unceasingly the stream of refugees flowed on.

Between the Hamadya, which contains the best bazaars, and the Street Called Straight which Saint Paul had once sought, all was fire and death. The French shells tore open the corrugated roofs and again flooded the damp thoroughfares with strange sun-shine. The Palais Azam, noblest of buildings, smouldered.

The battle in Damascus had started on a Sunday when 600 Druses, their typical turbans exchanged for those of conventional Arabs, had filtered into the native section to sound the call for revolt.

Two Cherkassian soldiers, irregulars employed by the French, were quarrelling in a bazaar. One drew a revolver and fired at the other. He killed an innocent bystander. The bystander was a Mohammedan. From the howling mob which gathered around the body and the soldiers, the cry of " Massacre " arose. Immediately the Druses appeared to lead the aroused fanatical Mohammedans. The riff-raff of the bazaars took up the cry, " Massacre." Within a few minutes the reeking overcrowded native quarter was in revolt.

The cry went up, " Death to the Armenians." The mob attacked and killed all they found, at least fifty. They pillaged and burned. The cry went up, " Death to General Sarrail." The mob rushed towards the Palais Azam, believing that Sarrail was staying that night in the wing which was his headquarters.

At the Palais Azam, now a museum, the sight of splendid carpets and of money, gold and silver coins of many ages, proved too strong a temptation. The mob broke the museum cases and grabbed the gold drachmas of Philip of Macedon and Alexander the Great. From the walls they tore priceless carpets.

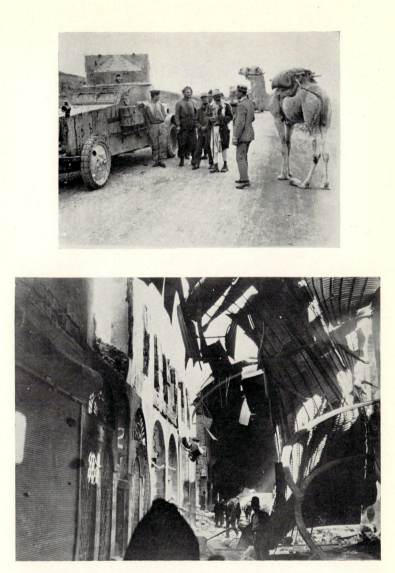

A camel may look at a tank, or the old and the new
meet in the Arabian desert.

Bombardment of Damascus: "The Street Called Straight" after the
French shells had torn off the roof and ruined the famous bazaar.

The Roman vases and old Syrian glass, buried a thousand years and resplendent as the rainbow, were crushed on the stones of the museum. Hittite antiquities fared no better.

At the doors of Sarrail's headquarters the rebels killed the guards, then stormed the building, pillaged it, and failing to find their victim set the house on fire. They roamed through the streets shouting death and destruction.

General Sarrail was faced with a great problem. He had inadequate troops to quell the uprising, and to use those he had in hand-to-hand fighting in crowded streets meant risking the safety of the Christian quarter. As a soldier his strategy was clear, and no one who ever saw the American army smash up a French village housing Germans can deny he acted for the best: he withdrew his men, ordered all peaceful citizens out of the rebellious district, and gave the order to bombard.

The night I arrived in Damascus it was a city of terrible silence. No prayers rose from the many minarets, only a few lights burned in the European section and not a soul was permitted to walk out of his home or place of shelter. Tanks and armoured cars stood at street corners and barbed wire had been wound on clothes-horses and placed at the openings to the Christian section. Sandbag barricades had been thrown up, behind which French soldiers whispered in the dark, making coffee and drinking red wine by the flickerings of pocket torches. The American consulate was crowded with foreign refugees, a few born Americans and seventeen naturalized citizens whom Mrs. Keeley had fed.

Sarrail had saved the city and the lives of all the Christians; for thanks he got curses from all the inhabitants, regardless of religion, and his eventual recall. I believe this was the result of the protest which arose in the press of the entire world a week after the bombardment.

This is exactly what happened. As I was the only newspaperman in the East, my dispatches, narrating the facts as here given, should have been sent to America and Europe. But French censorship, with the congenital stupidity of all censorship, believed it could suppress the news entirely. I had sent a dozen telegrams in one of which I estimated the dead at 1000. To this the French objected. They said there were no more than 500 dead, and a count many days later revealed 300 bodies. Undoubtedly there were more in the ruins. My thousand included 50 Armenians and the French military losses, and to this very day I am sure I was right.

But the French delayed and changed my telegrams. Meanwhile runners were sent by the Arabs to the Pan-Arabic Executive in Jerusalem. By the time the news reached Jerusalem the four blocks of destroyed houses, no more than 500, all of adobe — filthy hovels worth the price of mud — had risen to 10,000, and the dead were counted at 25,000.

The *United Press* had cabled to the Pan-Arabic Executive for news, and received this report; correspondents of the *Associated Press, The London Express* and *London Daily Mail* had also obtained similar reports from the same source. By the end of the week, thanks to the French censor, the newspapers of the whole world were flaming with lies.

These lies are generally believed to this day.

Chapter II

REVOLT IN THE FOREIGN LEGION

WHERE the Foreign Legion is today the big battle will be fought tomorrow. "Where is the Foreign Legion to-day?" Everywhere I went I asked and sometimes I came very close to it, but it was not until the end of my year as sole war correspondent with the French expedition in Syria that I became involved with the Foreign Legion.

"Involved" barely expressed it. It was my destiny not only to find the glorious regiment but to see it go into battle, to visit it in the captured capital of the enemy, to find my American hero, to be accused of causing a mutiny in the desert, and to be the instrument for saving a human life.

I knew the French had divided the Legion into its component two regiments, one to fight Abd-el-Krim in Morocco, the other to subjugate Sultan Pasha Atrashe whose stone capital lay in the hills of Syria, overlooking the Palestine frontier and the rolling desert to the south and east.

I sought the Legion because I was determined to find an American soldier in its uniform, and on this nail I could hang the whole dust-bitten tableau of the revolt in the desert. I needed just one American. Through him the Syrian war, the dreadful sunshine, the suffering and horror, victory and defeat, sacrifice and bravery, hunger and thirst, could be brought home to the millions of American readers.

* * * * *

277

First there was the battle of Rashaya. In the besieged citadel was a small part of the Legion which fought in the tradition of its organization. In a savage and bloodthirsty battle in which the French were forced into primitive barbarism by attackers who knew nothing of the codes and ethics which modern warfare had imposed, the opponents murdered the wounded and used teeth and nails in hand-to-hand encounters.

When relief came the Legion got drunk. They emerged from the charnel house and sang and looted. Into the eight neighbouring villages they ran sparing neither friend nor foe, they made no distinction between Christian Syrians and Pagan Druses. They killed and took.

Rifle shots could be heard all around as I walked down the road into the valley towards the cliff on which the Citadel of Rashaya was perched. The sun was low, the desert suffused in gold, the white cliffs gilded. Towards me came a bed walking.

It was covered with numerous feather quilts, sheets, two pillows; bed-clothes dragged behind it and from it protruded night lamps and candles. Under it a Legionaire could be seen as the motive force.

The soldier had a double load: he was drunk.

" Well, how goes it? " I said in French.

" Wass? " he replied.

" Who are you? " I asked in German.

" Wilhelm Bloemler," replied the Legionnaire, " aus Bonn, Rheinland."

" What have you been doing? "

" Helping myself to what the Druses left behind," he replied.

Then without any questioning he volunteered this bit of Legion information:

" The French officers are all right. We like them. They know how to treat soldiers. But our *sous-officiers* — non-coms — they are swine and devil dogs. They are all German non-coms. *Gott verdamt!* They have spoiled the Legion. Didn't I have enough of them during the world war? Would I have enlisted if I had known the *feldwebel* was going to be a German? Pfui! "

And he staggered merrily away under his bedding.

My next encounter with the Legion was at Moussifrey. It was here that all French forces were gathered for the great attack on Atrashe's capital, Soueida.

Commandant Muller, who had built the great Roman camp at Ezraa, had invited me to assist at an armoured car reconnaissance, to feel out the Druses. Some ten thousand of them were in the field. They had surrounded three French infantry companies, some artillery and some small units in the citadel of Soueida and were starving them to death. In turn the French were moving in from Ezraa, Deraa, Moussifrey and other towns. The Land of Job was again flowing with blood and tears.

The sortie was made with the usual grey-blue armoured cars.

" How far are we going? " I asked Commandant Muller.

" I don't know," replied the officer. " This isn't European warfare and all our means of information are not sure. In France we knew every outpost of the trenches, the position of every gun, the disposition of all the men of the enemy. Here it is like your wars against the American Indians. Guerrilla warfare. We shall proceed with our reconnaissance until we draw fire. When you see rifle bullets knocking up the desert sands or hear them clicking on your armoured car, you will know that the enemy has been located."

So we went first to Bors-el-Harriri, through the bad-lands flanking the Arabian desert, through nothing but sand and volcanic black stones scattered like seeds by a drunken sower, sometimes strangely stacked up like ugly idols in the fields.

There was a jackal feasting on a dead camel killed in the recent battle. Hot gusts of desert winds ravaged the car, blinding white dust penetrated everywhere, cutting our eyes and stuffing our throats. Occasionally the terrible stink of a dead horse came in with the sand. Obscene fat white birds waddled out of the carcasses of camels, rose heavily and settled nearby to await the passing of our motors.

Suddenly I saw a great lake stretch itself across our path, inundating our auto road. But we never reduced speed. I tapper the driver's hand. "Mirage," he said. We sped towards the lake and the lake sped towards the hills.

"Yes, we have to fight mirages in this damned country," commented the driver, "mirages and tribesmen, heat and sand and lack of water. Only yesterday one of our airplanes directing artillery fire had to quit in the midst of a *régelage* because the observer saw nothing but water which wasn't there. Lakes, river, oases suddenly appear before columns of marching men and aviators. Imagine setting guns for direct fire against the enemy and finding them pointing into an ocean covering the enemy in the midst of an infantry attack. *C'est la guerre.*"

Soueida with its black stone houses, its red citadel and its white barracks was just ten minutes to the east when the Druses spotted us and began firing from behind stone piles. Their bullets puffed the sand before us and our cars halted. Two old Breguet planes which had started behind us now flew overhead, each carrying fourteen small bombs. Hardly had the Druses revealed themselves with futile rifle fire when the aviators were upon them, using their machine-guns and releasing a bomb or two, which fell in the silent plain scattering

the stones, raising fountains of sand and scaring the tribesmen into the open.

The planes then radioed directions to the artillery and as
our decoy reconnaissance returned to Bors-el-Harriri the guns
were peppering the fields with steel.

At Bors-el-Harriri the sheik invited Commandant Muller
and me to dine with the elders of the village in the communal
hall. It was a strange one-room building, the outer walls covered with mud and dirt, the inner ones bearing signs of
Roman origin. The arches were unmistakably Roman. Some
red was smeared on the walls. A few odd things were
fastened on them. Although the Mohammedan must not
make a graven image or look upon one, there were some old
chromos held up by nails, a large coloured picture of Lillian
Russell in tights, and what was undoubtedly the " premium "
of a popular brand of American cigarettes of 1890, a little picture of " The Yellow Kid."

In the center of the floor a huge hole. It puzzled me at first.

The sheik clapped his hands and reed mats into which a
green and red design had been woven, in Aztec-Mexican
fashion, were brought us, and pillows. Commandant Muller
stretched himself uneasily on his mat which bordered the hole
in the floor. If this is oriental comfort, I did not realize it. Ill
at ease, I did likewise on my side of the hole. The main sheik
and the main priest occupied the two other sides of the quad-
rangle, and the food was brought in.

First we were given a circumference of damp flabby bread,
thin as a dollar and big as a barrel. Then came the pilaff.
It was an enormous plate, heaped with greasy rice, so much of it
that it hid a whole lamb. The lamb, head included, had been
cut into suitable pieces of a pound or two, and each man

rolled up his sleeves, dug his fist into the mess, worked his fingers around until he struck something solid and pulled. Whatever he found he had to eat to a finish, or he would insult his hosts. Bones were spat into the centre. The hole in the floor was the Arab garbage system.

Servants stood around helping us and waving fans at the thousands of stubborn flies.

The enormous bread, which resembled a Roman shield, we used as plates, napkins, knife and spoon, and table-cloths.

A vile, bitter, sour, aromatic coffee was poured into a cup and passed from mouth to mouth. "Take it at least three times," the Commandant whispered to me, " or they will be offended." Grapes came on another woven mat and date water, slightly fermented, turning sour and sickish, was served. Well, starvation in the desert sands seemed preferable.

* * * * *

The night at Moussifrey saw the bloodiest battle of the year. In slaughter it surpassed almost anything of the world war.

Knowing that the French had gathered the Foreign Legion there for the attack on Soueida, the crafty Druses came out of their capital and all the surrounding towns and attacked. Twenty-five loyal villages had answered the Pasha's proclamation, each with its war flag blessed in an imposing religious ceremony, each with its sheik.

At four in the morning when it was still dark, the vanguard of three thousand Druses galloped towards Moussifrey. Without a halt they charged the barbed wire and yelled. The horses caught. With flesh torn open they fell into the wire, struggling. Riders tried to disentangle themselves. Horsemen pressed those in front. They fired into the air. The gunners of the Foreign

Legion poured devastating bullets into the mass of men and horses caught in the wire. Horses screamed, men shouted and a clatter of machine-gunnery arose from all of Moussifrey.

Unable to break through the wire the Druses withdrew, consulted, yelled and charged again. Again they rode into the barbed entanglements and upon the dead and dying horses and men lost in the first fury. Again they caught and again the machine-guns perforated their struggling mass.

The sun arose revealing the horror.

From four to ten that morning, in intervals of about an hour, the Druses made six attacks, until they filled almost all the entanglements with their dead. In the last attack those who had lost their horses, but not their fanatical courage, stripped themselves, placed their bullets in a rag held in their teeth, and charged over the dead, naked, clearing the three rows of wire, to fall dead and wounded at the very edge of the machine-gun nests of the Foreign Legion.

An elderly bearded sergeant who had fought alongside the American Marine Brigade when the Moroccan Division, placed between the American First and Second Divisions, formed a spearhead for the memorable attack of July 18, the attack launched from the Villiers Cotterets which marked the turn of the war in France, said of this battle of Moussifrey:

"No one ever saw such bloodshed as we did last night. Realize that the entire attack was at one point; the Druses hoped to fill in the wire with their own bodies, and charge over them! My machine-gun crew bore the brunt of it. Look, here lie two hundred and fifty-seven bodies of men. Certainly the enemy took another two hundred and fifty dead with them because by their religion they must do so. That makes five hundred killed by one machine-gun nest. Then there are probably one thousand wounded. So it can be said one crew defeated an attack of three thousand and inflicted one thousand five hundred casualties. There was nothing like that in France. Think of the spirit of this enemy. It is beyond human belief. Now we must make ready to attack them. Au revoir."

Pagans, Romans, Mohammedans, Christian Crusaders and Turks have fought for Soueida. Caesar's legions had called the spot where they found water, Dionysus. Napoleon's emissaries had visited it when he was trying to stir up their traditional hatred of the Turk the time he made the campaign against Acre, near by. Now the Foreign Legion was to lead the victorious attack.

"The Druses fought like a nation released from a lunatic asylum," General Andrea said, as, during dinner in Soueida, he described the final battle. "For example, twenty charged one of my tanks, trying to stop the wheels with their bare hands. Five were crushed under the caterpillar tractor; ten were shot down by the machine-guns, but the remaining five still fought. Once another twenty charged a machine-gun. The crew killed or wounded nineteen but the twentieth never paused until he had entered the nest and cut the machine-gunner's hand with the only weapon he had, a knife.

"It is a nation committing suicide.

"Three hundred of these fanatics sacrificed their lives trying to kill me. They hid in a ravine, letting our advancing army of 12,000 men cross over. Then they appeared right in our centre. It was clever but futile. We had to turn our cannon, which had advanced, backward, and fire point blank until we had annihilated the three hundred."

The general described the tank attack on the city. It was remarkable. The little Renaults, one protecting the other, had crawled up the slope until one actually knocked at the gate of the citadel where the heroic garrison, commanded by a French major named Tommy Martin, had held out for two months on food and shells and radio lamps dropped by airplanes. Other tanks had attacked the rows upon rows of stone houses which, joined by common walls, had made one vast fortress of the city. Some walls they crushed; arches built by Romans which had resisted centuries and wars, crumbled under wheels made in Ohio factories.

If only the Druses had remained in their fortress city!

Six thousand of them, fighting in that stone wall labyrinth could have held up the French indefinitely and could have saved themselves. But they chose to leave their defences and race wildly and in circles, almost barehanded, against guns and shrapnel and all the inventions of wholesale slaughter save gas.

And they had almost won. Despite machine-gun fire, mine throwers, grenades, artillery shells, and bombs dropped from airplanes, 3,000 Druses, by an impetuosity born of religious fatalism, had succeeded in joining the battle. It was actually hand-to-hand fighting in the open, until the column under Colonel Duclos arrived, a bayonet charge was ordered, and confusion was turned into decisive victory.

The guns were being mounted near the citadel when I was taken to see it and the graveyard from which the corpses of French dead had been disinterred by the Druses, the rotten flesh given to dogs, and the bones placed along the roads as a warning to the foreigner. As the newly placed guns were trained on more villages, and intimidation by 3-inch shells began, white flags appeared over tall buildings and the elders came to Soueida to make deep submission to General Andrea.

I met one pasha, one emir and a dozen sheiks, each the father of a town.

" These are my guests," said the general. " They come here to discuss peace. I am inviting them to remain until other villages learn wisdom."

This was his way of saying the princes and sheiks were hostages, whose lives were in pawn for the lives of French aviators who were being fired on continually by " civilians " in " neutral " villages.

" Have you got an American in your Foreign Legion? "

" Yes," replied General Andrea, " and I hear from his commander he is a real soldier."

This one American was worth journalistically many times the victory of Soueida to me. So away I stumbled over the volcanic stones to find him and the Legion.

I presented myself first to Major Kratzert, who recalled with enthusiasm the bravery of the American First and Second Divisions in the battle of July 18, 1918.

" Is your Legion today as good as it was then? " I asked.

" The Legion is always as good," he replied proudly. " You may fill it up with the men from any country, old or young, strong and weak, and in the end it finds the spirit and the tradition and the glory of the Legion. The Legion is always victorious — in France, in Morocco, here."

I asked for " The American."

" Find the American — don't mistake him for the Englishman," the major commanded an orderly, and in a few minutes we emerged from the tent to talk to him. He saluted his commandant smartly, looked at my civilian clothes and got a nod of permission.

" God, I'm glad to see someone from home," he exclaimed,

The White Man's Burden, or How the Orient is Ruled. Arabs, accused of various crimes, hanged in the Merje square, Damascus, by the French military. The signs detail the crimes and warn the populace.

" Gilbert Clare " (Bennett S. Doty) photographed by the author, on the eve of his taking " French Leave " from the Foreign Legion at Soneida.

This caused the Syrian Revolution. French military exhibiting bodies of twenty-four men they killed. The Syrian nationalists claimed the dead were martyrs, not bandits and the uprising followed.

" when did you come over ? I've been in nine months — haven't spoken to anyone from home — "

" Where are you from ? "

" Memphis, Tennessee," he replied in an unmistakable accent.

" And your name ? "

" Gilbert Clare is my name. Yes, that's my real name. Most everybody here gives you a false name. Some of these fellows may be wanted for murder, some of them had a fight with their girls — oh, any reasons — they don't give their real names, but mine is my own — Gilbert Clare," he repeated as I noted it on an envelope.

His insistence on his " real " name puzzled me at once. It was only after I had started the work to save his life that I learned from the State Department that he too was giving a false name, the real one being Bennett J. Doty.

He wore the regulation khaki of the Army of the Orient and a pith helmet. He was bronzed and handsome: a blond moustache and a cheerful smile.

" Say," he continued apropos of nothing, " we just stole a sheep. What the hell do we Legionnaires care about orders. We stole, killed, roasted, ate that sheep before our officers could start an investigation. We steal, we fight like hell, we die, but we are always victorious. That's the Foreign Legion for you."

" How'd you come to join it ? "

" I was in the Thirtieth Division. We didn't get to France till late. I never saw much of war. Well, I was moping around in New Orleans, and one day, about a year ago, I decided to go to France and see some fighting. I'm glad I came. I came for adventure. Lots of fellows come for that. Harvey, that's the Englishman, says that's what he came for. Maybe. Some come because they have no jobs, some because they love France. The place is full of Germans and Russians who came because they had nowhere else to go. Nobody asks questions in this man's outfit."

" Did you get into the Moussifrey battle? "

" Yep. That was real fighting. So was Soueida. Not like France. No damned trenches here. You get behind a stone and blaze away at the enemy. Or you charge with the bayonet. Christ — ! "

He shook his head as if to drive a horrible scene from his eyes. Companions were forming in a little semi-circle behind him, envying his talk with a man from home. There were bearded men, unmistakable Russians, blue-eyed fair Germans, blond and nordic, dark Balkanites and not a few Frenchmen, who, to atone for a crime or a desertion, had joined as Belgians or Swiss.

" We pity the poor devils," continued Clare-Doty, indicating the Druses in the villages and the fortified extinct volcano craters beyond. " They are fools. They fight machine-guns, tanks, airplanes as they fought the Turks. Say, you know they believe in the transmigration of souls. They'll never die but reappear in flesh and blood after a fifteen year rest in a Chinese heaven filled with beautiful chorus girls or such.

" They fight to die. They want to die on the battle field so they can get to heaven quickly and honorably and enjoy themselves there for spell. I'd hate to be a tanker crushing them. We Legion infantry fight them fair.

" I thought they'd got me at Moussifrey. You ought to see them dancing as they dashed into the barbed wire which was full of their horses and men wriggling and kicking. Hundreds of dead. It only made them more furious. They are savages. They are good and crazy.

" When we were fighting around Damascus it was different. Those Arabs we fought didn't have one hundredth the courage. The Arabs did ambushes, dirty tricks, they never came into the open. Well, we were glad when our battalion got marching orders.

" This was a great show. We were getting all ready to storm the place — every house a blockhouse — when they burst out of it and met us in the open. The guy next to me got shot in the neck. Killed. We fought for six hours. I didn't get a scratch. We went at it with bayonets three times. Our losses were light. Funny thing, we didn't find any dead Druses. I shot one, I saw him fall, then we charged and I looked for him, but couldn't find him. Ask the men — " pointing to the eager group always expanding behind us — " not one of them could find a dead Druse. They take them away and keep their bodies in the open so their souls can take their time in making ready for the trip to China and heaven and chorus girls.

" The Legion takes no prisoners. Neither does the enemy. We enlist to fight; why ask, why grumble. Sometimes the food is bad. The water is bad. The heat is hell — and the fleas worse than hell. They could eat you alive unless you are tough — and we are tough.

" The Germans are the best soldiers of the Legion. Their sergeant-majors are sons of she-dogs to their own people. The Russians are the friendliest. Mostly Wrangel men, officers and wrecked noblemen among them. They are real pals. The Germans are so damned stingy. Imagine companions facing death every minute who won't lend you a needle.

" There's one Englishman, John Harvey. Glad I have someone to talk to. I guess Harvey is a fake name. But I don't ask him why or what. I guess I'm the only one who gives his right name. Our lieutenant, Vernon, speaks a little English, and now I parley-voo some too. I treat my officers decent. They can't make me out. They shake their heads and say ' crazy American ' and laugh. I'm an American and they've got to swallow me whole."

Bugles interrupted.

" Say I'll be glad to get back to the South," he said, shaking hands. " I'm homesick I guess. Send me some newspapers, magazines, something to read in English. You may think I'm tough, when you look at me here, you wouldn't believe I was a gentle student in the University of Virginia not so long ago. When you write that piece, tell them in Memphis I came for adventure and I'm getting my bellyful."

He departed with a smile after saying he had something very important to tell me at reveille, at 4:30, but whether he wanted to hear about the new skyscrapers in New York or the latest Broadway wisecracks, or to tell me of his plan to flee the Legion I never found out because early next morning I begged General Andrea to let me take the first plane out as I had no desire to add myself to the casualties at Soueida.

Three or four days later, in my hotel at Beirut a French settler in Tunis, a friend of General Andrea and a semi-journalist who had visited the Legion with me, came back full of fever and dysentery. While I was giving him some of my large stock of malaria and dysentery medicine, he remarked weakly and casually:

" Too bad your friend in the Legion will be executed to-morrow."

My first thought was, it is Sunday and there is no one at the consulate.

" Desertion," M. Brochier replied to my question. " Yes, desertion and mutiny. He led the others. And you — I, personally, believe you guiltless — but General Andrea holds you responsible for mutiny in the Foreign Legion."

It was Sunday and he was ill in bed, but when I sent in word that the life of an American was in danger Consul-General Paul Knabenshue came into action. He telegraphed to Damascus where Clare-Doty was imprisoned in the citadel, informed the state department, and went immediately to call on the High Commissioner of France, Henri de Jouvenal. I went to see the commanding officer at Beirut and prepared a statement to General Andrea, which follows:

" It was with great regret that I learned of the incident of the American Legionnaire, Clare, but I was greatly mortified to hear from M. Brochier that you held me responsible for the action.

" The facts of my interview with the American are just as I recounted them at dinner with your staff that night. I found Clare a real enthusiast for the Legion. He said he never regretted joining, loved the life, liked his companions, was proud to be the only American in the Legion in Syria and glad to be fighting for France. Not a single word he said indicated any dissatisfaction to me. He asked for some newspapers and I promised to send him some. Moreover, M. Brochier tells me he deserted the next morning, whereas it is a fact that I had intended staying another day in Soueida (were it not for the fleas) and that I had intended asking you permission to talk to Clare the next day, as he had asked to see me again.

" I have now discussed the matter with the officers at the serail here, and they are of the opinion that it may have been homesickness (" cafard ") due to his for the first time talking to an American, which caused the American to take the terrible decision to desert. While this may be true I must recount that in our talk Clare evidenced no great homesickness but his complete contentment in the Legion.

" Our interview was held in a group which included Major Kratzert and M. Brochier. They stood a little apart, but it was possible for M.

Brochier, who speaks English perfectly, to listen to everything we said. I want to assure you on my word of honour that not a single word was used on either side which could in any way be termed subversive. On the contrary, it was a patriotic discussion on both sides and I was deeply impressed by the loyalty and good spirits of the American soldier. A clipping of the interview I have already mailed to Captain Georges Picot.

"You have been exceedingly kind and generous to me, and I have already written you to say how much I appreciate it. Of my attitude to you and to France there can be no doubt. I want to add that I came to Damascus despite two threats received in Beirut from the rebels that they would disembowel me if I ever entered Damascus. M. Lapierre knows of this and even offered me a body-guard, which I refused. I have within the past three days received another threat from Damascus, this time I am threatened with either hanging or kidnapping until the war is over.

"I hope I have made my position clear and I earnestly beg of you to alter any unfavourable impression you have of me."

Through the secretary of the American Consulate at Damascus, Donal McGonigal, I obtained the only statement the American Legionnaire made before his second court-martial.

"'A few hours after you left our camp near Soueida citadel,' Clare said, 'I was speaking to Harvey, the only Britisher in the Legion. Harvey was sore that he hadn't a chance to speak English to some one. We got gassing about home and suddenly decided to get away. Some Germans and others asked us where we were headed. We said to Palestine, and they said they would go, too. So we headed.

"'It is not true that we all carried rifles. We took one for self-protection. Well, we needed it. After taking French leave we went south through the Druse mountains. At day-break we spied a bunch of men headed our way. They began shooting. They were Bedouins or Arabs and probably wanted to rob us. We fought for our lives. I had the gun at the time and killed two Bedouins and the rest quit.

"'We headed at another angle. Again the Bedouins attacked. This time it was a big group. We headed around the oncoming first band.

That night we tried to break through the encircling groups of Bedouins, all of whom were armed but couldn't shoot straight.

" 'The next morning the Bedouins were attacked by French and Syrian militia, which defeated them and captured us. When they came up we saw the uselessness of trying to beat them and the Bedouins, who were still cutting off our flight to the Palestine frontier, and we thought we might as well face death by court-martial as be cut to pieces by the Arabs.

" 'I am not afraid of death. I am told they do not kill deserters now as it is not wartime. I suppose I will get Devil's Island. Well, I have had my fling. I told you at Soueida I was getting a bellyful of adventure. Now I am fed up. Send me a tooth-brush and bed-bug powder. I am lousy. And tell the folks back home not to worry. I will get through somehow.' "

I had a consultation with Knabenshue twice a day. The officers at Beirut had said to me, " It was a case of mental suggestion, after talking with an American the Legionnaire got homesick. It is not unusual in the Legion where the enlistment is seven years and life is hard. But anyone who appreciates military necessity realizes that the court-martial decision of death for desertion and mutiny was justifiable. An army without discipline cannot exist."

I told this to Knabenshue, who had already engaged a lawyer for the rehearing in Damascus.

" Will you care if the lawyer harps on your visit to Clare — makes it responsible for his homesickness and his desertion? " Knabenshue asked me. The case was considered so grave only an order from the president of France could save Clare. The French had informed the consulate that Clare and his followers had fired on the French who rescued them from the Bedouins.

I went to Cairo to escape the French censorship and filed

the complete story of the desertion with the request that it be played up in the newspapers at home and in Paris so that a public opinion in favour of saving the man's life would be created and pressure brought on the president of France. All this was done. Clare, who had become Doty, was sentenced to eight years at hard labor, and after thirteen months imprisonment was reprieved and permitted to return to America. I never received a reply from General Andrea.

Chapter III

THEN UP SPOKE THE KING OF IRAQ

THIS is the story of a story I myself censored.

The French troops had marched out of Beirut and defeated the King of Syria, better known as the Emir Feisul, in battle outside Damascus. The British had been deep in political intrigue since the days of Allenby and Lawrence; now the French had given the Arabs a taste of superior grapeshot and a new régime came into power.

Feisul, crushed by French guns and left stranded temporarily by Lloyd George's diplomacy, moved out of the East to Italy where in 1920 all the oriental monarchs and would-be monarchs were intriguing with the secret aid of the politicians in Rome whose eyes were greedy for the Levant.

By that time the whole world knew of many secret treaties for the spoils of which Russia and France and Britain were fighting. There was a rumour that such pacts had existed for the Near East also, and that the Emir Feisul, in his chagrin, might do for Araby what the Bolsheviks did for civilized Europe; tell the truth for once.

Feisul had come to Lake Como not only officially incognito, but secretly. I was on a train which might and might not get to Milan, because revolution was reported from industrial Italy; the red flag was flying over the Fiat works; the "Red Flag" was being sung in the streets, and where "Evviva Wilson" had once appeared in black paint on house fronts now appeared the words "Evviva Lenin." (This was the Bolshevik uprising, please note, which ruined itself by early 1921 and which was dead and gone when Mussolini so bravely saved Italy from it at the end of 1922.)

On that train I got a tip from a British journalist who knew Feisul's whereabouts. The revolution proved bloodless and ineffective. An earthquake in Fivizzano was a diversion for three days, and returning via Pisa, Genoa, and Turin to Milan, and finding no bloodshed for the American newspaper readers' appetite, I took a day off and came to the marvellous Villa d'Este on Lake Como where the deposed Royal Majesty received me with an Arabic salute and guttural mumbles in French.

Tall, handsome, a dark Adonis of the withering Arab sun, faultlessly dressed in a blue serge pinched-back suit, Feisul sat in state surrounded by other dark men, several in more or less native dress, abbayahs and kaffeyas and agals in black and gold and colours in stripes. The aged Patriarch of Damascus, the head of the Eastern Greek Catholic Church, a man holding in many lands a position similar to the Pope in Rome, had the seat of honour at the emir's right.

" By the secret treaty of 1914," Feisul began, " Great Britain agreed to French Sovereignty throughout Arabia. Then came the British conquest, and a new secret treaty was drawn up by which France and Great Britain recognized the complete independence of Arabia, and agreed that my family were to be the future rulers.

" I now accuse Great Britain of failure to maintain this secret treaty so far as concerns my retention of the throne of Syria. I accuse France of instituting a reign of terror in Arabia and condemning 434 leaders of the Syrian people to death. I accuse the rest of the Allies, chiefly the United States, of failure to live up to their promises regarding the sovereignty of Arabia. President Wilson promised us complete independence, and today more than half the Arab lands are under Allied rule."

The deposed king continued his accusations gutturally. The Oriental chieftains nodded approval. Occasionally the emir looked hard at the Patriarch, who gave a hasty though tardy nod.

"The Allies today are treating the Arabs in a worse way than our proverbial enemies, the Turks," continued Feisul. "I am sure the French people do not know of the atrocities which French imperialism commits, nor do the American people know that the promises of President Wilson and the American Mission are forgotten."

I asked him his policy for the future.

"I shall insist on a throne," he replied. "I am the logical ruler — also the one ruler the people want. My program is peace and prosperity. I would restore liberty in Arabia, break the yoke of oppressors, let all the people live in peace and harmony, Christian and Moslem alike. See," he added in a more intense voice, "I, a Moslem, have with me the head of the Christian Church who has come voluntarily to testify that I am the right man to be king, that the people of all creeds want me, that the Christians especially trust me to keep them safe and happy in the future — isn't that so?"

He looked sharply at the Patriarch. The Patriarch came out of a reverie and approved in a manner which for one of his age was violent.

"Yes, yes, yes," the Patriarch spoke up. "I come to support His Highness. The Christians of the East, who have suffered much and suffer now, approve the candidacy of the emir for the throne of Syria."

When lunch was served in a private princely hall, Feisul came in wearing the uniform of a British officer of Allenby's staff, embellished with crescents in green and gold. As each course was served different wine appeared in small and large glasses which the oriental monarch raised to his lips but did not taste. The table became littered with wine glasses, all full but mine. Red and pink, yellow to red-gold, they stood in front of princes and sheiks like so many raised pools. Finally came the dessert, and just before he gave the signal to retire for coffee, the emir ordered a number of bottles of champagne brought in. These were opened and poured. Feisul raised his to his lips, set it down, and as abruptly rose again. We all rose and followed him out. Even my glass remained sparkling with the others.

After coffee I found I had an hour before train time. So I walked through the gardens of the Villa d'Este. Once or twice I saw the Patriarch, who had separated from his Mohammedan fellow travellers, skirting the trees furtively.

As I left the grounds there was a sound of heavy running and of a cassock flapping. Also a feeble shout. Behind me, waving a weak arm, and safe-guarding his enormous, black, churchly, stove-pipe hat with the other, panted the Patriarch.

" You know who I am? " he wheezed.

" Yes," I said, " the Patriarch of Damascus."

" Believe in me," he said, breathing fast, " believe in me. Look. Here is my ikon." From somewhere in the cassock he produced a small bronze bas-relief of the Trinity.

" I need no proof," I said.

" Good," he replied, and his old, red, watery eyes lit up. " This man," he whispered, " this Emir Feisul — he says I come to say all the Christians want him king. Do you know why I came?

Because if I did not come it might have meant death and suf-fering to my people. He — the emir — is a terrible man. But I had to come. Look at him, in his nice European clothes — civilized — eh? But see him in his oriental costume at home. Oh, dear God, what a difference. What a difference. Here he speaks as a benefactor of Moslems and Christians. Over there he is a terror of both his own and my people. When he wears those European clothes he is civilized — when he puts on his turban and draws his sword he is a barbarian, a slaughterer, an enemy of Christianity; Oh, I am afraid, I am afraid of him. Christians tremble before him. We fear him. What shall we do? I do not know. But you, young man, do not believe what I said in his presence. If he makes a deal with Lloyd George he will have to protect Christian lives, and that is why I am here to help him. If he makes no deal he may massacre us all. That is the truth. I cannot let you go away without telling you the truth."

With tears in his eyes he wrung my hands and walked slowly back to join the oriental monarch while, somewhat dazed by this sudden almost incoherent confession, I kicked the dust down to the railroad station.

I filed a dispatch giving Feisul's plea. I did not mention his claim of Christian support. As for the Patriarch, to protect his life I censored all he said. He died in Damascus when I was there about the time of the bombardment, and I saw many Mohammedans at the funeral, all of whom seemed to share the grief of the Christian population.

*   *   *   *   *

When I came to Bagdad I found that Lloyd George had compromised on his secret treaty. The family of Feisul was having difficulties in Transjordania and Nejd and in exile, but not in Mesopotamia. Here a throne had been created for the ex-king of Syria, and he was reigning over the people known as Iraqi. He sat on the throne and his ministers of state wore regal uniforms, but the R. A. F. did the bombing of the villages when revenue was not paid and Messrs. Smith and Jones and Brown from London were running the various departments of government.

There's oil in them deserts, stranger.

I went to the palace to interview the king of Iraq. Many years had passed and there was now nothing for him to talk about, no secret treaties, no throne to fill, no protection of religious minorities. Everything was running so well, thanks to British diplomacy and "imperialism."

I tried my best to make a story. I asked about the bombing of Sheik Machmud, about the oil dispute, about the army, about relations with neighbouring states.

"It is everyone's duty," said the King of Iraq, "to help his neighbour and his fellow people. If we all co-operate, in one common endeavour, we shall succeed. What the world needs is a policy of service —"

Emir Babbitt!

Chapter IV

" BRITISH IMPERIALISM," AND A NOTE ON MASSACRE

A RUMOUR of massacre reached America. The editor thereupon took his nice new atlas down and measured the
miles: somewhat over 600. Good. We have a man at Damascus;
he should reach Zakho in twenty-four hours, with due allow-
ances for the slowness of foreign trains, and in thirty-six hours
we should have a swell scoop.

It took just about two weeks to investigate that Turkish massacre of British subjects — Christians needless to say — and that
fortnight also gave me a small but compact picture of that
terrible nightmare of the chancelleries and bugaboo of Europe
and America: British Imperialism. Incidentally it showed me
that the glamourous orient is All Bunk.

When you get your delayed and censored telegram from
the lazy Syrian post office you find there are two routes to
Bagdad: the Nairn route and the Opposition. The opposition
bankrupts frequently and is replaced by a new lot of optimists
who dream fortunes out of the $125 fare per person for the 600-
mile desert ride. But the Nairn boys who first traversed the
northern Arabian desert, navigating automobiles like ships at
sea with the aid of stars and compass, have made the trip an
adventurous success.

Where the desert is hard and flat you run along at forty miles
or more per hour. The car behind with a burst of speed draws
up alongside, then the next car and the next, until the whole
convoy of ten or twenty is drawn up over a stretch a mile wide,

and a race begins. You do fifty, sixty, and more, flying into the horizon over a land which is a barren virgin, while behind you earth and sky are mingled in one vast cloud of universal dust. It is a thrill which comes rarely in a lifetime.

Sometimes you meet a gazelle. What is it doing out in the waste? How does it live? You catch up and run alongside the frightened animal. If your driver is good — and all desert drivers have to be good — you can climb out on the running board and stroke the gazelle. Sometimes you see a jackal.

Twice on the route you descend craters of old volcanoes, circle around, and ascend the other side, a fine sight at night with all the cars bumping up and down, shooting their head-lights into the air like so many search-lights on a Zeppelin raid night in Paris or London.

The trip lasts from eighteen hours to seven days depending upon the weather and the revolts in the desert. Eventually the Euphrates comes into view, a stale river, narrow and serpentine, going backwards almost as often as forward, like a drunken man unsure of any goal. Then in the distant haze the golden domes of Kademein on the left, and the Tigris, wide and dirty, and at last Bagdad.

✳ ✳ ✳ ✳ ✳

Bagdad! Bagdad the City of the Caliphs, the successors to Mohammed, the City of Haroun al-Raschid, the Thousand and One Nights, the city of poets, the vision of wondrous beauty, the glory of all the Orient!

Bagdad. A large Mohammedan village, built of mud and camels' dung, infested with flies and malarial mosquitoes, filled with oriental peoples in rags and patches, numerous cripples, children with the purple eyelids of trachoma on which their ignorant superstitious mothers have placed ordures and blue beads to exorcise the evil one; men with their faces eaten by syphilis; beggars — and beggars who try to touch you in humble piety and arouse fear and disgust instead of pity; sewage in the streets, the streets filled with nauseating stinks; shops where vile offal is displayed for sale, rotting and stinking and covered with thousands of flies and worms; streets crowded with men, women and children, dogs and camels, all equally filthy and many diseased; the town reeking with all that is low and horrible in humankind, while above it a devastating sun gives it life and death, selects for survival and destroys much of this flowing, palpitating mass which seems so shortly removed from the primeval ooze.

Bagdad in the valley of the Tigris-Euphrates, the scene of the Garden of Eden, the home of primitive man, the birth-place of civilization! The Orient is bunk. Beautiful Bagdad never was. The myth is kept alive by the " fortunate " who have spent much money to get to far away places. Of all travellers at least one, Aldous Huxley, has had the courage to tell the truth.

" Travelling gives one something to talk about when one gets home," writes Huxley, " the subjects for conversation are not so numerous that one can neglect an opportunity for adding to one's store. To justify this snobbery a series of myths has gradually been elaborated. The places which it is socially smart to have visited are aureoled with glamour, till they are made to appear, for those who have not been there, like so many fabled Babylons or Bagdads."

If the British had not occupied Bagdad during the war and kept it until this day I would have been at a loss for refuge in this repulsive capital. But British " imperialism " has been at work more than ten years. It cut right through the hovels, parallel with the Tigris, and built New Street. Two hotels with electric light and bath-rooms have been established, there is an officers' club, a newspaper, taxi-cabs, hospitals, schools, sanitary work on a vast scale, policemen, civilization, and — the British.

Cool men. Clean men. White men. The officers walk down New Street and the oriental mob parts and lets them pass. They do not have to rub elbows with trachoma and syphilis. They clap their hands and brown servants, clad in white and bathed because they have white masters, leap humbly to the bidding. They go to the post office where the brown Indian babu, the imported little officials who have brains and are efficient, scatter the mob of filthy Iraqi who are clamouring before the postage window, and ask for the white man's wants. They do it for me too, because I am a white man. When I go to the palace to call on the British general a guard of six men answers a bugle and stands at attention, and as I have left my book of etiquette behind me I am flustered by this homage. An officer comes along and puts them at ease. Everywhere I go I share with the military and British civilians the prerogatives of a superior race.

In the courts the British have brought justice in place of the tribal bloody sword. The government of King Feisul is largely a stage curtain behind which Britain works, but altogether it is not as alien or inimical a government as that of the previous régime, which was Turkish.

The British are in Mesopotamia by consent of the League of Nations. Of moral reasons there were none. But if all British imperialism is as terrible as this sample I have experienced, I am a convert to it, and so, I believe, would be any neutral who ever set a foot, hesitatingly, in this vile part of the world. And I

have seen the horrors of commercial exploitation also. When
the British came there was no industry. A little robbery, a little
murder, and dates constituted the fare of many individuals
and tribes. When the imperialist British government frowned
upon robbery and murder — when they put up gallows and
filled them frequently — many natives lost their occupation.
Then along came the exploiters of oil and cotton fields with
their offer of a rupee a day for labor, and so this Utopia was
commercialized.

But violence is by no means at an end. Internally and exter-
nally there is danger because there is an intense dissatisfaction
especially among the sheiks of powerful families and towns
who do not like to see a fine country where pillage and rapine
made living so pleasant, go the way of occidental law and order
and gold based on labour. The old order prefers the Biblical
times — of Chronicles and Kings.

*   *   *   *   *

My Iraq assignment was to learn the truth of these tribal
conflicts. Assyrians, Nestorians and Chaldeans, all Christian
tribes descended right out of the Bible, had been reported massacred by Turks.

I made a full investigation and told the first real story of
the atrocity. I really hated to do it, but I had a duty, and it was
to tell the truth. If Kemal Pasha has put me on the passport
black list, as fellow newspapermen have informed me, I can
only answer that I respect the Turk and believe that he has
never gotten a square deal; that I know that German generals
not Turkish diplomats were really responsible for the Armenian
massacres in war time; that Armenians massacred Turks when
they had the upper hand; and that the Greek massacres of Turks

in the Smyrna war were greater in number and cruelty than the Turkish revenge. But it so happened that I was the only man to get the evidence of a Turkish massacre of Christians and I told the facts without prejudice.

To get the facts was a difficult undertaking. From the Bagdad railroad station the "Berlin" railroad runs slowly into Sherqat and stops forever. I was lucky in sharing a sleeper with a Major Long, a medical officer who was returning to Mosul cured of rabies, and he fed me quinine after diagnosing my fever as malaria. At Sherqat, I paid $25 for a seat in a car for which Henry Ford should send $10 at once and put it into his museum. In Mosul I spent the night in the "International Hotel," which I recommend highly to naturalists who have never seen bedroom scorpions and eight-inch cockroaches, let alone the conventional mattress fauna of Europe and America. Early the next day another Ford took me to Zakho.

Outside of Mosul, at the suggestion of my Assyrian chauffeur, I stopped at Nineveh to visit the mosque. The Mohammedans, as is known, incorporated the Hebrew and Christian religions when their saviour announced that he was establishing a superior one which would include more sword-play and polygamy among its attractions. Jonah and Jesus are ranked as minor prophets to Mohammed, and the whale story goes as big in Mesopotamia as in Tennessee. Nineveh claims to be Jonah's old home town, and in the mosque they have a piece of evidence which the Fundamentalists overlooked at Dayton: they have the jaw-bone of the original Jonah whale. No less a person than Jonah himself brought the jaw-bone there. The souvenir is guarded closely.

We passed Gayara where the Germans put in three pumps which supply five barrels of oil daily. This is the only oil flowing

Turkish massacre of Christians. Archbishop Timothy listening to testimony from two Sheiks who escaped Turkish exile.

Bombardment of Damascus. Photograph taken by the author while shells were falling.

in all Mesopotamia. Of course there must be more, because the little streams feeding the Tigris are smudged and iridescent with oil seepage. The car wound through two mountain passes and was hailed by a thousand persons whose Biblical primitiveness had been disturbed by an advance telephone call.

*   *   *   *   *

They took me first to Archbishop Timothy, venerable and bearded, a priest of the Roman Catholic Church who looks every inch a Hebrew patriarch except for the flat round head-dress about six inches in height which seems to be more in the style of the Greek Orthodox Church. The Mohammedan Arab mayor, six priests, and various local dignitaries then conducted me into the courtyard of the local church which was packed thick with the refugees of the massacre. There were very few women and almost no young girls among them. Many of the men had bandages and reeked with iodoform.

Under the cool arches they had set some tables and asked me to take the centre seat. Before me they placed a large Bible. Then Archbishop Timothy arose and spoke while some two thousand victims listened in misery.

" I now call the mukhtar, the chief of Murga to testify," said the archbishop.

The mukhtar of Murga came forward, a man dressed in tiny rags. If he had been dressed in clothes made from a New England crazy quilt, and this uniform had been clawed to bits, it would have equalled the torn collection he wore. Yet there was a majesty about this Christian sheik.

He came to me, knelt, and kissed my hand as he would his priest's. He placed one hand on the Bible and raised the other to the sun-filled heavens.

307

"As God is my witness, and by the Blood of Christ I swear," he began in sing-song Arabic, which a priest interpreted into French, "I will tell you what happened on those sorrow-laden days. On the march north the first day the Turks killed five men of Murga, patriarchs of my village, who in their feebleness could not keep up with the younger. One by one they shot the elders and left them lying by the roadside.

"Three of our women who were ill and who sat down to rest from time to time they killed by stoning.

"On the first night we camped near a fountain, drank and were refreshed. The heavens were clouded and it was dark. In the Turkish camp lights were burning and the soldiery were merry. Their voices were loud with laughter. Before midnight Turkish soldiers came among us seizing all the young and pretty girls whom they carried off into the officers' camp. They violated our girls. All night we heard the screams. They clouded the skies with their mournful cries and it was like the Last Day of Judgment.

"On the second day two of our elders were shot when they lay down to rest.

"On the third day one of our women was prematurely in child-birth. The Turks stood around unmoved by cries and tears, until the child was born, and, seeing that it was alive, they gave it to other women, but the mother remaining on the ground, and too feeble to arise and march with us, they shot her.

"That night at the Ozozan mountains two women who tried to escape from the officers who were taking them to their quarters and two men who tried to run away were shot to death. Their young orphaned children were then killed.

"On the fourth day I escaped—"

Archbishop Timothy signalled him to go, and called the mukhtar of a neighbouring village. One after another five picturesque figures appeared, knelt, kissed the Bible, and gave their testimony. It was always the same. " The old men could not keep up with the march. A soldier came and bayonetted them." In one instance it was testified that three children were thrown over a precipice because they could no longer walk and there was no place for them on donkeys or carts or the shoulders of men.

When the mukhtars had finished I asked if there were relatives of those who had been massacred present, and many rose to give corroboration. I asked that children be heard and cross-examined them as to what they saw. Always the same: the old men lagged behind and were shot.

*   *   *   *   *

" Military necessity," said the British representative in Mosul the next day, " the Turks will plead military necessity. We know that the Angora government issued the order to clear the disputed Mosul frontier zone of all civilians, especially of those who might fight on our side. This has been done by the deportation of 8,000 Chaldeans, Assyrians and Nestorians. I am convinced that Kemal Pasha knows nothing of the massacre and will show his good sportsmanship by disowning it and court-martialling the major and other officers responsible. We, the British, have always called the Turk a fair fighter, but there is no telling what people will do when they can blame ' military necessity ' for their actions."

" You are absolutely convinced that the massacre took place? "

" The bodies are on the road. You can see them from airplanes. And besides, five thousand persons may exaggerate but five thousand cannot all lie. Don't forget that the people you saw have been released by their captors. Where are the missing two hundred?"

At Mosul there was no special preparation for the war with Turkey which then threatened. I returned to Bagdad, cabled the result of my investigation, found out that the British maintain a censorship in Iraq, all suspicious telegrams being sent to the high commissioner for inspection, and then I went to Hinaidi, the largest military air base in the world.

Here the British, with 350 planes and as many pilots, believe they can hold up the entire Turkish infantry and artillery. The men think so too, and were ready to try it. I found no one who hated the Turks. They did not especially care for a war just then. But they were keen on getting some action.

They showed me pictures of some of their recent work. Sheik Machmud was their only real enemy — he had killed British officers and they needed revenge. Several times they had flown over his town and set his palace on fire. On one raid they had succeeded in dropping four high explosive shells through the four corners of his solidly roofed citadel, then planting some liquid fire through the shell holes so that the building was burned out. Not a single mud hut nearby was destroyed.

On another occasion a tribe had revolted. Before one of the two regiments stationed in Iraq could be marched up it was likely the revolt would spread throughout the country-side. So the commander of Hinaidi sent ten Vincent planes with ten men and two machine-guns in each, landed all outside the rebellious town, and quelled the mutiny in a few hours.

Flight Commander Corballis of 55 Squadron took me up in his de Haviland 9 for a trip over the desert. I was impressed with the casualness of the thing. My previous flight had been in a French warplane in Syria, and previous to that I had had several flights with American aviators behind or over the front; on all occasions the tinkering and tuning had lasted for hours.

" Like a hop over town? " said Corballis.

" Yes," I replied.

" Climb in — any bus will do."

I climbed in. A motored steel arm seized the propeller in the middle and whirled it around. In less than sixty seconds after the invitation I was having a look at Bagdad from the air. From there, at least, it is not so bad.

From the north a sand-storm, like a great dragon rolling over and over, was coming towards the city. We flew over it and along the Tigris which cut numerous dark pretzel patterns in the golden-white waste. The golden domes of Kademein likewise were somewhat picturesque from above, where the surrounding filth could not be seen or smelt.

*   *   *   *   *

I went back to the hotel and heard Britons discussing the future of Iraq.

" Irrigation," said one, " will make this the Garden of Eden again. Only we will raise cotton instead of apples and snakes."

" What we need now," said another, " is a pipe line to Haifa, direct, all British territory, where the Syrian rebels can't break it, and then get at the oil — "

" This country," said a third, " has more mineral wealth and more agricultural possibilities than any on earth. Look what we British made out of Egypt. We'll beat that here some day — and probably get the same sort of thanks."

I went to see Gertrude Bell who told me fascinating stories

about the history of Mesopotamia. I went to see Reouf Bey Chadirchi, minister of finance, whom I had known in Berlin years before and who said that if Britain pulled out Iraq would sink a hundred years into her torpid past. I went to see the king and his younger brother who goes to Oxford sometimes and I tried my best to get a straight occidental yes or no about the British mandate, but got only a turgid oriental however and perhaps. But, after all, who wear the regal robes in Iraq? Imported kings. I did not ask the " man in the street." Keep away from him if you value your life and your health. If the " man in the street " in Mesopotamia objects to British " imperialism " I hope I'll never find that out.

Part V — The Truth about Mexico

INTRODUCTION

After ten years of investigating European affairs I went to Mexico, a land about which I knew nothing except what the newspapers reported and about which I am sure I had no emotions whatever.

I had read about a war between the Calles government and the Catholic Church; about Bolshevik plots; about American plans for intervention; about American oil troubles and always about acts of violence against Americans. I believe I came to Mexico as open-minded a journalist as ever visited a strange land. My one idea was to treat Mexico as a foreign country, a European nation towards which neither the reporter nor the United States had ulterior motives or propaganda-made prejudices.

But from the moment I arrived at the Texas frontier, every town of which I visited, I was deluged with propaganda, most of it, as I later found, as vicious as it was untrue. Catholic propaganda would have Calles the new anti-Christ and Ku Klux propaganda would install him in some hall of Methodist saints. The interventionists were roaring all along the border. Anti-Calles Mexicans were collecting dollars and talking about organizing armies. Mexico, many said, had gone completely Bolshevik and the time had come for intervention, war, annexation — disappearance of Mexico as a sovereign power.

In Mexico I heard much the same kind of talk from Americans. But I also found a new experiment in government as dangerous and as interesting as Bolshevism or Fascism. I found the

Catholic war with banners flying. I talked to diplomats, news-papermen, government officials and American business men who had lost their concessions or actually their shirts. I found friends of Mexico, " good-willers." But I also found censorship.

In the chapters which follow I have tried to tell some truths about Mexico as they appear to an objective ear and eye, accus-tomed to being disinterested and objective in all the political hurly-burly of the European scene. Owing to the press cen-sorship I made no attempt while south of the Rio Grande to send any messages; whether all or part of the following would have been suppressed I cannot say, I can only suspect. But cen-sorship or not, I know that certain chapters could never appear in the American daily press. The reader will quickly discern why.

Chapter I

Our Diplomacy in Mexico: A Heritage of Hate

IN the belief that our diplomatic and newspaper representation is largely responsible for misunderstandings between the United States and Mexico, misunderstandings which have led to violence in the past and may still lead to war, I intend to disregard the so-called "code of journalistic ethics," a code which is just about as immoral and hypocritical a collection of unwritten taboos as has ever been imposed upon an art or a profession by a mobilized bourgeois Babbittry.

I have met American diplomats in thirty-seven countries. I make the statement that, with an occasional commendable exception, they did not impress me as wholly representative of America. It may be a personal reaction, a prejudice, but this fact stands out: in Europe, Asia and Africa I have never met a diplomat who whole-heartedly hated the country to which he was accredited. I found many who were not satisfied, who longed for a change even if it were not a promotion; true, but they had a kind word to say for at least the climate, or the beer or the sea-coast or the sun-shine. When I went to Mexico I had my first experience with an American diplomatic corps which was so imbued with enmity for the country to which it was assigned that it could not or would not see nor admit the beauty of Popocatepetl or Indian blankets, or the picturesque peon, let alone the significance of a new experiment in social progress.

The advent of Ambassador Dwight W. Morrow (closely followed by Lindbergh) has been acclaimed a Mission of Good-

Will; there have been other times of great mutually profitable friendship, notably that during the Maximilian incident following the American Civil War, but generally speaking, for a hundred years our embassy in Mexico City has housed a heritage of hatred for Mexicans and Mexico itself.

Ambassador has followed ambassador, the rare, open-minded, objective, friendly man making a failure of his job; the prejudiced, small-calibred state department agent seizing his inheritance greedily, saturating himself with the ever-present spirit of malice, and propagating it at home and in Mexico.

Oil, mining, banking and plantation interests, which to this very day scorn and curse the land which gives them wealth, and the diplomatic corps, have worked together without friction, each renewing and feeding the other's hatred. Since the Diaz overthrow in 1910 a new element has entered further to intensify this attitude: the old native aristocracy and the ousted Cientifico, or big business interest, which grew fat with Diaz. Naturally the newly arrived ambassador and his assistants look up the " best people " in Mexico as they do in Europe. They find no broken nobility, no tarnished golden royalty to invite and to consult in Mexico, but there are always the remnants of " good " families which surrounded Diaz, which have little taint of Indian blood and which are eager and implacable co-operators in the hatred against the upstart democratic régime.

Diaz, the captain for Juarez the Liberator, had surrounded himself in the beginning with a group of idealists and liberals. Gradually the material trend of Diaz's political scheme of life led to the elimination of these idealists and their replacement by a group of hard-headed, practical, rapacious individuals who proceeded for a generation to rule " scientifically." Diaz the

Liberator became Diaz the Dictator, and the Cientificos in their later days grew rich and powerful, while Mexico sold concessions to Americans for almost all the natural wealth of the nation. Not a single business was carried on without graft and corruption. The contracts and concessions, according to an American lawyer in the University Club of Mexico City, would, almost all of them, be invalid if made in the United States.

The Madero-Carranza-Obregon-Calles régime announced agrarian reforms, an attempt to restore the lands and their wealth to the people and the nation, and the confiscation or semi-confiscation of property, if necessary, to carry out this policy. The Mexican Cientificos suffered as much as the American interests.

And the policy of the American embassy has always agreed with American business interests and the Cientificos. The new type of Mexican official, who perhaps carries a revolver on his hip and much more explosive experimental sociological matter in his head, has never had a welcome in our embassy. He has been hated without being seen or heard.

The American business men who have surrounded and influenced the official acts and attitude of the embassy are almost one hundred per cent. Mexico-haters and interventionists. If it is the duty of an ambassador to work for the interests of his own country, and if he sees his fellow expatriates as representatives of American public opinion, it is obvious that the diplomat believes himself to be in the right when he lends his position and his power to the views of all those Americans he finds surrounding him.

In my three month Mexican assignment I was able to discover only one centre of American opinion which was not anti-Mexican and which expressed itself much more unqualifiedly than I do regarding our diplomacy. This centre was the University Club. In this pure one hundred per cent. American institution I found no politicians, no grafters, no big oil concessionaires, but successful young American business men, engineers, professional men, who spoke the first words I had heard in the country for fair play and sportsmanship in dealing with Mexico. In many cases they were Americans who were employing Mexican labour or co-operating with Mexican employers, in other words men who really had contact with Mexico, and their attitude was friendly. They saw the mistakes and failures of Calles but they did not hate.

The Americans who have influenced the embassy, however, are not of the University Club type. They are largely the interventionists and the possessionists. The old cry, " The United States, from Alaska to the Isthmus of Panama," born during the honest, expansionist, pre-Civil War era, can be heard here. Among the interventionists is one type which cloaks the issue in moral sackcloth, which says that we should occupy Mexico for its own good and for noble reasons of civilization. Another type displays no sackcloth hypocrisy: it says, " Take Mexico for our own good."

The atmosphere of the American embassy before and during my visit, was openly interventionist.

Then there is a little resident group in the capital which opposes intervention or occupation and its attendant bloodshed, also an occasional body of American pacificists or clergymen which pays a visit and reports favourably for Mexico. All these elements are derisively labelled " good-willers " by the embassy and newspaper corps. (They will have to invent a new word now that the Morrow-Lindbergh Missions have been termed " good-will visits " by the world.)

Of the resident or semi-resident group I met Dr. Ernest Greuning who was at work on a history of Mexico; Roberto Haberman, an organizer for the American Federation of Labour; Carlton Beals, a brilliant young writer, the author of " Mexico; an Interpretation," and " Brimstone and Chili "; Frances Toor, the editor of *Mexican Folkways;* Howard Phillips, the editor of *Mexican Life,* each with a friendly, fair word about the Calles régime. I met them after weeks of listening to the same song of hate which starts on the Texas frontier and never ends in the south. So many hundreds of persons had assured me that Calles was a Syrian, a Bolshevik, a cheap grafter; that his régime was pure Bolshevism and corruption, that Mexicans hated the United States and were preparing for war, that they delighted in the murder of Americans, so many, indeed, that it was difficult for me to get over the shock of an entirely opposed view.

The " good-willers " were not blind to Mexico's shortcomings nor her acts of censorship and terrorism, nor her electoral corruption, nor her extremism in dealing with business and the Catholic Church; they saw mistakes and suggested calmness, tolerance, patience, a square deal and friendly watchful waiting.

One day when diplomatic officials were repeating the charges of terrorism and Bolshevism, I mentioned the views of the " good-willers."

" Skunks — liars — traitors," thundered the embassy speaker. " They are all paid agents of the Mexican Bolshevik régime — pay no attention to them — anyone who says a friendly word for the Mexicans is a traitor to the United States."

There was such passionate fury in the American diplomatic official's eyes and voice that I found myself saying:

" How can you call them traitors, — even if they work for

Mexico? — I find hundreds of Americans working for foreign governments in Europe — "

" But it's different here."

" We are not in a state of war yet."

" But we may be any day. And anyhow for an American to work for Mexico, with relations as they are at present, is treason. The Americans you named ought to be hanged."

I mentioned the American senators who favoured friendship instead of intervention.

" They are traitors, too — they are subsidized by the Mexicans," was the reply.

Later, documents were offered me by Miguel Avila, former military secret service operative, whose bona fides were approved by both embassy and consulate. These documents, which were proved false at the senatorial inquest, had pretended that Calles was giving money to senators who were friendly to Mexico. This incident I mention elsewhere; what I want to underline here is an embassy attitude so violently prejudiced that it gave its approval to vendors of false documents, forged for the purpose of discrediting not only Mexico but all " good-willers " who stood in the way of an officialdom's unanimity for war, intervention, occupation.

One reason for such passionate hatred of the " good-willers " is that they were all more or less making favourable publicity for Mexico. The embassy has failed to control them as it has the representatives of the regular press. The latter are offered anti-Mexican poison from the day of their arrival and very few fail to drink from the bottle bearing the official label, the guarantee of their own government.

The American ambassador at the time of my investigations and President Calles made a fine contrast, although both were fanatics. Calles was the warm, sometimes violent radical fanatic; our ambassador the cold, phlegmatic, unemotional fanatic whose god is property and whose saviour is the law of vested interests.

Our ambassador manifestly understood absolutely nothing about the new era in Mexico; he seemed congenitally incapable of understanding Change. Everything that wasn't done according to previous formulae was Bolshevism.

Men of this type who were alive when George Washington led a revolution remained Tories, not because they liked a tax on tea but because it was bolshevistically wrong to throw property off a wharf.

When Calles spoke of ideals in government our ambassador could see only violations of property laws; when Calles explained his reforms, our ambassador saw Bolshevism and when Calles asked for co-operation he received nothing but threats. The entire attitude of the American embassy can be summed up in the words of one of its minor officials who said: " We can't do business with the dirty crooks."

In all fairness it must be said that the Calles authorities, while not adding electric light to the fountains of mutual hatred, did not show any too friendly an attitude to the American diplomatic group nor try too hard for a peace of mutual concession and understanding. The few Calles politicians I met — they were not many because my paper was openly opposed to the régime and I was not particularly *persona grata* in Mexico — expressed the historical hopelessness of dealing with U. S. officials. Frequently I heard them revive stories of our diplomacy at the time President Madero was assassinated and two conspirators allowed to take over the country and plunge it back into political chaos.

" Complete confidence between Mexico and the United States can never be re-established," they say, " until this whole Madero affair is explained and atoned for to the satisfaction of our people."

Once it is admitted that the assassination of President Madero was made possible by the negligence of the diplomatic service of the United States, it follows that Mexicans have a right to ask what indirect part American diplomacy played in the tragedy, and it makes it easier to see why so much distrust of our diplomacy still persists in Mexico.

I produce elsewhere Madame Madero's statement, sworn and attested at the American consulate, giving her version of meetings with the ambassador, and their conversations. Madame Madero declared she had the assurances of Mr. Wilson that her husband's life would be spared.

It was not. Madero and his vice-president were taken from prison and murdered by the men or agents of the men who plotted a revolution, accomplished it, then met in the American embassy and, with the assistance and countenance of the ambassador, organized a government to replace that which Madero had headed. The revolution and the assassination could have been prevented by the United States, say Mexicans today. They want the telegrams between the president and the ambassador published, they want to know if Ambassador Wilson's telegram reporting Madero's downfall was sent before or after the fact, and they want to know, first of all, what advance knowledge Wilson had of the conspiracy. These desires do not seem unreasonable.

Whenever there is seated in Washington an American administration which desires peace and has no *arrière pensée* for intervention, it can exchange explanations with Mexico; the

United States would not humble itself even if it apologized for the use of its diplomatically immune building for planning the setting up of a government founded upon treason and assassination. And a word might also be said about the American oil companies which subsidized Mexican counter-revolutionaries so that they were able to raise whole armies to fight a government which the United States had recognized. And similar breaches of neutrality or international morals. Mexico, of course, might have a few apologies to offer also.

Do we really want to understand Mexico? To understand is to forgive; to forgive is to forswear. Could we march in and take Mexico if we understood the new experiment? Can any nation fight another without ignorance and hatred?

For the moment it looks as if the era of good-will has really arrived. But one can never be sure about events in Mexico. Ambassador Morrow and President Calles were succeeding admirably in replacing hatred with friendship, suspicions with mutual trust; the oil troubles were settled much to the applause of our state department and our oil interests, and even the religious conflict was approaching a peaceful end.

Suddenly an assassin's pistol removed Alvaro Obregon who was to spell Calles in the presidency and continue with him the one modern dictatorship which really works for national progress through emancipation, physical, spiritual and material, of the masses. Obregon's death revealed serious conflicts among the important political units of Callesism: the Obregonistas, the labour movement which made Calles, the agrarian party and the radical labour associations. When Morrow arrived Obregon and Calles had disputed the amount of concession and compromise which was the price of friendship with the United States. Obregon had won. The labour unions, led by

Luis N. Morones, continued to attack and were in turn attacked by Obregon, so severely in fact that Morones was later accused of encouraging the assassin.

However, the progress of Ambassador Morrow continues and in Mexico many hope that he will be retained by whatever administration is in power. To return to the old ambassadorial policy of ignorance and hatred would be to prepare an eventual and final war. The good imperialists are still hoping for it. If Morrow fails, and if Mexico is ever annexed, a monument should be set up, not for a president, a general or an admiral, but a massive statue in solid concrete, of a man with a silk hat, a morning coat, a silver-headed cane, spats perhaps, but with no individual face. The legend would then be: " Ambassador Babbitt — whose ignorance, stupidity and mediocrity added a new State to the Union."

gained nothing excepting the Ambassador's assurance that the President would not suffer bodily harm, and his promise to send the message soliciting the intervention of President Taft to save the lives of the prisoners.

Q.- Was the Ambassasor's assurance carried out?

A.- Two days later the prisioners were assassinated.

Q.- Did you converse with the Ambassador in Spanish, or in English?.

A.- In English.

Q.- Is it your opinión that the lives of the President and the Vice President could have been saved by the Ambassador?

A.- It is my belief that had the properly energetic representations been made by the Ambassador which it was reasonable to expect him to make, in the interest of humanity, not only would the lives of the President and the Vice President been spared, but a responsibility would have been averted from the United States which was thrust upon him by the acts of its then diplomatic representative in México.-

México, D.F. Agosto 15 de 1916.-

Sara Perez de Madero

Last page of document signed by Mme Madero, wife of the assassinated Mexican President.

Chapter II

THE STATE DEPARTMENT, THE EMBASSY AND THE ASSASSINATION OF A MEXICAN PRESIDENT

IN the night of February 22, 1913, Francisco Madero, president of Mexico, and Pino Suarez, vice-president, were assassinated. A counter-revolutionary plot fathered by Victoriano Huerta and Felix Diaz was temporarily successful. Huerta and Diaz had met and come to terms in the American embassy. Mr. Henry Lane Wilson, the ambassador, was in touch with the state department before, during and after the *coup d'etat*.

To the present administration, for almost all citizens of the United States and for the tabloid press this episode is dead history. But for Mexico, and for Central America which is beginning to look to Mexico for leadership, and for South America, which also lives in the shadow of the Monroe Doctrine, the assassination of President Madero and the part American diplomacy played, is a subject still alive and demanding explanation. The Mexican charges may be summed up as follows:

1. That Ambassador Wilson is proved by his own dispatches to the state department to have possessed prior knowledge that Huerta was to seize the government and arrest Madero.

2. That despite the fact that this knowledge was in the possession of the state department, despite the fact that it knew its representative knew all about the plot, it did not warn him to keep his hands off conspiracy and to discourage Huerta and other traitors.

3. That the facts clearly indicate that Huerta's coup could not have succeeded without the assistance and approval of the ambassador and

indirectly the state department, because Huerta could not have taken any action unless he knew he had American support.

4. That it was not what the ambassador and the state department did, perhaps, but what they did not do, viz: take good care that no harm came to Madero by warning Huerta resolutely and in unmistakable terms — that earned for them, according to opinion in Latin America, a moral responsibility for the fate of Madero and Suarez.

5. That through the actions of its ambassador, the United States incurred moral responsibility for the entire episode, the downfall of the Mexican government and the assassinations, from which it has not yet freed itself, which damned it in the eyes of all Latin America, and which still operates to the disadvantage of the protagonist of the Monroe Doctrine.

In the following remarkable *j'accuse,* which was written by Mme. Madero, August 15, 1916, and sworn to by her before the American vice-consul in Mexico City, April 29, 1927, American diplomacy in Mexico is arraigned before the world — at least the Latin world. This document has been refused publication by several big American newspapers whose editors admitted its importance but believed it to be somewhat " old," because American interest had somewhat subsided and it wouldn't do to reopen old wounds. The document, with its original errors in spelling, follows:

Q. Before going into detail on the subject of your personal experiences with former Ambassador Henry Lane Wilson, between the day of President Madero's arrest, on Tuesday, February 18, 1913, and his assassination on the night of Saturday, February 22, when you with other members of the President's family were vainly entreating the American Ambassador to utilize the power of the United States government and his undeniably potent influence with Victoriano Huerta to save the lives of President Madero and Vice President Pino Suarez, is it not true that the attitude of the American Ambassador toward President Madero and his government was regarded as unfriendly?

A. By President Madero and virtually all the members of the government it was firmly believed, and apparently with reason, that the attitude of the American Ambassador, not only toward my husband's government, but toward the Mexican Republic and the Mexican people was unfriendly — actively unfriendly. I am not in a position to say positively to what extent this feeling toward the American Ambassador was justified by the facts, but it is true that this feeling did exist and that foundation for it seemingly was warranted by the evidence which almost daily came to the attention of my husband.

(The following question and answer are written on the margin of the first sheet of the statement in the handwriting of Mrs. Madero.)

Q. Was the desirability of requesting the United States gobernment (sic) to recall the Ambassador ever suggested to the President?

A. President Madero was repeatedly urged to ask the government at Washington to recall the Ambassador.

Q. Why did he refuse?

A. He said: "He will be here only for a short time, and it is best to do nothing that will antagonice (sic) him, or his government.

Q. Were the actions of the Ambassador during the events which took place between Sunday, February 9, when the rebellion against President Madero's government began, and Tuesday, February 18, when Huerta seized the government and made prisoners of the President and his cabinet, regarded as frieldly (sic) and helpful to the federal government?

A. In answer, let me suggest this question: What evidence is there to indicate that during this interval the Ambassador exerted himself to do one proper, friendly act, or say one friendly word in behalf of the legal government of Mexico which was beset by rebels and traitors? Does any honest, unprejudiced person believe that had the American Ambassador set his face against Huerta and his plot that Madero government would have fallen? Does any honest, unprejudiced person believe that had the Ambassador made proper and sufficiently firm representations to Huerta the lives of the President and the Vice President would have been sacrificed?

Q. Were you with the President during the revolt?

A. I did not see my husband after he left Chapultepec Castle to go

329

to the National Palace on the morning of February 9. He remained at the Palace and I was at Chapultepec.

Q. When did you first become aware of the seizure of the government by Huerta and the imprisonment of the President and his cabinet?

A. Early in the afternoon. I tried to get in communication with the President over the private telephone. No one replied. I grew apprehensive, and called the Department of Communications. I asked them if anything had gone wrong. They assured me that everything was progressing favourably, thta (sic) the fighting that day had been in favour of the government and that the army and the people, as a whole, remained loyal to President Madero. While I was talking, three of the President's aides, Captains Garmendia, Montes and Cæarin, who had escaped from the Palace, came to me. They told me what had happened at the Palace — that Huerta had seized the government, that there had been an attack upon the President in his office; several men had been killed; that the President had escaped the bullets and fled to the lower part of the Palace to hanange (sic) the soldiers, where Blanquet arrested him.

Q. The Ambassador in his dispatches speaks of murders having been committed by the President, of men whom he had shot during the mêlée in his office. Is this true?

A. It is not true. He never carried a weapon.

Q. Where did you go from the Castle?

A. Immediately after the President's aides had told me what had happened I took refuge in the Japanese Legation.

Q. What were the conditions under which the President and the Vice President were induced to resign?

A. By agreement with Huerta and upon his pledge that they were to be allowed to leave the country and proceed to Europe, it was arranged that they should resign.

Q. Did you attempt to see the President?

A. Yes, several times without succeeding.

Q. When did you have your interview with the Ambassador?

A. That afternoon. Mercedes, my sister-in-law, was with me. The Ambassador was not in when we entered the Embassy. Mrs. Wilson received us, and caused a telephone message to be sent to the Palace, notifying the Ambassador that we were there.

Q. What was the manner and appearance of the Ambassador?

A. . . . His manner was brusque. At times Mrs. Wilson tugged at his coat, apparently to try to induce him to speak diffwrently (sic) to us. It was a painful interview. I told the Ambassador that we had come to seek protection for the lives of the President and the Vice President. " Very well, Madam," said he. " What is it that you want me to do? "

" I want you to use your influence to protect the lives of my husband and other prisoners."

" That is a responsibility that I do not care to undertake, either for myself, or my government," replied the Ambassador.

" Will yoy (sic) be good enough, then," I asked, " to send this telegram to President Taft? "

I handed him a message addressed to President Taft, which had been written by the President's mother and signed by her. It was through the Ambassador that our only hope lay in obtaining communication with President Taft. We supposed that the cable was in the hands of the government, and that it was useless to expect that a message of this sort would be allowed to pass. This is a copy of the message:

" Mexico, D. F., 20th February, 1913. — To the President of the United States, Mr. William H. Taft: I pray you to intercede in order that the agreement mede (sic) with my son and his friends with General Huerta to permit them to go to Europe may be carried out. Their lives are in danger, and above all, they have a right to their liberty because they were honourable men, and this is the expressed condition on which he resigned, as is known to some of the foreign diplomats who intervened. I address you as a mother in trouble, who appeals to the only person whose influence can save the life of her son and assure him his liberty. MERCEDES G. de MADERO."

Q. What was the reply of the Ambassador to your request, after he had read the message?

A. " It is not necessary to send this," he said. But I persisted. " All right," promised the Ambassador, " I shall send it." He put the message in his pocket.

Q. Did he send the message?

A. You can see the answer I received from the State Department:

"April 30th, 1913. Mrs. Sara Perez de Madero, New York city; Madam: Your letter of March 2nd, addressed to the Honourable William H. Taft, then President of the United States, in which you request to be informed whether or not the message, of which you enclose a copy, with your letter, came into the possession of President Taft, reached the Executive offices after Mr. Taft's term of office had expired, and was referred to this Department. The records of this Department show that this message was brought to the President's attention. Instructions in the matter had already been given the Embassy and the action it took on behalf of ex-President Madero and ex-Vice President Pino Suarez was taken with the knowledge and under the direction of the President. The Ambassador states, in reporting to the Department in connection with the death of the ex-President and the ex-Vice President of Mexico, that the action on their behalf could not have been more energetic than it was. I am, Madam, your obdient servant, JOHN B. MOORE, Acting Secretary of State."

Q. Did you put forth efforts to ascertain if the message ever was received by President Taft?

A. When I was in Havana, on my way to New York, I sent this letter to President Taft:

"Havana, March 2nd, 1913: To His Excellency, The President of The United States, Honourable William H. Taft, Washington, D. C.; Sir: I address these lines to Your Excellency in order to enclose a copy of a telegram which my mother-in-law Señora Mercedes G. de Madero, directed to Your Excellency on February 20th last, through the United States Ambassador, Honourable Henry Lane Wilson, and which telegram I personally delivered to him with the request that he be kind enough to forward same in code. As Your Excellency will see by the contents, we implored your influence to save the life of my husband, Señor Don Francisco I. Madero, so dear to us. As events transpired, and we received no reply from Your Excellency, we desire to know whether or not this telegram came into your possession. Anticipating my thanks for the attention my request will receive from the hands of Your Excellency, and awaiting your kind reply, I am, Respectfully, Sara Perez de Madero."

332

(The following question and answer were written and then crossed out by Mrs. Madero.)

[Q. What reply, if any, did Mr. Taft make?]

[A. His reply, which came a long time afterwards, contained nothing to indicate if my mother-in-law's message had, or had not, been received by him on time.]

Q. What followed after you had delivered to the Ambassador the message directed to President Taft?

A. The Ambassador said: "I will be frank with you, Madam. Your husband's downfall is due to the fact that he never wanted to consult with me." I could reply nothing to this, for I had gone there to ask a favour, to plead for my husband's life, not to discuss questions of politics, or policies with the Ambassador.

Q. What else did the Ambassador say?

A. The Ambassador continued: "You know, Madam, your husband had peculiar ideas." I said: "Mr. Ambassador, my husband had not peculiar ideas, but high ideals." To this the Ambassador did not reply, and I proceeded to say that I asked the same protection and assurance for the life of Vice President Pino Suarez as I asked for President Madero. The Ambassador's manner grew very impatient. "Pino Suarez is a very bad man," he said, "I cannot give you any assurance for his safety. He is to blame for most of your husband's troubles. . . . he is one of the leaders of the 'Prra' (sic)," (meaning the popular name given to one of the political factions which favoured the Madero government, "The Porra," which means stick, or club).

The Ambassador used the common designation of the Progressive Party which President Madero had founded during his political campaing (sic).

Q. . . . .

A. . . . I then represented to him that Mr. Pino Suarez had a wife and six children who would be left in poverty in the event of his death.

Q. What did he say to that?

A. He merely shrugged his shoulders. He told me that General Huerta had asked him what should be done with the prisoners. "What did you tell General Huerta?" I asked. "I told him that he must do what was best for the interests of the country," said the Ambassador.

Here my sister-in-law interrupted and said: "Why did you say that? You know very well what kind of men Huerta and his people are and that they are going to kill him."

Q. What did the Ambassador say?

A. He made no response, but turned to me and said: "You know that your husband is unpopular; that the people were not satisfied with him as President." I asked: "Why, then, if this is true, is he not permitted to go free and proceed to Europe, where he could do no harm?" The Ambassador replied: "You need not worry; the person of your husband will not be harmed. I knew all along, that this was going to happen. That is why I suggested that your husband should resign."

"But why if you knew of this in advance, Mr. Ambassador," I Asked (sic) him, "why did you not warn my husband?" " "Oh, no," he replied, "that would not have been good policy, for then he would have prevented it."

Q. The Ambassador is quoted in an interview in *The New York Herald* on March 21st, 1916, as saying that you had requested him to ask Huerta to "put your husband in the Penitentiary for safekeeping." Did you make such a request of the Ambassador?

A. No. We discussed only his personal safety and the urgency of Huerta being compelled to keep his promise to allow the President and the other prisoners to leave the country. I speke (sic) of the uncomfortable accommodations they had. "He seems to be getting along all right," said the Ambassador. "He has slept for five hours without waking."

Q. What was the outcome of the conversation?

A. When the interview terminated and we went away, we had gained nothing excepting the Ambassador's assurance that the President would not suffer bodily harm, and his promise to send the message soliciting the intervention of President Taft to save the lives of the prisoners.

Q. Was the Ambassador's assurance carried out?

A. Two days later the prisoners were assassinated.

Q. Did you converse with the Ambassador in Spanish, or in English?

A. In English.

Q. Is it your opinion that the lives of the President and the Vice President could have been saved by the Ambassador?

334

A. It is my belief that had the properly energetic representations been made by the Ambassador which it was reasonable to expect him to make, in the interest of humanity, not only would the lives of the President and the Vice President been spared, but a responsibility would have been averted from the United States which was thrust upon him (sic) by the acts of its then diplomatic representative in Mexico.

Mexico, D. F., Agosto 15 de 1916,

(signed) Sara Perez de Madero.

Chapter III

MEXICAN DOCUMENTS TO ORDER

THE Hearst Mexican documents and many others were offered to me, some the second evening of my stay in Mexico City, others almost every day for weeks. The document vendor was Miguel Avila. He was introduced to me by fellow newspapermen who hated the Calles régime. At the American embassy and consulate where I went expressly to get advice about buying documents from Avila, his reputation and integrity were affirmed.

Despite the approval of American diplomacy I advised against buying the documents which eventually became the property of the Hearst press, caused a senatorial investigation and a complete exposure of the crookedness of the deal. On one other occasion I had been offered documents and when the agent was approved by the American consulate, I bought them. One was a letter about $25,000 sent by the Third International for Bolshevik work in Buenos Aires. The man who sold me this document confessed forgery (according to the Moscow press), but American newspapermen in Russia say Drushilowsky always was and is now a secret agent of the Chekah. I suppose the documents were his forgeries but I cannot understand the excitement in the radical press about them because in open sessions of the Third International Congress of 1922 I heard announcements about the sending of money for Bolshevik enterprises in South America. The document may have been a forgery; the forged words, however, relate historic facts.

There were several reasons for my dropping negotiations with Miguel Avila.

I have dealt with secret agents, detectives, terrorists and spies, some of whom were quite big men in their way, but I got a very bad impression of Avila from the following incident.

The day Avila offered me the first documents I was invited to dinner by an American I had met once in New York. When I came to his apartment I met three or four Americans known as " good-willers," or friends of Mexico. Early the next morning Avila came to my room in the hotel, furious:

" You had dinner with our enemies," he cried, " I know what you had. Both beer and wine. Chicken. Six courses. They are trying to buy you over: they told the cook you were important and to spend money freely — twenty pesos! "

By the end of the week in addition to my dealings with Avila, the following reports were made to me:

From the good-willers: " Avila offers to spy on you and sell us a report on your daily activities."

From a Calles official: " Avila claims you are a state department spy and is willing to report on you."

From an American official: " Avila says you are in the company of traitors and Bolsheviks " — (meaning, of course, good-willers).

From an American newspaperman: " Avila is willing to sell me the documents he offers you."

The Hotel Regis became a beehive of espionage. The buzzing was enormous. It was complicated one day by the arrival of a secret agent from the Ku Klux Klan who wanted to work hand in hood with Calles and refused to be disappointed when Calles turned him down. Then came a secret agent for the Knights of Columbus.

He had a strong German accent and credentials for a Catholic weekly in Iowa. He seemed hard of hearing and he shouted his whispers.

"I'm a newspaperman myself," he yelled to me in the crowded lobby, "I'm a big secret agent for the Knights of Columbus —"

"Are you sure it is a secret?" someone asked.

"Sure!" he replied.

"Then you might remove your Knights of Columbus pin from your lapel."

"Oh my God," he exclaimed, terrified, and tore the pin out of his coat. He took out a pill box and placed the pin among. He came in once a week to exercise his calling. The Ku Kluxer disappeared suddenly. But Avila, who claimed to represent various elements, kept negotiating with me.

It was a bad season for documents because some three hundred had mysteriously passed between the American embassy and the office of President Calles, and both governments, after the original shock of publicity, were reticent about them. Avila claimed the whole three hundred genuine. But it was not from him that I obtained a copy of one of them. Next to alleged documents of military invasion, this one is believed to be largely responsible for a diplomatic crisis which almost brought on a rupture of diplomatic relations. It is in the form of a circular letter allegedly sent by Calles to the governors of the twenty-eight Mexican states. It was sold as an original, bearing on it the name of the governor, rubber stamps showing date of receipt at the state capitol, and initials of the governor. Not only did the American embassy obtain the alleged original but copies were offered by the dealers to other persons.

According to the Calles followers the first part of the docu-

338

ment, the letter sent to all the governors discussing Mexican internal and external politics is genuine. They, however, claim that the sensational part of the document is apocryphal. The date is January 1, 1927. The first part deals with the progress of agrarian reconstruction, road-building, school system, irrigation, land bank developments, etc., and the apocryphal part follows:

" This progress has had as a consequence, the natural resistance and lack of confidence which meet all social innovations and has met internal and external resistance which I am accustomed to in carrying out my policies and in enforcing the application of the fundamental laws of my country. Unfortunately the application of the laws has provoked such a situation on the exterior and such an agitation and resistance in the interior as to endanger the fundamental peace and public tranquillity. It has led to the formation of groups of discontented, especially to activities by the fanatical Catholics, enemies of my government, who have begun a rebel movement, supported by American money and attempting to destroy our institutions.

" Unfortunately many of the means taken by my government for the protection and betterment of the social interests of the Mexican people have been wrongly interpreted in foreign countries by selfish elements who have given them the appearance of dissolvent social actions. They have found a badly interpreted echo in the capitalist American press which has wished to present Mexico as desirous of sustaining imported doctrines and as propagandists of these doctrines in Latin America, and as desirous of bringing into our national life a political system absolutely foreign to it.

" To this is added the fact that some foreign diplomats, among them the ambassador of the United States, abusing the diplomatic immunity with which they are invested, have made common cause with the enemies of my government. He has manufactured all kinds of intrigue in order to create international difficulties between Mexico and the United States and to bring about a state of lack of confidence and bad understanding which would necessarily lead to the rupture of diplomatic relations between these two countries, and this in turn would give an opportunity to the enemies of my administration to organize and to make possible the realization of their iniquitous and dastardly plans."

In the original Spanish document, according to the spokesman for President Calles, there are errors of spelling and grammatical construction. These facts and the whole style of the allegedly inserted paragraphs, according to the spokesman, point to a forger whose knowledge of the English language is better than of the Spanish.

Regarding the whole series of documents treating of the military invasion of Mexico, little was said because officials realize that every nation in the world prepares such plans. But there was considerable excitement over several other alleged documents of President Calles in which orders are given the Mexican war department to send arms and munitions to the Sacasa faction in Nicaragua. Naturally the Calles spokesman claims that these were also forged. Whether forged or not, it is the understanding of the Mexican government that supposedly originals were forwarded by the American embassy to Washington and were accepted by the state department as genuine.

While there is no doubt that an American embassy employee had trafficked with the Calles government, there is also considerable belief that numerous Mexican employees have sold genuine documents, directly or indirectly, to the American embassy. No one doubts this because it is a usual method for Mexican government employees who are disgruntled with the régime for which they work, and who are always glad to take silver on the side.

When the Hearst documents, thanks to the senate's actions, became a public scandal, I received a cabled request for a statement of my relations with Avila. Following is the reply intact:

" *Immediately on my arrival in Mexico, Miguel Avila offered me various documents allegedly stolen from El Sol Petroleum Company, the only oil concern co-operating with the Mexican government.*

" *According to Avila the Mexican government was unwilling to issue checks directly to politicians, writers, journalists and others, for propaganda and other efforts in the United States but authorized El Sol to pay vouchers which the Calles Government would reimburse.*

" *Avila produced a document stating the above idea.*

" *On this document the words ' department treasury' were typewritten over ' department education' which aroused my suspicion. When I showed the document to Americans knowing Spanish, the latter pointed out that the document was badly spelled, was bad in its grammar, which showed it to be the work of a non-Spaniard, presumably an American, because the expressions were direct translations from English.*

" *At the same time, Avila offered a document claiming to be an original letter which Calles dispatched to each governor, wherein Mexican-American relations were discussed and the American ambassador called a trouble maker.*

" *This document was declared an absolute fraud by officials*

341

who gave copies out as a sample of the alleged three hundred forged documents which figured in the news last spring.

"Simultaneously two Americans told me Avila had offered to spy on me for them, and another claimed he paid Avila twenty pesos to report on whom I was meeting in Mexico.

"Finally when Robert Murray informed me that Avila was willing to sell him a statement that the documents all were forged and give the name of the forger, I decided to end all dealings because I was convinced that everything was crooked. Avila then said he would sell the documents to other interests."

About all that need be noted about the whole tawdry affair is the approval which our diplomacy has given so easily when its policy is furthered, and which is accepted as pontifical by newspapermen even when it concerns forgeries which may lead to the most serious international events.

Chapter IV

AMERICAN REPORTERS AND MEXICO

THE day we got the news of the attack by the Catholic rebels on a train with its civilian and military passengers, a slaughter paralleled in modern times only by some sanguinary exploits of the Druses and Arabs in Syria, almost the entire American press corps was gathered at the Western Union office in Mexico City.

There was a new sign up: " Censorship today."

I was fresh from the French Army of the Orient and I had seen similar guerrilla warfare. I said:

" Why the devil doesn't the government do what the French are doing in Syria: mount two machine-guns on airplane swivels, one fore, one aft, and stop attacks on trains? The attackers have only rifles and revolvers and would be beaten off easily."

" For God's sake," replied one of the men representing Mr. Hearst's papers and news-agencies, " don't repeat that. The government might hear it, and do it."

I had no more interest in the Mexican war than in the Syrian war; my viewpoint was that of a potential civilian train passenger. I was shocked.

" You don't seem neutral in this war," I said to my colleague.

" No, I'm not," he replied. " If you had lived in Mexico as long as I, you would not be neutral either."

Five minutes later I was walking up the street with another representative of the American press in Mexico.

"The Hearst man," I said, "told me that the rebels will be victorious in three weeks."

"He is too much of an optimist," replied my other colleague, "I am hoping for victory in three months."

At this moment his "hoping" has lasted more than a year.

To a third colleague, the representative of a great New York daily, whose attitude is friendly and anti-interventionist, but whose reporter's name was joined with Miguel Avila's in testimony before the senate committee which was investigating forged documents, I said:

"I want to hear both sides of the Mexican question."

He replied:

"There is only one side: we are all anti-Calles."

The rest of his declaration was a series of oaths.

A fourth colleague had a pocketful of forged documents and was begging his paper to recall him to Texas.

"I'll blow this government to pieces when I get out," he said.

We were only nine or ten Americans in the Mexico City press corps and I have quoted four directly to illustrate the general anti-Mexican, anti-Calles, pro-Catholic revolutionary attitude of the majority. With one or two exceptions the press corps with, to my knowledge, only one member a professed Catholic, sympathized with the rebels whenever it was safe to do so and on many occasions tinged the news dispatches to favor them. Yet I find in the New York Catholic organ *Commonweal* the following editorial comment:

"Necessarily, therefore, American public opinion has not merely the right but even the duty to expect that those upon whom it relies for information will supply it with the facts. And it has been distressing to note with what inert indifference the American press has accepted the exile or the gagging of its correspondents, and has hastened to publish without comment whatever the Calles government offered it for consumption."

This comment followed a report of the views of Pope Pius XI who, also under the impression that the reporters in Mexico were favouring the Government, not the Catholics, " abandoned the official manner of speaking through encyclicals and allocutions " and addressed the American press as follows:

"Again and again the voice of the Pope has been raised both in solemn allocutions and encyclical letters to tell the truth about Mexico to the world; but the carefully laid plans of the persecutors of the church have prevented it being heard by all in its entirety; indeed, sometimes it has not been understood at all.

"Nothing like this persecution has ever been known in history, not even in the first centuries of the church. For then, even under Nero, Caligula and Domitian, there was no general persecution of private religion in homes, the catacombs or the cemeteries. But now in Mexico nothing that is Catholic is tolerated, not even the private celebration of the Mass and the administration of the sacraments, punishment for which has, in many cases, been the death penalty, and always fines, imprisonment and murderous outrages. . . .

"Notwithstanding their noble resistance — the admiration of ourselves, and of the whole world that knows the facts — this people of confessors and martyrs finds hardly a soul to respond to their cry for aid to save them from utter ruin, and to save all civilized nations, and indeed the whole human race, from the infamy of a savage persecution now being tolerated in the twentieth century, the boasted era of civilization and progress. If the whole press, the whole nation, of the United States can find an opportune remedy for this disastrous social catastrophe, it will merit glory in the history of civilization and religion."

Again *America,* a journal of Catholic opinion, declares the American press " does not try to find out and publish the facts connected with the present (Mexican) régime, and not only displays no curiosity as to what is happening in Mexico but absolutely refuses to consider publication of the facts as attested by an experienced and impartial newspaperman." The writer in *America* believes this is the dark work of " unseen powers " which exercise a censorship.

It would be useless here to discuss the rights and wrongs of the Catholics in Mexico or the possible justification for the violence with which the government has attacked the church, or the violence with which the Catholics have replied. My point is that the American reporters in Mexico as a body are pro-Catholic, not because they care for the church or the rebels, but because they hate the Calles régime so much that they will support anyone who fights it, be he Ku Kluxer or Knight of Columbus, oil man or priest or ambitious, treasonable, Mexican general.

As best proof of this statement I can recount another detail of that afternoon in the Western Union office. Everyone, including myself, was protesting the censorship. But most of the press telegrams were put through. An official who sat at a desk with the Western Union clerks said:

" The main object of today's censorship is to stop internal telegrams: we have evidence that the bishops here are communicating with the rebels regarding guns, ammunition, trains, and future attacks — and also with enemies of the government in the United States."

He said also that President Calles had prepared a press statement on the train massacre and, knowing that the Mexican editors would write headlines or editorials giving an opposite impression to the one he wanted spread, had forbidden changing a word or comma, and for headlines permitted only the use of his first paragraph in larger type. The American re-

346

porters, the first day of the news, had to content themselves with Calles' meagre report.

This was a very astute move on the part of the president. He had laid the blame for the deaths of one hundred men, women and children on the train, on the three priests whom he named, who had led the attack! In Mexico this caused no astonishment. Ever since Archbishop Orozco, for whom the government offered a reward of 10,000 gold pesos, dead or alive, raised the standard of revolt and placed the Guadalupe Virgin on the red, white and green flag in place of the Eagle and Snake, the priests have led the smaller rebel groups in the field.

Leading Catholics considered the train attack a big victory in the new revolution; but the American newspapermen, mostly Protestant but mostly anti-Calles, realized the bad impression that would go through the world when the details of that fight became known. Right as they considered the Catholic effort to free itself from the Calles persecution, they were afraid that the cause they were so eager to defend would get a set-back if they printed the fact that three priests had led the mob which, while fighting (Catholic) soldiers, had murdered one hundred (Catholic) passengers.

" I do not believe priests were present," said one American correspondent.

" Nor do I," said another.

A third, who had a relative on the train who told him of seeing the priests leading the attacks, said:

" Well, I am sorry to say I know it is true priests were present, but we need not play that up in America."

With one exception, I believe, the press corps in Mexico favoured the Catholic rebellion and I cannot for the life of me see any reason for the Pope or the church press to complain of *news dispatches;* as regards the editorial attitude of the American papers themselves, that is another matter.

I repeat that almost all the news sent out of Mexico by American correspondents during my stay was pro-Catholic because the press corps is anti-Calles, anti-government.

One reason for the general anti-Calles attitude was the American embassy. Here in Mexico City, where I found so many contrasts in the relations between diplomacy and journalism to those in Europe, I also found the embassy leagued with the press corps. Here, for the purpose of spreading ill-will, I found that perfect co-operation which I had sought in Europe, never found, and proposed to Secretary Hughes and Secretary Kellogg on my visits to Washington.

The second great contrast was the relations of the Mexico City correspondent to his editor as compared with the relations of a European correspondent to his editor.

In Europe, thanks no doubt to the fact that America is still uninvolved in Transatlantic politics, the newspaperman is almost entirely free from editorial political instructions. In my nine years with *The Chicago Tribune,* for example, I never received an order from Colonel McCormick to support or attack any party, system or cause. When I was expelled from Italy, Colonel McCormick stood by me as gallantly as when I was deported from Russia by the Bolsheviks; I could and did describe the failures of Republican Germany, the stupidity of Monarchist Germany, the ribald and ridiculous actions of the Hohenzollerns, Ludendorff, d'Annunzio, Mussolini; the failures of France in Syria; victories and defeats in the temperance movement, Socialist movement, dictatorship movement. No office policy bound me nor does it bind the big majority of foreign correspondents, nor are we chosen and promoted because of the tacit understanding that we will support any petty local policies in our dispatches from abroad.

In Mexico quite the reverse.

To begin with there are powerful newspapers in America which want war with an annexation or occupation of Mexico, and these papers pick men who believe in this policy or who sell themselves to it. Another small section senses the newspaper owner's views, — ingratiates itself by playing up to him, and thereby corrupts itself. The rest are influenced by other forces. Where the editor and paper are liberal or open-minded, the embassy and the Cientifico influences come in to pervert the news. Or there may be unfortunate dealings with Mexicans, such as gun smuggling or document forging, which influence the reporter. Most of the correspondents rank in intelligence, cultural background and appreciation of the fundamentals of the Mexican situation with a $35. a week police reporter in Chicago. Most of them are too young for the job and are certainly paid so little that there is no incentive to take it seriously. It appears that newspaper owners in the United States refuse to pay the price necessary to staff themselves in Mexico with first-class men. Despite the seriousness of Mexican-American relations and potentialities — more important to our own political future than those of any European country, for, to a highly intensified extent, our present and future status and understanding with all Latin-American states depend vitally upon the outcome of dealings with Mexico — the people and editors of our country are content to have events in Mexico interpreted by ill-paid or incompetent or prejudiced reporters. All are ill-paid and there are few who are not compelled to engage in outside enterprises and to enmesh themselves with interests alien to their profession in order to produce those extra dollars which cover the expense of living. Two of the foremost and most prosperous newspapers in New York refuse to pay fixed salaries in any amount to their correspondents in Mexico City. They are served by " string men," that is, reporters who are compensated only for the dispatches which are ordered, accepted or used by the papers. Cheapness seems to be the principle which governs the employment by the press of the United States of men who cover the developments in the most fundamentally and permanently important international news source in which the United States as a nation and as a people is concerned.

In connection with this exposition of the news situation in Mexico City it was revealed at the senate inquiry into the authenticity of the Hearst Mexican documents that one New York newspaper, the name of which is awfully regarded as a synonym for journalistic respectability and righteousness, had provided money to its correspondent in Mexico City to bribe men to steal for it documents from the files of the Mexican government. The correspondent who did the bribing admitted it under oath. This same gentleman while employed by the newspaper which boasts daily of the integrity, independence and accuracy of its news dispatches, also was proved, while employed by the newspaper in question, to have importuned the Mexican government to hand out to him a valuable petroleum concession. He did not receive the concession, and the anti-government tenor of most of his news dispatches clearly showed his chagrin.

Also — and this is important for it concretely indicates the extent to which only one-sided, biased Mexican news is fed to the American public — fully 90 per cent. of the news dispatches from Mexico depict only the darker side of the picture: fighting, executions, government raids upon Catholic schools and lay institutions which violate the law of the land, train wrecks and hold-ups, financial and economic depression, all destructive not constructive news.

There is a vast amount of constructive work under way in Mexico. Much has been accomplished and much is being done to clear away the revolutionary wreckage. Hundreds of miles of highway are being built, huge irrigation projects are being completed, the popular educational system is being extended and modernized, the army has been reorganized and greatly reduced in size and cost, agrarian seizures and outrages are being halted, and so on. But it is seldom that a line about this work of development and rehabilitation sees light in the American press. The editors excuse themselves by saying that this is not sensational, not " spot " news, not material for circulation building headlines. But the reporters tell the truth when they say they send no constructive news because the editors refuse to print it. American editors demand that Mexican news meat must be excitingly gory. If it doesn't drip blood and sensation they don't want it and they won't have it. Editors are not interested and they insist that their readers are not interested in a Mexico that is thriving, peaceful, productive, in a Mexico that is working and earning money with which to swell the volume of American trade and provide employment for American workmen and profits to American manufacturers and exporters. Many of these editors would prefer to see these same thousands of American workingmen carrying guns on their shoulders, marching to Mexico, rather than manufacturing stoves and automobiles and chewing gum and radio sets for the Mexican people. Show some of these editors a fighting

Mexico, with blood on the landscape presaging a war of intervention, a sick Mexico with all the dramatic news possibilities symptomatic of national sickness, and they will whoop and cheer, leap in the air, crack their heels together and if necessary make room on the first page between the local murder and the big " national " murder stories, for evidence that their nearest neighbour on the south, the neighbour in the fortunes of which the United States is more vitally concerned than in those of any other country on earth, is weltering in a supposititious and hopeless morass of civil strife, economic ills and implacable national doom.

Between the American editors and the American reporters, Mexico has not had a square deal. I did, however, meet two press representatives in Mexico City who were simon-pure honest reporters, who did not involve themselves in Mexican politics or concessions or religious disputes, who had a sense of humour, who reported events as they actually happened, who, in other words, worked in the same free spirit as the European corps works in every capital. No Calles propaganda, no embassy intimidation, no subservience to newspaper office policy can be read in the dispatches of these two men. Incidentally they have had a pretty hard time of it.

If the United States wants peace and understanding with Mexico our editors and the State Department will both have to make a big change. If Ambassador Morrow is the herald of good-will, as he seems to be, then it is necessary to have a newspaper attitude changed to conform to the new times. Police reporters are out of place in Mexico; so are adventurers who engage in journalism as a side line to gun running or trafficking in oil concessions or document forging or document dealing. There have been changes in the past year. No doubt those newspapermen who can adapt themselves to veering editorial policy will catch any suggestion from their home offices for a return to honesty and objectivity.

Not until our diplomacy and our journalism are purged of all corrupting influences can the Mexican problem be rightly understood and solved.

Chapter V

THE CASE FOR INTERVENTION

A MEXICAN lady of purest Spanish blood, descendant of a prime minister, made the most illuminating remark on the Mexican state of mind:

" For generations," she said, " we Mexicans have been brought up from childhood in fear of the judgment day, the eruption of Popocatepetl and intervention by the United States."

A member of President Calles' staff supplemented with: " In five years or fifty years or five hundred years, we do not know just when but at present five seems far away, the United States will intervene in Mexico. We will be conquered, or annexed, or just policed. Calles and Obregon are of this opinion; so are most government officials, but they hope to postpone that day."

It is generally admitted that almost one hundred per cent. of the resident Americans and almost fifty per cent. of the articulate Mexican people believe in the inevitability of intervention. All they ask is, what sort of intervention?

There are different opinions. Some want a U. S. protectorate; some want to be incorporated as several states of the Union; some want merely an entrance of American troops at once and a stay just long enough to put the Mexican house in order, and still another group favors the Cuban plan.

A leading American citizen, of long residence and a big figure in the Chamber of Commerce and in American business life, is the chief exponent of the last system. He has been asked

by previous administrations to come to Washington and out-
line his plan and has done so and found approval there. Secretary Kellogg knows his views. His plan is not for permanent
occupation of Mexico nor for incorporating that nation into
the United States as an inevitable result of the Monroe Doctrine
and the necessity for peace and trade on the North American
continent. He believes eventually Mexico will be able to govern
herself.

At the same time this leading American citizen, who has
lived long in Mexico and knows the situation so thoroughly that
his advice is frequently followed by our secretaries of state, is
against a military occupation which would straighten matters
out only temporarily.

He suggests something like the Platt agreement with Cuba.
He wants the United States to come into Mexico peaceably, to
end the present militarism which he says is ruining the country,
to settle the church strife, then to restore the old constitutional
guarantees of personal property, and to aid Mexico in building
up a political control. He suggests that a body of twenty-five,
more or less, leading citizens not one of whom is a general or
military opportunist, or a high church dignitary (who would
restore the church as ruler), or a red radical (who would replace church or army dictatorship with labour dictatorship), be
formed under the ægis of the American occupation. Up to
now such citizens have had almost no say in Mexican public
life. Such a directorate, provided it had the support of the U. S.,
would soon restore Mexico to peace and prosperity.

Naturally the routed elements, labour, the military and the
church which has had more than 400 years of undisputed rule,
would seek to overthrow such a régime, therefore it would be
necessary for the United States to have an agreement for the

355

peaceful re-entry, at any time, of its special agents or military forces for the maintenance of the directorate.

A great percentage of the Mexican upper classes favour intervention because they see that the Calles labour dictatorship is growing stronger every day, and that with the education of the Indians and ex-peons there is almost no hope for the restoration of the rule by the white race. At the time Diaz was overthrown it was estimated that 80 per cent. or 12,000,000 of Mexico's 15,000,000 people could not read or write. The present régime claims that the number of illiterates has been reduced to 60 per cent. It must not be forgotten that the Mexican system of education, like the Bolshevik, includes the teaching of propaganda with the teaching of the alphabet. As the peons become articulate they also seize the land of the big landowners.

There would be even greater co-operation among Mexicans in favour of American intervention were it not for the fact that Mexico can never forget the part the United States played in the Huerta-Diaz coup which resulted in the assassination of Madero, the Lincoln of Mexico.

Mexicans believe that the pact for the overthrow of Madero was made in the embassy and had the approval of American diplomacy — even to our representatives recognizing the new rulers in suspicious haste and urging our consuls to work in their behalf. This one incident rankles in the breasts of Mexican patriots and Mexican friends of America. The war of 1845 and the Pershing expedition do not stir up one-tenth of one per cent. as much feeling as the Madero assassination affair. The greater part of the distrust which has characterized American-Mexican relations since 1913 is due to unsatisfactory explanations of this incident.

A great number of American business men believe intervention is the sole means of saving Mexico from Bolshevism. They claim the American investment is approaching two billion dollars. In other words Americans own more than half the value of Mexico and have little protection for such an enormous investment. They face retroactive laws and confiscation. They do not believe in the Calles promises to give them 50-year leases for the oil lands in exchange for their present outright ownership. Why should they believe Calles, they say, when Calles might be overthrown in three days, and another régime take its place, even more radical, which would not recognize the Calles leases?

Other Americans declare themselves frankly as honest imperialists. " Why not? " they say. The American prospectors came upon a great wealth which Mexico did not know it had and could not use. In the exploitation of this mineral wealth Americans say they have brought employment, higher wages, sanitary conditions, schools, education and civilization. They have been a godsend to Mexico and at the same time made their fortunes. They see all this work ruined now, and believe intervention would be good not only for themselves, but for Mexico itself.

I made notes of individual opinion from the moment I got into the Pullman until I left Texas for Chicago and Washington. In the manner of an inquiring reporter, I asked men to express an opinion on intervention, the religious troubles, Calles and Bolshevism. Here follow some genuine interviews as samples of American opinion.

Business man No. 1 of the Smoking Car: " Mexico has fallen into such a bolshevistic state that it is impossible to do business with either the government or with individuals. If you own a ranch the government will probably take the richest part for distribution and offer you bonds for it which may or may not be paid. Or the peons may seize it and the government cannot put them out. The oil business is going to hell."

Business man No. 2 of the Smoking Car: " The trouble with Mexico is we Americans want to do business our way not their way. We sort of think we are the bosses and they should obey our laws, not we their laws. Another important fact, according to my view, is that the internal trouble is fundamentally economic, and the religious trouble which is making all the noise is merely covering up a big economic problem."

An American scientist who is writing a book on the Aztecs: " When Cortes came to Mexico there were 30,000,000 persons living in this country. They had a great civilization even if their religion did include human sacrifice. The Spanish Conquerors brought disease and slavery. The population is now 15,000,000. Epidemics and slavery killed more than 15,000,000. Civilization fell into decay. Some blame the church. The fact is that the first Catholic leaders, after destroying the Aztec civilization, began teaching the Christian civilization. The Aztecs made such great progress that the Spanish rulers were alarmed. They saw their régime would not last if the people became educated, so they ordered the priests to stop teaching the natives. For hundreds of years the Spanish aristocracy held the people in subjugation. Then came the modern successors, the big haciendados, the ranch and mine and oil landowners, who imposed chattel slavery. In the silver mines the mercury system of working killed every workman within three months. Hundreds of thousands were killed. The system of taking mountain men to the tropics and vice versa killed hundreds of thousands. A noble civilization perished and a fine people were degraded. It will take many years of freedom and free schools to uplift the people a bit."

An American geologist working for a big oil company: " The Mexican people are not Christian. The majority are pagans disguised. I will give you an instance. In Yucatan recently there was a drought. The peasants wanted rain. They went into their Catholic church and took out an image they called Saint Isidro. They placed the image in a cow yard and threw dung at it. They danced and screamed and prayed. Although they called the image by a Christian name it was actually the ceremony of Tlaloc, the Aztec god of rain.

" About the fourth day of this awful ceremony it began to rain. There was more dancing and more rejoicing, and the filthy statue of Saint Isidro was taken out of the cow yard and washed and painted red, just as the old Tlaloc statues used to be, and placed in the Catholic church again.

" What Mexico needs is a little Christianity."

One of the big American bankers: " Calles is an atheist. They say he is a Mason. Now I am a 33-degree Mason myself and know that an atheist cannot be a Mason.

" Calles is trying to do what Henry VIII did, establish his own church to supersede the Catholic church. Calles is an honest man but he is wrong-headed.

" The trouble with this country is it is absolutely bolshevistic. Capital is afraid to do business, to invest money, because it may be confiscated. Bolshevism in Mexico is a great danger to the United States.

" I once said to Obregon, let U. S. capital come in, let industry and agriculture flourish under our system, and in five years Mexico will be the richest country in the world. You can then double your income from taxation, the government will grow rich and you will be able to put through Calles' fine sounding program of reforms which no one doubts are needed. But you know that until they are educated up to it, the peons don't want the land you give them for nothing. They are not yet capable of taking the risks of being farmers, they prefer to work for others. And you have no capital to work with. Let the U. S. supply that and postpone your reforms a few years.

" Politics is back of most of the troubles. Politics are causing the economic depression, the worst in history, and the religious war too."

An American oil man, one of the newer arrivals: " I'll tell you the whole truth about Mexico, if no other American will: it is the best place to make money with the least effort. That's the only reason we have for being here. Otherwise we could remain at home. I'm here to make a million. I don't care a damn for Mexico, and neither does any other American resident here. I want to make my million quick and easy. That's why I'm here. When I make it I'm getting out and never want to see this country again."

One of the big lights of the American Chamber of Commerce: " The American investment in Mexico, which approaches two billion dollars, gives us some rights of protection. If some of the oil leases were obtained through fraud and graft and corruption during the Diaz régime, each case should be tried in court individually, but the rights of property under international law should be protected, and confiscation should not be permitted.

" At the present moment I see no protection unless through intervention of American forces."

An American newspaperman long resident in Mexico: " Calles is venting a personal spite against the church. He is

360

not a Mexican nor a Catholic. The Catholic church is the salvation of these poor people. It is the bulwark against Calles' system of Bolshevism and Calles is seeking to crush this spiritual force among the masses before putting through the whole bolshevistic program."

An American good-willer, or friend of the régime: "The old order, the Diaz crowd of grafters and slave-owners, cannot realize that a new day has come, and that idealism is replacing the exploitation of the people by the army, the church and big business."

So there you are. You pay your money and you take your choice.

Chapter VI

Calles

BEFORE going into Mexico and during my stay there I heard the following statements about Calles from otherwise reputable persons:

" Calles is an Arab, a Syrian, and not a Mexican."

" Calles is a fanatic against the Roman Catholic Church. He is a high degree Mason. He is a leading member of the Ku Klux Klan and is working with the American organization."

" Calles is a Bolshevik. He gets his orders from Moscow. He is the American head of the Third International. He studied Communism with Lenin and Trotsky in New York."

" Calles is the only honest man in Mexico. He is the Messiah of the Mexican workingman."

" Calles is a crook. All he is doing is making millions which he is investing in mines and in land in Sonora. He doesn't give a damn for the Mexican people."

Every man, Mexican and American, whom I met on the Texas border and in Mexico, had a definite conviction about Calles.

These facts, however, are obvious: (1) Calles is the only big dictator on the North American continent. (2) He is a fanatic against the Roman Catholic Church of Mexico and seeks to destroy it utterly. (3) He is a fanatic for the dictatorship of labour.

Is Calles a Bolshevik? Here is the testimony of Peter W. Collins of Boston, a lecturer who recently made a tour of Texas and caused great interest in his talks on Mexico. Collins, lecturing under the auspices of the Knights of Columbus, said: " Calles is a red dictator who desires to subjugate Mexico to Soviet rule. The present constitution of Mexico is taken from the Bible of communism written by Karl Marx."

Colonel McLemore, who publishes a paper in Texas, told me that Calles went to Moscow just before he became president, and received Bolshevik instructions and was made head of the American branch of the Third International.

Mr. X., one of the leading American bankers of Mexico City, said: " Calles is a Bolshevik. This country is absolutely bolshevistic. It is like Russia."

If Bolshevism means dictatorship by one man or one minority group then Calles is a Bolshevik, and so are Mussolini and Admiral Horthy and half a dozen others. If Bolshevism means dictatorship by one man or one minority group with a certain definite program based on Marxian doctrines, then neither Mussolini nor Calles are Bolsheviks.

Mussolini is a dictatorial product of peculiar Italian circumstances and Calles is a dictatorial product of peculiar Mexican circumstances. Calles has denied ever being in Russia; the time of his alleged trip was spent in Berlin, where I interviewed him and where he got the greater part of his plan for the co-operative farm system he is fostering. Calles never met Lenin or Trotsky in New York, as his enemies claim.

But that Calles is profoundly impressed by red radical ideas there is also no doubt. He is using them just as Mussolini is using them.

Russia produced Bolshevism but the present system is being called Leninism. Italy produced Fascism, but the present system is becoming so different that its leaders call it Mussolinism.

And Mexico is producing something which has no name but which might be called Callesism.

The Soviets have tried hard to destroy all religion; Calles has passed laws prohibiting any priest or minister to function and has deported all foreign-born ministers who are Roman Catholics, but has smiled encouragement upon Bishop Creighton of the American Episcopal Church and encouraged other Protestant ministers.

The Soviets have destroyed the liberty of the press, public assembly, political action and free speech. Mussolini has destroyed the liberty of the press, public assembly, individual rights and free speech. Now comes Calles and destroys the liberty of the press, public assembly, political action and free speech. Only Calles is not half as strong as his guiding stars, and does things only half way.

The Soviets make it treason, punishable by death, for a workingman to strike; Mussolini follows with a so-called labour charter which makes the Italian workingman less than a free citizen, and Calles works for the complete dictatorship of the workingman. All three systems are dictatorial, but there are vast differences in each, and one name cannot cover the three.

Calles' radicalism is directed chiefly against the Roman Catholic Church because he blames the church for everything that has been wrong in Mexico. In a pamphlet published in the United States the present Mexican régime has stated first of all that the church of Mexico is no more like the Catholic Church in the United States than Mohammedanism is like Christianity. It blames the church for participating in every rebellion and war since the time of Cortes. It accuses the church of everything evil, including slavery, peonage, ignorance, the illiteracy of the masses, the lack of civilization, etc., etc.

364

Calles believes all this and it has made him a fanatic. He is out to end the domination of the church in state affairs and his followers point out that Juarez, the George Washington of Mexico, deported the priests, confiscated the wealth of the church, and was even more bolshevistic than Calles when he (Juarez) refused to pay the foreign debts.

Calles has had offers of help from the Ku Klux Klan of the United States and has refused. The Ku Kluxers, however, once opened up headquarters in Mexico City. One day the leading newspaper, *Excelsior,* published a satirical attack on them, saying that Mexicans could not join because of the high cost of white sheets. The Kluxers sent a death threat to the editor. He attacked them again. The Kluxers marched on the *Excelsior* offices.

Now in Mexico everyone who can afford a revolver carries one. The Kluxers marched on the office and every editor and reporter went to the window and began a fusillade. The leader and two followers of the Klux idea fell dead. The K. K. K. organization, which thought Mexico, owing to its anti-Catholic campaign, was ripe for it, went out of business. Some headquarters in Alabama is still sending out wild propaganda in which a death-mask always appears in the Pope's tiara, but even fellow fanatics of Calles refuse to have anything to do with the K. K. K. They have nothing against the Catholic Church of the United States or Europe, they say, and they even draw a line between the church which has the white Spanish educated following in Mexico and what they term the Pagan-Aztec-Catholic church which the Aztec and Toltec and Maya Indian masses of Mexico worship today.

Calles has three great fanaticisms. He is determined to give the Mexican Hierarchy a death-blow and to establish a dictatorship of labour. His third complex is agriculture. He does not care as much for the vast oil and silver and gold deposits and the other easy means of refinancing the Mexican state as he does for making the peon into a farmer. Roads, irrigation, agricultural schools, land banks, farm co-operatives, land distribution, all these are part of the program for restoring the ancient peasantry, and Calles' followers are even trying to replace the religion of the people with a moral code based on agriculture.

In this, however, Calles has been less successful than in his destructive program. He has taken the land away from the absentee landlord, divided the estates which ran into the million of acres, handed out farm implements, given away rich acres, sent out teachers and done everything humanly possible to bring the old peon back to the land, with but slow results.

The Indian has become accustomed to being either a slave or a hired man. He has never faced responsibility. He has never earned more than enough for corn, meal and pulque, the alcohol of the highlands. Everywhere you go you hear tales of disaster to the Calles agricultural program. The Indians have failed to cultivate the soil, or they have tilled some of the land and taken small profits and spent it on drink, or they have sold the hoes and spades and farm tractors and lived on the money.

Altogether Callesism has worked out more like Bolshevism than Fascism: it has been more successful with destroying old systems than in creating new ones. The church, the military system, the Cientifico or Spanish nobleman rule, are being hard hit in Mexico, but the constructive program has gone along very slowly.

* * * * *

Calles and the Catholic Attack

Immediately following the battle in the Spring of 1927 between the Catholic rebels and the Federal troops at Ocatlan in the State of Jalisco, President General Calles threw aside the pretences of democratic, republican government in Mexico and announced his dictatorship. This is one of the most vital facts of the situation in Mexico which the censorship has suppressed. The circumstances as related to me by one who was present were:

President Calles, furious when he learned that priests had participated in the battle, called in the editors of *Universal* and *Excelsior,* the two big Mexican papers. He handed them an official statement concerning the battle.

"You will print this statement, without change, without editorial comment, and without any headlines whatever," Calles ordered them. "In case you want any headlines, you may set the first paragraph in large type. Otherwise no change, no comment."

The editors protested.

"Gentlemen," replied Calles, "I accept no protests. From this day the presidency of Mexico ends: the dictatorship of Mexico begins."

Immediately following this open declaration of dictatorship, President Calles ordered a mobilization and clamped on a censorship. This censorship, which enraged the American and other foreign press representatives, was, according to the Calles' spokesmen, put into effect because the Roman Catholic Hierarchy in Mexico City had been sending military instructions to the rebels in Jalisco and other states where the fighting was going on.

The archbishops and bishops then resident in Mexico City, and who had been forced to register with the police every day, were deported. Hundreds of priests were placed under surveillance. Many have since been deported. It is estimated that almost 1,000 of the 4,000 resident Mexican priests were deported or have fled the country.

In carrying out his dictatorship, Calles ordered a meeting of his chief supporters, the labour council, which then voted the following program for their chief:

1. That priests be put on all trains crossing the war zone.
2. That the Knights of Columbus members holding government positions be fired.
3. That all Knights of Columbus be expropriated.
4. That the two big papers, *Excelsior* and *Universal,* on account of some or all of their stock being owned by the Catholic Church or by Catholic sympathizers, be taken by the government.
5. That so-called " Red and Black " or labour battalions be recruited for a final battle between church and state.

So far as the censorship of news to foreign countries is concerned the action taken by Calles has been accompanied with the same stupidities which has marked Bolshevik and Fascist censorships. To begin with it has been impossible to keep the real news from leaving the country, and on the other hand, with everyone doubting the news in the newspapers, the wildest and most sensational rumours have found credence.

As dictator, Calles also set about strengthening his internal position. One of his strangest and most unconventional actions was to call in members of the cabinet and other big leaders and lay down the law to them. They must either support him to the end or get out. Among the leaders called in were the Minister of Agriculture, Leon, and General Alvarez, Chief of Staff. According to information which had reached the dictator many leaders and cabinet members had been spending all their time with their mistresses in cabarets and private drinking parties, one of which took place regularly in (of all places) an American-Mexican dairy. Calles said: " You will either give up your mistresses and stand by me in this war with the church, or you can leave the government and devote yourselves to your women."

Calles began weeding out the pro-Catholic officers from the national army immediately following his declaration of dictatorship. Many minor officers were shifted or let out. Generals in command of troops were changed. Governors of states whose loyalty was doubted were being supplanted just when the Gomez-Serrano revolt broke out. In short, the whole régime was furiously at work strengthening all positions, material and moral, for war to the end.

" If the Calles-Obregon régime goes down," said one of the unofficial cabinet, " it will be with flying colours. It is a fight to the finish. The church has ruled for 400 years. It has been said that no one can break its power. It is true that even the president's closest friends have told him that he made his biggest mistake when he attempted to enforce the anti-church laws which have been dormant for so many years. But Calles is a fanatic in his war on the church and is risking his and his party's fate on it."

* * * * *

The Catholic Peace Plan

While blood was being shed daily in the war between the Catholic rebels and the government troops, who incidentally are also Catholics, a plan for peace between church and state had been drawn up, approved by the Pope, and placed in the hands of General Obregon, then military master of Mexico.

This plan was given to me by Archbishop Leopoldo Ruiz y Flores of Michoacan, acting secretary of the Episcopate from the time Archbishop Diaz was expelled until he himself was expelled last summer.

I found Archbishop Ruiz in hiding. It was before the Ocatlan train massacre. Yet despite the fact that he knew that the consequences of giving information to an American newspaperman would be punishment for himself, Archbishop Ruiz consented to permitting his name being used with this statement.

Archbishop Ruiz' opinion of the situation was this: " Calles has taken certain steps and the Roman Catholic Church has taken certain steps. Neither can retreat, for moral and spiritual reasons. But we believe that the Calles party has realized it has made a mistake. Its pride, however, makes it maintain its attitude. Within a short time, however, there will be a change in government. The leaders of the church feel that General Obregon will see the way to an amicable peace settlement, and therefore we have drawn up the plan which General Obregon requested us to, have obtained the approval of the Holy See to our action, and have placed the plan in the hands of Obregon." The document follows:

" The program of the bishops, clergy and conscientious Catholic people is clearly set forth in the petition presented to the Congress of the Union.

If this be examined dispassionately it will be seen that it limits itself in indispensable liberties.

"Until the reform of the constitution is brought about in the sense of that petition the bishops believe that the Holy See will approve the resumption of services in the churches only if things return to the state of *de facto* tolerance which existed in January 1925.

"If the government does not accede to this tolerance it behooves it to indicate the points of regulation which it does not believe prudent to cede so that the episcopate may bring them to the attention of the Holy See.

"We believe the Holy See would permit the registration of priests in charge of churches, especially if the prelate in charge of each makes it, it always being understood that this registration does not mean a licence from the civil authorities to exercise the functions of minister, that its object is purely a matter of record.

"We believe that the Holy See will tolerate the exclusion of foreign priests within certain limits, reserving for itself the right to have an apostolic delegate in Mexico.

"We believe the Holy See will tolerate the limitation of the number of priests, always with the understanding that there will be sufficient, in the judgment of the prelates, for the necessities and rites of the faithful.

"We believe that the Holy See would ask immediately liberty of instruction, worship, of association, of press, etc., etc., as well as respect for the property of the church and of its necessary edifices.

"This memorandum unsigned and with the approval of the archbishop of Mexico, Michoacan, Aguascalientes, Zamora and Saltillo, will be transmitted by the priest who, charged by Signor Obregon, requested it from the bishops.

March 20, 1927."

"When Obregon becomes president," was Archbishop Ruiz' comment on the plan, "we believe that the way out will soon be found. Peace between the church and the government may be expected shortly after either Obregon's election as president or a revolution which will place him in power above Calles.

"You will see from the peace plan that we cannot cede the principles of the church. The Holy See has instructed us to make no agreement without the approval of the Holy Father."

Another important reason which Archbishop Ruiz had for believing in an early peace was the admission made by Obregon that the United States was exerting its power to bring it about.

"In the meeting between the bishops and Obregon," continued Archbishop Ruiz, "the general said that great pressure was being brought on Calles through diplomatic channels and upon himself officially and unofficially by the American government and by influential Americans. The American government and the American people will therefore be largely to thank when peace is made."

Archbishop Ruiz, when I saw him in hiding, was dressed in simple civilian clothes. Other church dignitaries called upon him during the interview. They too, according to law, wore plain clothes, but when they entered the house they produced their birettas and put them on. Archbishop Ruiz spoke in English and in his own hand corrected the translation of the peace plan.

The Archbishop later went to Rome. The peace movement was interrupted by the assassination of Obregon, but what is now known as the Calles-Ruiz plan has been submitted to the Vatican and will probably be accepted by it and the Mexican government.

*　　*　　*　　*　　*

372

Mexico a Dictatorship of Labour

The United States must be prepared to face on its southern frontier a nation which is a complete labour dictatorship.

If the American Federation of Labour were suddenly to organize a political party whose one aim would be complete domination of American politics, and an army whose aim would be to supersede the United States Army, our home situation would parallel Mexico's.

In the Calles plan for the dictatorship of the labour unions the political arm is already functioning, although it is not complete, and the military arm is just being organized.

This is the most important movement in Mexico today, and to understand the Mexican situation it is necessary to recognize the fact that the Calles régime is building an economic, political and military dictatorship of labour.

Calles still is dictator. Morones was czar of labour. Obregon controlled the old army and had another army of 20,000 in the State of Sonora. But the more important fact is that while Obregon was the big military chief both he and Morones and Calles were simultaneously building up a new military organization in which the old Cientifico or Spanish officers will be absent and in which the soldiers will be not the soldiers belonging to some *jefe* or chief, some captain or colonel or general, but the labour soldiers of the labour dictatorship, who will be class conscious and nationalistic.

The present military situation in Mexico is amazing. There are 28 states each controlled by a *jefe* and each state has its troops and each military commander can start a civil war and try to capture the government. The history of Mexico from

1910 to the present day has been the conflicts between the troops belonging to generals, not to the Mexican nation.

Only among the savage tribes of Arabia is this situation paralleled. In Europe the system of troops belonging to dukes and princes, and the system of hiring troops to states or cities, passed away with the Renaissance. Nationalism came into being. In Mexico the feudal army system still exists but Calles is killing it.

To begin with, Calles has built up a federal army with better discipline and *esprit de corps* and equipment than has ever existed in Mexico since the days of Cortes. General Winans, the commander of the 32nd Division at Juvigny and now commanding Fort Bliss, told me that on his recent visit to Torreon he was amazed at what Calles had done with the national army.

But even this national army cannot be relied on too much to fight for the Calles régime. What happened when General Gomez marched west from Vera Cruz? What would happen if the Catholic Rebellion obtained the support of two or three generals of the west coast and marched east with their men? Would the national army maintain its national discipline? Nobody knows.

But the Calles régime does know that a new army, built from the labour unions, and imbued with the spirit of a labour dictatorship, would stick to the régime through all vicissitudes, political and religious. There have been " labour battalions " in action before. Only recently when the religious troubles reached a climax, the labour organizations volunteered to form labour battalions should Calles need them.

The nucleus of the labour dictatorship is the Confederacion Regional Obrera Mexicana, the C. R. O. M. or Mexican federation of labour. Morones told me that it has 1,800,000 members most of whom pay a few cents dues each week. Actually the body is sustained by the government. The Partido Laborista, or labour party, is the political arm. The military arm is still not organized well enough to have a name.

A great number of the men in the C. R. O. M. have been in the army at one time or another. During the uprising of de la Huerta the armed workingmen came into action. De la Huerta had among his troops small bodies of Communists. When de la Huerta was on top his army killed numerous labour leaders, and this led to the C. R. O. M. organizing its own men, equipping them with arms, and placing them at the disposal of Obregon.

Since that time armed labour groups have remained in Mexico. At one time, so Morones' office informs me, Samuel Gompers helped the C. R. O. M. obtain arms from the United States. Moreover, the C. R. O. M. today completely controls the munitions plants, and its heads are prepared to call a general strike in case any general attacks the labour government, and to turn over all munitions on hand to the labour party troops.

The C. R. O. M. today is openly opposed to the 28 generals who rule the 28 states of Mexico. This opposition has had its effect not only on the various divisions controlled by these *jefes,* but also on the national army, where, according to officers who have confided in me, there is a seething undercurrent of rebellion against the C. R. O. M. In fact, when I asked Morones to discuss various questions of the relation of the labour organization to the military organization, he was loath to answer these points.

" Peace depends on the workers organized politically and militarily," was all he would say.

In the new labour college, which began functioning last year, there is a course of military training for selected members of the C. R. O. M. These men will be trained to become officers for the new labour army, just as at present there is a military academy creating officers for the nationalist army.

The present handicap of the C. R. O. M. is that, of its membership of about 1,800,000, 80 per cent. of the peasants are illiterate and at least 40 per cent. of the industrial workers are illiterate. However, a great educational effort is being made.

Part of the C. R. O. M. is organized on the syndicalist basis. For example, one union, the graphic arts, includes everyone having to do with printing and publishing, from the men who cut the trees for wood-pulp to the artists and editors, and newsboys who sell the papers on the street. This, it will be noted, is an I. W. W. idea, although the I. W. W., founded by the Magon brothers, has practically disappeared in Mexico.

The program of the C. R. O. M. is " the socialization of all means of production and distribution," which is a program borrowed from Karl Marx, but just as Lenin had his " retreat from Communism," when he established the N. E. P. or New Economic Policy, and permitted private enterprise internally, so Morones has announced his " armistice in the class struggle." In other words, no matter what the program of labour dictatorship is, the leaders realize it cannot be enforced under present conditions, and are willing to postpone its radical tenets to some unspecified future day.

" The program today," said one of Morones' spokesmen, " is evolutionary, not revolutionary. The revolution in Mexico smashed the feudal system of 400 years and it would be foolhardy to try to undo a 400-year-old system in two or three years."

As evidence of the " armistice in the class struggle," the C.

R. O. M. offers the treaty signed between the 160 textile mill owners and the textile workers' union. Strikes are outlawed for a period of three years. A system of amicable settlement has been found satisfactory to employers and employees. No suspicion of labour dictatorship remains here. The employers are told they may now buy new machinery, modernize the industry, engage in large scale production, reduce prices below the present cost of imported fabrics, and otherwise engage in business for three years without fear of government confiscation or other acts of dictatorship.

The leaders of the C. R. O. M. from Morones down, emphasize the point that although their eventual aim is the dictatorship of labour, the C. R. O. M. is not bolshevistic. It has made its choice between Moscow and Washington, and has accepted Gompers and Green instead of Lenin and Trotsky. Any suggestion from the American Federation of Labour is law to the C. R. O. M.

So they say. Yet at the same time, militarily and politically, the C. R. O. M. is leading Mexican labour towards the goal of complete dictatorship.

* * * * *

Mexico, the Land of Corruption

Political, business, military, and some say, the old religious life of Mexico were or are infested by corruption and graft on a scale unheard of in any other country in the world, with the possible exception of Marie's Roumania.

One of the secretaries of President Calles got about $20 a week and is building a half million dollar house. It is said that Calles knew nothing about it, but that certain interests which want things presented "right" to the president have made the house possible.

Members of the chamber of deputies get $500 per month. Most of them have no other income, or very little. Yet almost every man after becoming a deputy buys himself one of the best American automobiles, which in Mexico costs about $10,000.

It has been customary for the director of the military factories to leave his post after six months several times a millionaire. Five thousand dollars a month graft is supposed to be the right thing for assistant directors to accept.

The four gambling houses in Mexico City, I am informed by friends of the present régime, pay 1,000 pesos or about $500 a day to each of the following officials: the chief of police, the general in command of the state, the governor of the state and a minor official in the president's office.

In San Antonio, in New York and in Paris there are thousands of Mexicans living on millions made quickly and easily through graft in their home towns.

To be appointed general or governor of one of the 28 Mexican states means to have the right to make a certain number of millions by graft and corruption.

Some of the graft goes to the upkeep of the troops under command. The troops get paid just so much, and must keep themselves. That is why the wives and children of Mexican soldiers live with them and accompany them on the march. Battles and victories mean loot for the soldiers, graft for the general.

All this is so because there is still no national spirit in Mexico. The soldiers belong to their feudal lord. They fight for money.

In industry, Calles is trying to supplant the graft system by decent pay and patriotic sentiment. But according to hundreds of persons, Americans as well as Mexicans, one man cannot change a system of centuries, a system which reached its greatest corruption only recently, when Diaz, the companion of the liberator Juarez and the idol of Mexico, grew old and fell into the hands of the most notorious group of grafters that ever sold out a nation.

Astonished by almost incredible histories of graft and corruption from Diaz' day to this, I deliberately asked one hundred persons the same question: " Is there one honest man in Mexican political life? " I asked this of every American beginning with the American ambassador and winding up with a busted adventurer in a second-class hotel. I asked this of every business man, every American official I met, all the newspapermen and their wives, all the Mexican officials and business men I met, the hotel help and the few American so-called " goodwillers."

Eighty said Calles was the only honest man in Mexican political life today, ten said Morones, then minister of labour, nine said Obregon, then the power in the army, and one said Soto y Gama, one of the old revolutionary leaders, now not much in evidence.

" If you can get to Calles you can get justice," was the slogan of the Americans. But they pointed out how hard it was for thousands of American business men to bring all their problems to Calles. Most of the time they had to pay graft or abide adverse conditions.

The head of an American international industry pointed out a case. His workmen belong to a union of their own, not affiliated with the Mexican labour federation. One day a new employee was found to be a radical agitator. According to the agreement he could not be discharged. He was let alone. Soon he began agitating a strike. At the same time he approached the American director of this enterprise with a blackmail proposition. He was turned down. He then resumed his agitation, and within a few days a committee waited on the American with notice they would strike the next day.

The American, being an American, went directly to Calles' office. He said:

" Mr. President, I have received notice that my men are going on strike tomorrow. I am not here to argue their rights or mine, or wages, or working hours. I have here the contract which says that the union must give ten days' notice of a strike. I want justice."

Calles replied:

" I am always on the side of labour when there is any compromise to be made. I favour labour against capital when there is a question of justice. But I will not stand for labour breaking its contract. Go back to the works and tell this union that if they strike I will outlaw them. I will permit you to employ non-union labour. I will help you to break the strike, and if the union attempts violence, I will call out national troops to fight them."

The American, a one-time high officer in the American army, went back to the plant. He told the men exactly what had happened. They confirmed the facts. There was no strike and the American company found that it met no opposition when it got the agitator beaten up and driven out of the state.

In another case a workingman suing a company applied to the national board of conciliation, which promptly handed down a decision in the workingman's favour. The company had a suspicion that the man had paid graft to a member of the board. It appealed directly to Calles. Calles held an investigation and heard from a secret agent that the usual graft and corruption were at work, this time in Calles' own pet board of conciliation. He ordered the order revoked. The company was saved several thousand dollars, the board of conciliation got a shake-up, and again it was shown that when it was possible to get even a minor dispute before Calles there would be justice instead of corruption.

Chapter VII

THE BOLSHEVIK PLOT

IN Mexico there is a Bolshevik movement against the United States. It may be called a plot, because it is a part of the Third International's plot against bourgeois governments the world around. In Mexico Bolshevism is taking a small revenge against America for our non-recognition policy.

But before I write another word about the red activities below the Rio Grande I must express the opinion that the action of the state department in calling in the representatives of the American press in Washington and delivering to them a harrowing tale of wild plotting to make the United States communist and arm Central America and the Antilles against us, is probably the most fantastic stupidity perpetrated by a foreign office in modern times.

On November 18, 1926, America was alarmed by headlines in thousands of papers which told of Russia's plot. The news itself, though not as sensational as the headlines, was exaggerated, unfounded in fact, unsupported by evidence. The column began:

"Washington, November 17 (A. P.). — The spectre of a Mexican-fostered Bolshevist hegemony intervening between the United States and the Panama Canal has thrust itself into American-Mexican relations, already strained."

As regards Bolshevik activities in Mexico I can give here the results of my three months' investigation:

There can be no doubt that the Third International (which is of course a part of the Russian communist movement) is concentrating upon Central and South American nations, trying to league their public opinions against the country which promulgated the Monroe Doctrine. With their congenitally profligate use of words, the Soviets promise financial and moral aid. They carry on their intrigue according to instructions from Moscow, as outlined in open and secret sessions of the International each November, and in the same way as the work is done in Berlin and other European capitals and as it may be done some day in Washington. The orders are to use the embassy, consulates and trade missions, all diplomatically immune centres, for propaganda and for furthering the international communist movement (or plot if you so prefer to call it).

Mme. Kollantay was Russia's ambassador during my visit to Mexico. In her high-minded, cultured and charming way she was directing the communist plot in a dozen countries. There were sixteen departments in her office, each devoted to a Central or South American country or group of islands, or to a special function such as press propaganda or to supporting leagues or clubs or movements anti-United States in aim or spirit.

The Russian embassy is second only to that of the United States in size and number of employees. The United States does the largest business in Mexico; the Russian does almost no business. Its only real function is anti-United States activity.

During the ambassadorship of Petkowski the Third International openly subsidized the communist organ, *El Machete,* which started with 3,000 circulation. Under Kollantay's supervision this propaganda sheet which continually attacks the Mexican federation of labour (C. R. O. M.) and the United States, reached a circulation of 70,000, a remarkable figure in a country where some eighty per cent. of the population is illiterate, and where the big Mexican papers have about half that number of buyers. Of course almost no one buys *El Machete*. It is paid for by Moscow and given free to anyone who sympathizes with its cause.

The Russian embassy, consulate and other official agencies are sending agitators throughout the country. They are concentrating at present on the oil camps, the textile factories and the railroad unions. I have talked to American oil men who have found Bolshevik agitators coming into the camps as workingmen, or attaching themselves to the camps as hangers-on. In every case these men dominate the meetings. They make the speeches and they read the inflammatory matter from *El Machete* to the hundreds of workers who cannot read or write but who, in these unsettled times in Mexico, are good listeners.

Russian agents, disguised as peddlers, go through the country-side ostensibly selling cheap goods but really preaching red doctrines. Sometimes when a peasant says " I cannot buy, I am too poor," these Moscow agents reply, " Arise and take. Take the land. Take the factories. Prepare for the dictatorship of the proletariat." Frequently such agitation has led to excesses; at all times it has led the ex-peon to sympathize with the views of the agent.

Occasionally, when there is a big strike, there is a little money from Moscow. The railroad workers, who are called the " aristocrats of labour," and who refuse to join the C. R. O. M., received 30,000 roubles from Russia. The embassy denied transmitting it, saying it came direct by mail. Nevertheless there is no doubt the embassy was the instrument for obtaining it.

The day I arrived in Mexico I thought a revolution had broken out. There were crowds swarming the streets and marching on the palace. Agitators were making speeches and shaking their fists at Calles' office. A friend translated. It turned out to be a meeting to protest the Schick diphtheria vaccination.

The importance of the demonstration lay in the fact that two elements immediately got possession of the mob, the anti-government element and the Bolshevik element. Agents of the latter were soon gathering signatures to a circular *contra el imperialismo Yanqui,* " against Yankee imperialism," and even blaming vaccination deaths on the United States.

Communist literature, proletarian dictatorship literature, anti-church literature, is flooding the industrial camps, especially the oil districts. In movie shows, labour meetings, and at parties where the great feature is a magic lantern, the Soviet agents are preaching. They also teach their listeners how to read and write. There is a great wave of emancipation sweeping through Mexico and the Bolsheviks are among the first to capitalize it for their own interest. They are even trying to substitute Communism for the religion of the waning church.

A large hatred but small success against the United States, that is Moscow's portion in Mexico. Why no success? I think this is the vital answer: Labour has refused to become Russianized. The C. R. O. M. leaders declare the American Federation of Labour has promised and is giving full support, and would even aid the Calles régime with shipments of arms and ammunition, on the one condition that the Mexican Government discourage the spread of Bolshevism south of the frontier.

The Soviet embassy grits its teeth and seeks other ways to attack the United States. If it cannot control the C. R. O. M. it can control other labour organizations in Mexico and it believes certainly that it can organize other Latin-American States.

While most of the bolshevising is done secretly, there are times when the movement comes out in the open. For a year now the Soviet embassy has been trying to hold a congress of all Latin-American communist parties. The delegates from almost every state had actually arrived in Mexico City, and had actually held their first meeting when they were exposed by American newspapermen. This publicity forced the government to act. The government found it couldn't afford to offend the A. F. of L., and outlawed the meeting. Another attempt followed. This also was exposed. If the congress has actually been held within the past few months, it was done secretly.

The Liga Anti-Imperialista de las Americas, fostered by Russia in Mexico, is not much to worry about. Even the Bolsheviks there confess the United States is a wall they cannot scale. They would like to use Calles as a step-ladder but so long as the A. F. of L. stands by, and Calles and his successors stick to the A. F. of L., there is no danger of Bolshevism gaining labour control. The slogan "Down with American Imperialism" may sound dangerous, but it is only a festive firecracker.

For reasons best known to herself Mexico prefers the United States to Russia.

Chapter VIII

I Report on Mexico to Secretary Kellogg and Mr. Green

ON my return to Chicago from Mexico City I was requested to make a report to the secretary of state. Accordingly I went to Washington and had a long talk with Mr. Kellogg whom I found extremely well informed on all developments, but as extremely prejudiced, I felt, as any of his embassy reporters. Mr. Kellogg believed just what Mr. Sheffield and his assistants wanted him to believe. I suppose the state department cannot do otherwise. What are diplomatic representatives for if they cannot be entrusted absolutely to mould international opinions?

I did not hesitate, however, to express mine. It was simply that I believed both the press and political agencies of America unfair in their general attitude to Calles and Mexico. I repeated what I considered the one outstanding difference between the other countries in which I had travelled and worked and Mexico: in these thirty-seven some American reporters and some American diplomats find at least some few things to praise: in Mexico it is all hatred.

Mr. Kellogg registered surprise.

The next day he called me at my hotel and questioned me for more details, then asked me to visit Assistant Secretary Robert E. Olds. Mr. Olds was particularly anxious to know about Bolshevik activities in Mexico and gratified to hear that they existed and were dangerous to the policies of the United States in the Caribbean. He wanted to know particularly about the relationship between the C. R. O. M. and the Bolsheviks, and I told him that to the best of my knowledge and belief the C. R. O. M. was loyal to its agreement to fight Bolshevism in co-operation with the American Federation of Labour and with the understanding that the A. F. of L. would support Mexican labour and advise the Coolidge régime to support the Calles régime.

(One of my indirect rewards for all this was the accusation by the attorney for the Soviet government, later, that I had been sent to Mexico as a state department spy against Calles.)

On arriving in New York a week later I was asked by a representative of the president of the A. F. of L. to give him a report of my trip to Mexico. He asked if I would care to repeat what I told Mr. Kellogg and Mr. Olds. I offered to do so and later was asked to make a written report for use at the coming convention of the unions, when their Mexican policy would be discussed. The report, which is dated June 1, 1927, follows:

In making this report to you I would like to preface it with the opinion that the state department, Washington, seems to be completely mis-informed on the situation in Mexico. This, I believe, is due to the reports from the American ambassador, Mr. Sheffield, and his staff. The attitude of the American embassy in Mexico City can best be illustrated by this statement made to me by one of its secretaries, who said:

" Anyone who is a friend of Mexico is a traitor to the United States."

This same secretary continued by calling Messrs. Roberto Haberman, Robert Hammond Murray, Dr. Ernest Greuning and other Americans who are friends of Mexico " skunks." He further stated that it was treason to work for any Mexican organization, etc., etc. In fact, the tenor of my interviews with embassy officials was a song of hate. I got the impression that we were actually in a state of war with Mexico, or about to declare war. This attitude of the American embassy is retailed to most all American residents of Mexico, and especially to the newspaper corps, so that all you hear in Mexico from American sources is anti-Mexican. This is an unusual situation. In every country in the world there are some Americans, from the Ambassador down to the adventurers, who find something to like or admire in the country to which they are sent officially or where they are earning their living. Mexico is the exception.

There seems to be no doubt that the Mexican government, the Partida Laborista and the C. R. O. M. are one and the same thing, just as the Third International, the Communist Party and the Politburo and other organizations ruling Russia, are one and the same. Technically, of course, they are separate. But with what might be called " interlocking directorates," the direction of all organizations, official and lay, by the same people or the same clique makes them one company.

I did see Morones and although he promised Haberman a written reply to the set of questions I left with him, I never got a reply, thanks to Haberman's procrastination. However, I did have a talk with Morones, who cheerfully explained how the labour movement, the C. R. O. M., the Calles government and the official labour party were working together to establish a labour dictatorship. I questioned him on military plans for the labor party. He seemed shy on answering this orally but said that any time the Calles régime would be threatened by anti-labour forces, the labour movement, the C. R. O. M. etc., would supply labour battalions, just as they did during the Huerta affair. He said there were thousands of men in the labour unions who had retained their rifles and would fight when necessary. He also said that when the new labour university would open next year there would be a course of military training to make labour men officers, so that they could rely on class conscious officers whereas they cannot rely on the present officers from the regular military academy.

The religious revolt for the moment is dying down. The Calles government has occupied all the important strategic points and so far no general commanding a state has joined the rebels with his troops. That, of course, is the pivotal question. The rebels are at present led by a few soldiers, a few officers and a few priests. They have no real leadership.

However, there is pride instead of secrecy regarding the part that Bishop Orozco and scores of priests are playing. In Mexico they boast of the fact the priests are leading all the rebel bands. Why shouldn't they? It is a civil war and they will be heroes if they win. It is only in the United States that Catholics deny the military activities of the church.

I will not attempt to express an opinion as to who is right. But you must realize that the Catholic Church of Mexico is no more like the Catholic Church of the United States than the latter is like the Mohammedan church. The Mexican masses are not half Christianized. They are more than half pagan. They worship Catholic saints with the same excitement and the same ritual they worshipped Quetzacoatl and other Aztec gods. Another big point: the church in Mexico has since the year 1520 or so been engaged in temporal affairs. The church has been on one side or another in every war and rebellion. Hidalgo and Morales I believe were priests who fought for the masses; in other wars as in the wars against Diaz, the church supported the Spanish rulers. But the fact I must emphasize is that *the church has participated in every war*. The Calles régime also blames the church for the terrible ignorance and poverty of the country at present and for its indulgence of chattel slavery, peonage, and all the horrors of the past 400 years. The present troubles arose when the Calles government instituted public schools to emancipate the masses from terrible ignorance and poverty, and the church refused to let its communicants attend the public schools. One act led to another. The church declared a boycott and Calles ordered the expulsion of the Spanish-born foreign priests. The church called a strike and Calles called for the expulsion of the bishops. The priests led the attack on the train, a horrible massacre almost unparalleled in modern history, and Calles declared himself dictator and vowed fanatically to destroy the Catholic church completely.

There are two sides to this question; it would be foolish to say one is right, one wrong. The church and Calles both have acted without moderation. Fanaticism features both sides. However, the few moderate liberal people I saw believe that after the 1928 election, when Obregon or some other liberal will be elected, it will be easier to patch up a peace, because Calles on the one hand and the leaders of the church on the other have gone too far to retreat and compromise. Regarding Gomez:

I Report on Mexico to Secretary Kellogg and Mr. Green

Arnulfo Gomez, governor of Vera Cruz, is the anti-Calles candidate for president. He is backed by the Catholics and the American oil interests. The big American oil companies are supplying the money. The K. of C., according to one of their Mexico City men, will supply an unlimited amount.

However, I do not believe much in the Gomez or other factions. I think that the Calles-Obregon-Morones régime will survive. Calles has his grip on everything. Obregon has 18,000 of an army of 20,000 he is raising in Sonora in case the regulars (Federales) do not stand by Calles. Calles has rejuvenated the regulars. General Winans, who saw the manœuvres in Torreon recently, says Calles has the best army ever seen in Mexico.

My personal opinion is this: I believe that the United States government should support the present régime in Mexico. Calles is a fanatic, but there are other men, liberals, not radicals, just a few, but honest, who want to save Mexico from continuation in the 400 years of ignorance, slavery and terrorism. If we change our attitude to friendship, instead of ambassadorial hatred, we can do more than by intervention. Even Calles would listen to some friendly gesture. They would repeal the confiscation oil laws, compromise with the church, and live at peace with us if we showed the least indication of wanting friendship instead of military intervention.

Part VI — The Rest of Europe

Chapter I

AMERICAN AMBASSADORS AS CENSORS

WHILE Henry Morganthau was occupying the building in Constantinople, an American newspaperman chalked under the sign " American Embassy " the words " All interests served here except American."

This sentiment is a genuine reaction felt by thousands of Americans who visit many of our embassies, legations and consulates, and then go to the newspaper offices, sink despondently into arm-chairs and voice patriotic indignation.

What are ambassadors for, they demand. Are they sent abroad to represent America and to be of service to Americans abroad, or are they social parasites who bow charmingly over the perfumed finger-nails of pseudo-countesses and slightly decayed old-world nobility? Are ambassadorial duties chiefly entertainment and one annual Fourth of July oration at the American Club?

They certainly shine on that day. If anyone is under the impression that travel is a liberal education and residents abroad are different from all the Rotarians, Kiwanians and Babbitts at home, let him attend a banquet and listen to the average American ambassador pull the eagle around by his tail feathers, refer to the United States as " God's own green foot-stool," use such new and grand expressions as " greatest country on the face of the earth," preach " service " and " a little co-operation " in the same gorgeous platitudinarian manner which characterizes similar meetings in all the go-getter metropolises of the home country-side.

What the American abroad really needs, strange to say, is actually a little Rotarian service. He is a stranger and is always being taken in. The Rotarian idea of service, which he has begun to be a little ashamed of, and of which there may be a surfeit at home, is completely missing abroad, so away goes the victim to the embassy, legation or consulate to seek advice and help.

But most of our diplomats abroad are unaccustomed to being of service to anyone, let alone just plain citizens. Many of them are very wealthy men who have never come in contact with the people and do not intend to lower themselves now that they live in a civilized nation where class lines are sharp and " it just isn't done." And they certainly did not come to Europe to be bothered by Americans, they would tell you if they could tell the truth.

Their chief activity, as is well known, is to represent America in things America doesn't give a good tinker's damn for, namely, social functions. Here they believe they fulfil a noble mission. They call themselves " the better Americans " and tell British (especially British) and Italian and Lettish and other society to judge America not by the loud business man, the non-spat-wearing reporters, the cane-less tourists, the rather rough sales-man who knows only his calling, or by all the nasty reports about bootlegging and Chicago and lynchings, but by them, the diplomatic representatives, " the better Americans," who are better, they believe, because they have given up being Americans and adopted all the soft hand-kissing ways of civilized Europe.

" What disgusts me most here," said Mayor Walker of New York in one of his amazing speeches at a foreign banquet, " is to find that the ambassador to a foreign country in a couple of years gets more British than a Britisher, more Spanish than a Spaniard, more French than a Frenchman. They seem to be ashamed of their Americanism when they come into the courts of Europe."

They are. And they wear out their figurative knees cringing and crawling before such men as Mussolini, de Rivera, Lloyd George, Poincaré and other dictators and strong statesmen. They have fallen so low in the diplomatic gutter that they have not only ceased to defend their own citizens, but have let their own colleagues in the service suffer insults and broken skulls without much protest. There was a time when the state department was young and strong and could startle a world with its cry, "Pericardes Alive or Raisuli Dead." Today it seems to cringe and whine, "Long Live Mussolini, no matter how many American consuls are bloodied by Fascisti."

In fact American diplomacy is so cowardly, so hypocritical, such a bootlicker of Fascismo, that it not only has accepted insult and assault, but it has suppressed the news in both Washington and Rome. Let me be more specific: The assault on acting Consul-General Franklin C. Gowen at Leghorn was reported several weeks after it happened and the diplomatic agencies had thought it history, when someone accidentally or intentionally carried the report all the way to London. The attack on Earl Brennan, vice-consul in Rome, came to light just a week after it happened because another American vice-consul, angry that his own service had failed to publish the facts, told them to a reporter in Paris, so that *The Chicago Tribune* in Chicago was able to print this Fascist victory. (Incidentally the Paris edition of *The Chicago Tribune,* which obtained the story, refused to print more than a line or two because it had already lost considerable Italian tourist advertising through my deportation from Italy.)

Acting Consul-General Gowen stood on the curb watching a blackshirt parade. He had saluted the Italian flag when it passed, but apparently failed to salute a private black flag of the Fascist organization. He was clubbed, beaten to the ground, later taken to a hospital.

Mussolini apologized to Ambassador Fletcher. Weeks later Mr. Fletcher had to explain to the press corps. Mussolini had said it was a regrettable accident; Mr. Gowen had been mistaken for an Italian; Mr. Gowen's hospital bill of 200 lire, $8 then, would be paid by the Italian government.

I tried to get more facts from Gowen. His letter to me is marked " private and unofficial," so I regret not being able to publish it. I telegraphed our Washington bureau to find out what the American government meant to do. The reply sent by the man who went to the state department with my telegram read: " Kellogg announced Gowen incident settled satisfactorily." (The hospital bill of $8 had been paid.) The Fascist foreign office asked all Italians representing American newspapers to pass over this " unfortunate affair " lightly and easily, and to forget it. It was forgotten. Mr. Gowen was transferred from Italy.

The case of Consul Brennan is much more serious because, take it from a fellow consul, it was premeditated and in revenge for Brennan's activities in enforcing the emigration law, so that numerous Fascisti, guilty of political terrorism and civil crimes, such as murder and robbery, found it impossible to get visas for America.

Brennan was attacked by uniformed Fascist militia, members of that vast organization which Mussolini has made superior to the regular army and by which he has intimidated the king, the nobility and their army. Among the attackers was a member of Mussolini's body-guard. Mr. Brennan had gone into a shop to buy a film. On emerging he was identified as the vice-consul sought, was clubbed and stoned until he was unconscious. The next day *Chargé d'affaires* Warren D. Robbins, in the absence of Ambassador Fletcher, sent a protest to Mussolini's office. But the facts were withheld from the press. Later when newspapermen tried to cable a few mild words, the telegrams were suppressed by the foreign office.

Mussolini eventually apologized to the embassy. The state department eventually reported the incident satisfactorily settled. Mr. Brennan in due time recovered from his wounds, and it is assumed that his hospital bill of perhaps another $8 was paid by the Fascist régime. And, I have to state, the fact that meagre reports of both these incidents were published long after they happened made them lose their value, so that terrorist Fascism was not much hurt nor did its terrorists learn any lesson of respect for American citizens. Thus terrorism and censorship have made aides and abettors of American diplomacy.

In scores of other cases where Americans have been assaulted by Fascisti our official agencies abroad have acted in the most half-hearted fashion. When a British subject gets into trouble abroad it is wonderful to see the way the British government flies to his rescue and many Americans, including many of my newspaper colleagues, have frequently obtained aid from the British. The British diplomatic view-point seems to be: " He is a Briton, therefore he is probably right "; the American view-point: " He is an American, therefore most probably he is in the wrong."

The "better Americans" who represent us abroad have better things to do than to serve plain Americans.

My first disillusioning experience with American diplomats in the rôle of protectors of American liberty was in April, 1920, when Paul E. De Mott, a youth of twenty-one, whose home was in Paterson, N. J., and whose record as a Quaker relief worker in the Argonne was highly satisfactory, met his death in a German prison. De Mott had been riding around in the Ruhr district in that murderous month which followed the capture of Berlin by the monarchists under Dr. Kapp, and the subsequent republican victory.

In the Ruhr district, which was also my assignment, the civil war lasted until May. With the defeat of the monarchists there sprang up a sort of socialistic proletarian army which was promptly denounced as Bolshevik. No doubt there were Bolshevik agents among them, but we who had joined the republican forces at Essen saw no change in their colour as they continued fighting, and the poor devils of soldiers were under the impression that they were fighting monarchists, and not Ebert's republican troops.

These last captured De Mott and shot him. De Mott had made three mistakes: he had come in a grey Quaker uniform which was not unlike that of the workingmen rebels; he had ridden in an automobile in which some of the rebels had concealed rifles, and he had carried letters written to Lenin and Trotsky, because he had intended going to Russia to obtain an interview for a small American newspaper and a still smaller magazine.

When De Mott was murdered by the German reichswehr we had no ambassador in Berlin but a diplomatic mission headed by Ellis Loring Dresel. To the American correspondents who made inquiries the mission replied, "Nothing to bother about, the man was a Bolshevik." Whereupon most of the Berlin correspondents dropped the matter.

I went to Wesel and came into the courtroom in time for the sitting of the military court of inquiry. De Mott's effects were spread on the major's desk. Evidence was given. From the letters, papers and evidence it was quite plain that De Mott was no Bolshevik and that he had been murdered in cold blood. The best the reichswehr officers could say was that he took the wrong turn in the hall while looking for the prison lavatory. The German authorities had never notified the American mission of the capture, let alone the murder. The mission greedily swallowed all German explanations, because the moment the letters to Lenin and Trotsky were mentioned the red flag of Bolshevism had stampeded them, and to this day, so far as I know, there have been no reparations to either the American government or the Quaker family of the deceased. And all this took place at a time when the French were getting a million gold francs and a salute for the death of one of their men in Berlin.

My last experience with diplomatic censorship was in December, 1927, when refugees in Budapest told of the assault of an American, Captain Winfield Keller, at Oradea Mare (formerly Grosswardein) in the Hungarian land occupied and annexed by Roumania after Hungary had been made militarily impotent.

Captain Keller saw service with the American army in France and later did some organizing work for the Young Men's Christian Association; he married and engaged in business in this frontier town which became the scene of serious anti-Hungarian and anti-semitic outrages. Roumanian young manhood, the flower of the Roumanian universities, five thousand strong, girls as well as men, rioted and looted for three days, stabbing or clubbing several hundred persons, but always when they outnumbered their victims twenty or eighty to one. Thus they showed Roumania's moral right of occupation.

Captain Keller was one of the most dangerously injured victims. He was part-owner of a printing-press which was hired by Hungarians to publish their paper. He was atrociously beaten and knifed by Roumanians who knew him and who had pretended friendship until the university men and women joined them in the attack. Mrs. Keller telegraphed to the American minister in Bucharest, Mr. Culbertson, and when the Roumanian authorities refused to forward her telegrams, for which they had accepted money, she came to the capital to ask help.

The legation concealed the fact of the attack on the American so cleverly that the American newspapermen knew nothing about it until their Vienna and Budapest co-workers, who had had the news from refugees, informed them by coded telegrams or by letter. When they protested, the legation declared its business was to take matters up diplomatically for settlement. Interrogated by the American press representatives, it admitted that one of its duties was to protect American interests and enterprises, and that the American newspapers came under the second heading, which showed rather rare perception, because many of our foreign officials hold the old-fashioned view that the newspaper is a parasite rather than a legitimate business. Nevertheless the legation thought that it was best to keep the news out of the public prints.

One more incident of a different character involving a financial not a physical violence: During one of the recent Polish upheavals the Warsaw censorship tried to prevent two Ameri-

can reporters from telling the world how Pilsudski had mobilized troops for the purpose of intimidating or ousting Parliament if they refused his budget. This time, fortunately, there
was no list of dead and wounded, so the Polish embassies in
Washington and Paris protested " exaggerated reports in the
American press." Then followed an amazing incident. One
of our several minor officials called the American reporters to
his office and said:

" The Polish government has floated several loans through
American bankers. The representatives of one of these big companies has cabled to say your dispatches have bent the market.
The bonds are down several points. In the future you must
send out only news favorable to Poland."

The reporters answered in three short, well-chosen syllables
and later tried to complain to the minister, but they obtained
no general satisfaction.

With the exception of one member (the *Associated Press* correspondent who is an employee of the legation) the American
press corps in Poland is (in 1927 and 1928) in conflict with the
American minister. The newspapermen feel with Mayor
Walker that here is a case of an American citizen becoming
more Polish than a Pole. During the early days of the Pilsudski
dictatorship in 1927 the press was anxious to obtain certain
facts which it believed the legation could give; especially during the Zagorski kidnapping (and probable murder). One day
a Warsaw newspaper was confiscated by Pilsudski because it
declared that the general's nephew had talked " with the minister of the greatest foreign power," who had confided to him
that Zagorski had been assassinated and his body destroyed by
the unofficial Chekah which flourishes under Pilsudski.

Attempts to obtain a statement from Mr. John B. Stetson, the American minister, were futile. A secretary informed the representatives of one New York and one Chicago newspaper that "Mr. Stetson is not satisfied with the anti-Pilsudski news you have sent out."

In every capital in Europe there are colleagues who could swell the list of incidents. Behind them all is the obvious fact that there is no co-operation between American diplomacy abroad and the men who help make public opinion. How important the foreign correspondent is, is a matter of opinion; that he is important is undeniable, and while a visitor like Lindbergh performs an act of amity very rarely, the American reporter functions day in and day out as an agent for friendship and good-will between peoples and nations.

On two occasions I have had the opportunity of pleading with the secretary of state for greater co-operation between diplomacy and the press. I found Secretary Hughes intelligently and enthusiastically interested. He assured me he was in favour of complete confidence between the official and private agencies of public understanding. Mr. Kellogg also seemed under the impression that the sublimated international reporters who serve him as ambassadors and ministers were working hand in hand with the newspaper representatives.

But there seems to be no fixed state department policy to encourage such relationships.

Journalists of all European governments especially the British and French and Italian, co-operating completely with their diplomatic representatives abroad, are entrusted with the political policies of their nations; their advice is sought and they are completely in each others' confidence.

The United States, not having a permanent foreign office

which functions for the benefit of the country, whatever the political party in power, has no permanent policy and no especial need to keep the press in alignment. Wherever American diplomats and American newspapermen happen to co-operate, the reason is personal; in the majority of countries the press representatives frequently oppose the ambassador or minister. No American reporter feels the European journalist's patriotic debt to his foreign office — on the other hand he does feel and resents his being left out of things by the diplomatic agent, usually a petty-minded, frequently a rich, almost always a prestige-seeking, second-rate politician and social climber whose job is the reward of heavy contributions to the national campaign strong-box. The career-men have not yet made their ideas predominant.

The new ambassador soon finds that he cannot control the press; it is the first fly in his sweet diplomatic ointment. He can neither bribe with money nor with social prestige by inviting the reporters to his select affairs. He finds that even political pull doesn't work because while the newspaper-owner back home may be a friend, a member of the same party and involved in fifty political enterprises, he gives his man abroad *carte blanche,* even to criticizing the ambassador. The latter becomes chagrined. The reporter continually assumes the attitude against the embassy of the Irishman wrecked on a desert isle who on recovering consciousness and being told by a dark native that there was a government there declared himself against it.

The European system has its drawbacks also. Too frequently the journalist becomes the tool of the foreign office; he loses his objectivity and writes to suit his ambassador, suppressing some truths, giving false value to others, becoming in short a press agent instead of a free and untrammelled publicist. This is diplomatic censorship *par excellence.*

Most deplorable is the European system of semi-official news bureaus. They are subsidized by the state and controlled by the party in power. In cases like the Tass in Russia and Stefani in Italy they are corrupt to the extent of making propaganda for political factions and suppressing all news which is not favourable to the violent political régime. Reuter in England and the post-war Wolff Bureau in Berlin are the only ones free from suspicion, but the same cannot be said of Havas in Paris. Those controlled by Poland, Roumania, Bulgaria and other small states are only too patently propaganda spreaders.

Unfortunately a great part of the news served to the American people is this tainted news of semi-official agencies because the *Associated Press* has an exclusive exchange agreement with them all, and while the *Associated Press* is innocent of evil intent, it transmits a lot of this " agency " material. To give a concrete example, the *Associated Press* in Rome used the Stefani reports about many acts of Fascist violence, these reports being written in a tone to defend and apologize, instead of giving actual facts. Thus the news is pre-censored.

Recently there has been a movement both in Washington and in Europe to treat the *Associated Press* as a semi-official American agency which it is not, although it may be giving that impression abroad as many officials in several foreign offices and certain American officials have expressed themselves as being of that belief. Frequently the *Associated Press* man is called in by an American diplomat who discusses " policies " with him. " Policies " can mean only one thing — what to write and what to suppress — in other words, to censor. Fortunately the *United Press* and the smaller agencies are hot on the trail of the A. P.

in these later times, and being more liberal minded, they are glad to go the limit on any A. P. "policy" story. Should the A. P. attempt to "tone" a story of revolution in Warsaw and the "opposition" discover it, you may be certain the "opposition" will make it so hot for the A. P. that the latter will get orders from New York to send in full and to explain. This is what happened, for example, when some small non-agency men and I sent 500-word cables on the Pope's address to a pilgrimage during the Holy Year in which he denounced Fascism for its anti-Catholic attacks. Stefani agency and the *Associated Press* did their best to suppress or minimize the sensational seriousness of such a move by the Pope, but the "opposition" cables exposed them quickly.

Somewhere between this European system of creating semi-official bureaus or of taking journalists too much into the functioning of embassies, and the American idea of indifference and antagonism, there must be a golden mean. I know there is no more patriotic body than the press corps abroad. Its attitude is to serve its country by sticking to the truth. I wonder if the same can be said so unreservedly for the diplomatic corps! The latter's patriotism is too much the spread-eagle style; too much Fourth of July and not enough a five-hour-day service. Diplomacy may think itself possessed of the one and only truth, but there is too much consorting with monarchists and nobility and officials who represent factions and not nations to tinge the diplomatic reports. In most cases the resident newspaper representative knows much more about the country than the new ambassador. The reporter at least sees the situation whole; a labour upheaval interests him more than the precedence in seating arrangements at a foreign office dinner; he has contacts in all strata of society and can be sympathetic to all classes and keep his ear to all social tremors. American diplomacy can only gain by observing a policy of honesty and fairness in dealing with American newspapermen. But the policy should be originated in the state department. It should, in short, be the same policy which Washington, from the president of the United States to the clerks in all departments, holds towards the Washington correspondent. The present system of American diplomats acting as censors or trying to control the American press is as vicious as it is ridiculous, egotistic and futile.

Chapter II

MARIE'S ROUMANIA

BOUNDED by Russia, Poland, Bulgaria and the Black Sea, lies the Land of Corruption. Bucharest is its capital and until quite recently its queen was Marie. The queen has been summed up in two words: "Poor Ferdinand." He is dead and she has lost her power. But the national corruption of Roumania remains, secretly, behind a massive bulwark of terroristic censorship. All of us who have tried to pierce it have been hounded by the police or arrested or expelled.

From the royal house, from the office of the dictator, Jon Bratianu, down to the smallest functionary in the newly occupied territories, graft has ruled the country for the greater part of the present century, until a peaceful revaluation in November, 1928, placed the Peasant Party in power and promised reforms. No doubt it will take years to change an inherited system.

There is, for example, the case of the station-master of a little Transylvanian village, to whom a man in the guise of a cattle merchant came one day and asked for two freight cars.

"No cars now," said the station-master.

"Reserve me two for next week," pleaded the dealer.

"All gone."

"Next month?"

"All gone."

"Next year?"

"All gone."

The dealer looked very hard at the station-master and said in a new voice:

" How much? "

" One thousand lei per car."

" Taken," said the dealer, and 2000 lei changed hands. Then the dealer stammered and hemmed and said:

" Look here, I'm only the agent for a big cattle and sheep man and I must account to him somehow for this graft — "

" Easy," replied the government station-master and taking an official blank he wrote out a full receipt. The cattleman seized it triumphantly and shouted:

" Now I've got you, you grafter. I'm not a cattle dealer at all, I'm an agent for the police. I'll put you in jail for this or you'll come across handsomely."

" You won't put me in jail — and I won't come across," said the railroad grafter stubbornly.

" But I've got the goods on you — a receipt — and on official paper, too."

" Say," replied the government crook, " don't you think that when I bought this job from the ministry of railroads that I got with it the right to make good my big expense by taking in smaller graft? "

The cattleman-detective lost his crest.

" You win," he said. " Well, I'll be going. I've no cattle. Give me back my 2000."

" Two thousand? I'll say not. You bought these two cars and you'll take them."

* * * * *

Now for the heads of the police system:

The Sunday morning of King Ferdinand's funeral there arrived at the main station Mr. Ross White, a photographer for a Chicago company. He was late. So late in fact that he could step right out of the depot, unlimber his camera, and shoot the whole procession more successfully than those who had waited for it three days.

Flushed with victory he boasted a bit that night.

"I'm on tomorrow's plane for Vienna — I'll probably beat the world on this," he said.

"How about your exit visa?" someone asked.

"Exit? I've got a $10 visa all right."

"How about registering with the police? How about special permission to go on the plane? How about special permission to take out pictures?"

Well, we put Ross White in the hands of a native son who said, "Count your money," "Good," and "Come along."

They called first of all on the inspector of police in charge of foreigners and told him their troubles.

"It's as much as my life or my job is worth," said that high dignitary reaching down in his low pocket where he carried a duplicate of the official rubber stamp which was locked over Sunday in his office. As he got it ready by breathing on it hotly, as all economical Europe does, he eyed the money counting, and as he saw the pile of 100 lei notes mount, he stamped and signed.

Then to the home of the police chief in charge of exit visas, and the same performance. And another 2000 lei.

By midnight White had amassed dozens of rubber stamps in assorted shades of purple mixed with spittle; passes, papers, notes, and revenue stamps. And so to bed.

He was early at the aviation field. There his troubles began all over. It seemed nothing he had was worth anything. He was lost in a forest of itching palms.

The first official got 1000 lei and stamped something; the second got 500 and stamped something; the next two got 100 each and stamped nothing; it was becoming monotonous. Others came and were sent rejoicing with 60 and 40 and 20. Ross White got in the airplane and the motor started. A full hour had been lost and now the airplane company was demanding extra money.

Just before the final signal to depart a gold-braided official came up and confiscated all of White's work.

"Undeveloped films and plates must pass the censorship — ready in three days," said Goldbraid.

"Darn," or worse, said White, "how much graft do you want?"

"I need eleven 20 lei notes," said Goldbraid.

"Why eleven — why not an even ten?" asked White.

"Because," said the government official with a smile, "because a ten per cent. tip is usually added on service bills in Roumania."

He got it.

* * * * *

We now pass on from petty provincial officials, from chiefs of police, to the Bratianu dictatorship itself.

I was present at a short session of Parliament when, in the presence of one or two score of soldiers armed with rifles and bayonets, a bill was introduced to place the national natural resources in the hands of a commission of four.

The minority opposition, after listening to Jon Bratianu's request for unanimous action, left the chamber in indignation. By actual count 86 members remained. When the vote was counted, the official tellers announced:

For the Bratianu measure 124
Opposed 2
Total votes cast 126

Outside the cruel humour of this Balkan corruption, there was important news for America and England in this bill. The "natural resources" meant oil. The four men were presumed to be the premier, Jon Bratianu, the premier's brother Vintila, (later premier), the premier's son-in-law and favourite of Queen Marie, Prince Barbu Stirbey, and another related accomplice. In other words the politicians were voting themselves absolute mastery of Roumanian oil. When I expressed the opinion that such raw crookedness was unparalleled in modern history, I obtained another light on Roumania, because my American oil agent said:

" It is better this way; we will have only four persons to bribe. If oil had remained in the hands of Parliament we might have to bribe two hundred."

My duty, however, was to report the graft. Accordingly I wrote a telegram giving exactly what had transpired in Parliament under my own eyes. Three days went by. I knew nothing of the secret Roumanian censorship until the postman arrived at my hotel with a formulary by which I could get 1618 lei for a " returned telegram." The post office later refused to return the original, but a little graft obtained a view of it with the orders of the censor, a colonel of the army, to suppress *in toto*.

As news is always fresh until it is printed, I sent the three-day-old telegram by mail to Budapest, whence is was telegraphed and appeared in the American and European press. The political police immediately moved after me. They came to my hotel to arrest me, but the porter, who got a bigger bribe from me than he got from them, misled them and gave me the tip to leave the country.

* * * * *

Other newspapermen have had similar experiences and tasted Bucharest jails. Among them is Lorimer Hammond who reported one of the numerous Carol crises. The Royal Household had ordered the censors to suppress telegrams in which the name of Mme. Lupescu appeared. Lupescu, daughter of a little shopkeeper of Jassy who trembles his life away in terror, had been the wife of a " shavetail " aviator, then the mistress of another. Captain outranked lieutenant and colonel outranked major, so that she stepped forward to the heights of courtisan-ship until the fatal night of the Army Aviators' ball when Crown Prince Carol, as commander-in-chief of all aviation, outranked the then possessor of Mme. Lupescu and made her his No. 1 mistress. This is a typically sordid story which the newspapers call " romance."

The censor who was ordered to suppress her name spoke " the English." Ah, those wonderful men, those small European officials who " have " English (including the press attaché of Admiral Horthy who took us to a Budapest theatre party and introduced his wife as " my husband "!).

Pride was the ruling complex of the Roumanian censor: pride plus a secret dictionary. When stumped he would retire and read the unabridged. Mr. Hammond learned of both the queenly order and the censor's vice. Accordingly he sent ten thousand words about the political crisis caused by Carol's " flame," Carol's " broad," Carol's " skirt." Never a name. And our proud censor looked up flame and read fire, looked up

414

broad and read wide, mistook skirt for shirt, wondered a little, but saw no harm in anything.

Mr. Clarence Streit of *The New York Times,* who was in Bucharest at the same time, was expelled after twenty-four hours notice by order of General Nicoleanu, the prefect of police, who wrote and said that Streit's article had contained " gross exaggerations and insults addressed to the Roumanian crown and country."

The Times offered its columns to the Roumanian government to disprove a single statement of Streit's but the government preferred silence, although Queen Marie and lesser members of the court requested three foreign correspondents to write some counteracting propaganda for them. This they refused to do. It was before Marie's trip to America, when a touch of the royal hand made many democratic editors her slaves, so the American press and its foreign correspondents (who are braver than their editors in the fight for journalistic freedom) supported Mr. Streit. *The Chicago Tribune,* stating the whole case, said:

" He (Streit) had printed the truth as he saw it, about a country controlled by a minority as domineering as it is reactionary. . . . A conniving oligarchy such as rules Roumania lives by secrecy, not by the truth as American newspapermen have a habit of writing it. *The Tribune* has had the same experience in Russia and Italy. Neither Mussolini nor the Soviet Government wanted the truth about their activities sent to America. Now Roumania joins these two countries, and makes it a threesome of suppression."

In reply to my request Mr. Streit has sent me a full report of the incident, saying in part:

" I did not emphasize the scandals (both about Carol and

about Queen Marie) but I showed how grave a matter the abdication was and how lightly it was accepted and its effect on the crown and the general political situation. I emphasized most of all the responsibility of the king. I also paid special attention to the Bratianus and showed how the king's policy coincided with their selfish interests. From all I have heard since, the series really frightened the king and queen and the governing clique. However, if I had written the series at another time it is doubtful if I would have been expelled. It was on the eve of the elections. . . . "

The last sentence is the key to the action. Time makes an irony out of an ideal. The Liberal party was founded to fight the reactionaries, with a program similar to the British party of like name; in the hands of the Bratianus it became the party of censorship, suppression, selfish exploitation and terrorism. Since the war there has not been a single honest election in Roumania. Although it is no longer necessary to indulge in much violence, because the masses are so generally terrorized that they would always vote a Liberal majority, no election takes place without cracked heads, and frequently there is murder. Kidnapping of Opposition candidates is frequent; assault of Opposition candidates and their voters is common; patrols keep thousands from approaching the ballot-boxes, and in cases where an Opposition majority is feared the boxes are stuffed or broken open and false ballots put in. And the name " Liberal " remains to fool newspaper readers.

The election terrorism is one of many scandals which the drastic press law of Roumania neutralizes by silence. A fine of $100. and four years' imprisonment is provided for persons who " by mail, telegraph or telephone sends out news offending the king, the queen, or the crown prince, or who attack the constitutional government or the established order of succession to the throne."

This law was enacted after Gregory Phillipescu had had the courage for the first time to attack the scandal of the Royal Household. In his newspaper *Epoca* he told Queen Marie to behave herself and plastered the walls of Bucharest with a likeness of Prince Stirbey with the captions: "Our Hero," "The Man Behind the Portieres," and "The Rasputin of Roumania." Now Phillipescu is a refugee in Paris.

* * * * *

The Carol scandal is revived about twice a year. In the Manoilescu affair, the arrest of Carol's agent was kept out of the Bucharest papers until the government had prepared all its propaganda for the military trial. The oil scandal and the agrarian reform scandal, by which the Bratianu clique evaded losing agricultural lands by planting occasional miscellaneous trees on them and calling them "forests," were never reported in the press. The scandals following anti-semitic pogroms, which occur frequently, are suppressed or diminished or mentioned in terms of excuses.

One of the worst outbreaks in recent history occurred in Oradea Mare. The rioters were sent with governmental aid to hold an anti-Hungarian demonstration in a Hungarian town ceded to Roumania without plebiscite. For three days the university men and women, the future intelligentsia of Roumania, assaulted Jews and Hungarians, looted shops for silk stockings, stole candles from a church, desecrated the synagogues, tore up scrolls of the Bible, and in the name of Nationalism and Patriotism acted generally like a lot of swine.

I have elsewhere told why the American reporters in Bucharest, there for political events, knew nothing of all this until some foreign newspapers arrived. Eventually the Roumanian press was forced to say something of the affair. The government inspired news items saying that the students had been "provoked" by "thousands of Hungarian Communists," an obvious lie as since Admiral Horthy suppressed the red régime in Hungary in 1919 there are no longer "thousands of Communists" alive or resident.

Incidentally the Roumanian student body is not the only one which engages in violence and supplies the backbone to reaction. In Germany, Austria, Hungary and Bulgaria I have seen the young intellectuals at work. Unlike the American and British student who uses up his high spirits in sport, the Continental student lives and breathes hatred. He is ruling-class conscious. He is brought up to replace his reactionary father as an army officer, privy councillor, exploiter of labour, controller of the economic and political life of the country. Whenever monarchism and anti-liberal movements are under way the Continental student gives them a fillip of violence. How mean-minded, cruel, corrupt and gluttonous the university man is has been shown clearly by Harry Domela, a middle-class youth, who, once mistaken for a younger son of the Kaiser, attended Heidelberg University as a prince, lived with the students, attended duels, orgies, secret meetings where hatred of the middle and lower classes was the chairman, and then wrote an amazing book, which in any country possessing a greater sense of humour than Germany would have made a laughing stock of the university fraternities.

The further down the Balkans you go, the less does university life mean culture. And Roumania, which likes to think of itself as a part of civilized Europe, and not a part of the

Balkans, is at present the most balkanized country in Europe — balkanization in the European vocabulary meaning violence and corruption.

As it is the custom of American news services to employ native journalists for "protection" during dull times, I once made inquiries for a suitable man. One was recommended to me by an American official.

"He is one of only two native journalists," said the official, "who does not pay the weekly visit to (Jon) Bratianu. On these occasions the premier invites them to have two cigars from the drawer of his desk. There is a 1000 lei note as a cigar band on each."

Chapter III

German Censorship: Einst und Jetzt

THE liberty of the press in Germany was abused by Bismarck with such great success that even today the newspapers are in large measure corrupt or subservient.

During the war Maximilian Harden was the only editor who was not a slave of the military machine. The military machine enforced almost absolute discipline. In addition to the press conferences where general instructions were issued, as today "general suggestions" are given to the assembled editors, the foreign office handed out slips of papers with warnings or orders. These were later printed in books for confidential circulation. Here are typical excerpts from a copy I was able to obtain:

August 7, 1917: The press is requested not to represent the South American Republics as nigger and monkey states as it has been doing lately.

Sept. 18, 1917: A representative of the press has asked how many American troops have landed in France. The answer is, about 40,000 of which half are labour battalions.

Nov. 20, 1917: There are 40,000 Americans in France of which 20,000 are technical formations.

May 17, 1918: American troops in France are officially estimated at ten divisions of which only four are near the front.

Oct. 26, 1918: Regarding President Wilson's note: The press are requested not to direct questions at Wilson's note and not to demand the Kaiser's resignation. Nor must it be said that the President demands the Kaiser's resignation. None but chauvinists in England and France are

420

doing that. The German press under all circumstances must avoid do-ing it.

The disillusion which followed the military collapse in Ger-many embraced the press. All intelligent, liberal-minded, honest Germans whom I have spoken to in the course of the past eight years blame the corrupted newspapers for much of Germany's sorrow. "They lied to us," is the almost universal judgment on the behaviour of foreign office men and the newspapers during the war.

Bismarck had not hesitated to lie. Says Emil Ludwig:

"No one ever rivalled Bismarck in his use of the press. By day and by night (literally) his underlings have to work for the press, preparing, suggesting, summarizing, contradicting. He shows the utmost mastery in the dosage of his poison. . . ."

The dosage of poison today is homeopathic. The editors are called to a conference in the foreign office where the big political campaigns are planned for them. One day it is: "Go strong on the war-guilt lie," and there follows a campaign to prove that Germany was the sweet, innocent, white lamb among the blood-stained Poincarés and Sazanoffs. Another day it may be: "Everybody, to the attack on the Dawes plan," or suddenly: "Lay off Dawes — say a kind word for it or keep quiet." During the Genoa conference the press was instructed to paint carmine pictures of German commerce with Russia — all to embarrass France and coerce the latter into better terms for a future German-French commercial pact. One day it may be: "This report is true, but it would be better to deny it or suppress it, as it would embarrass important negotiations under way."

Press instructions cover the whole world, now that Germany

has again become an international power and plies her trade overseas. Thus, during the 1927–8 American invasion of Nicaragua when the liberal press spoke of the United States as " imperialistic " and referred to our " protectorates " in Central America and the West Indies, the foreign office, jealous of its good relations with Washington at a time when revision of the Dawes plan was becoming a booming subject and when full restoration of German property seized in America was impending, warned the liberal editors to print no comment on Nicaragua which would make a bad impression.

There was a time, during the inflation period (when German journalists and editors were living on starvation wages), when I obtained from several members of this foreign office conference a good summary of what happened every day. On one occasion I published something about the foreign office having ordered the editors to suppress some item. Immediately afterwards *Zeit,* the official organ of Stresemann, then chancellor, published a denial which attacked my veracity.

The same afternoon Stresemann invited the press to tea. Of course I could not tell him that I had obtained my information from one of his own foreign officials. So I said:

" But I got the news from a geheimrat — a privy councillor."

" Sometimes," replied the chancellor, his blue eyes sparkling and his double chins moving with laughter, " sometimes you think you hear the voice of Almighty God, and it is only a privy councillor."

The success of the German foreign office control of the press is due to the general belief that patriotic impulses not party politics actuate its suggestions. The German newspaper therefore is unlike the American newspaper which editorially sees party in every move of government, and attacks accordingly. About the only thing an American newspaper respects in a politician is his moral history. In New York in 1919 I was present at a conference of newspapermen with politicians including one who said he was the agent for a Republican National Committeeman, at which a proposal was made to buy some love-letters of Woodrow Wilson then alleged to be kept in a bank vault in Newark. Later the representatives of the R. N. C. lost all interest because it was agreed not to use "personalities" in the campaign. In like manner the story of President Harding's "romance" and illegitimate child was known to Democratic newspapers throughout the country but no use was ever made of it. Cleveland's personal affairs were also left untouched. On the other hand nothing in the past political or business life of a politician is held sacred.

In Germany newspapers do not stoop to attack the politician's affiliation with a trust, or his religious convictions, or his class loyalties, but they confine themselves to his actual political achievements. Their sense of patriotism is invoked by both public and officialdom, because a man in office is a part of government, and government is held sacred. Thus the foreign office says suppress this or encourage that not because it will help the chancellor in his present policy, but because it will help Germany, of which the chancellor is only a temporary agent.

The result is unctuous servility. Blinded by the belief that they are acting for the nation's good German editors are the saddest examples of self-deluded prostitutes of patriotism. This is especially true of the nationalist press, which has the added corruption of big business ownership. Stinnes has been replaced by Hugenberg. The part-owners of the steel and iron trusts and the scores of lesser trusts, more aggressive and domineering than any that ever faced Roosevelt, these men control news agencies, hundreds of Berlin and provincial newspapers, the Nationalist Party, a large part of the People's (Stresemann's) Party and have a big influence in the Centrist (Catholic) Party and even some in the Democratic Party. Big business, when it is reactionary, as it is to a large extent in Germany, also controls the Stahlhelm and affiliated or similar nationalist, armed, illegal organizations and their newspaper organs. In many instances officers of the Reichswehr, the national army, are in their pay. Public opinion, force, commerce, steel and coal are in the hands of a few men in Germany, a combination of power unheard of in any other country, and because the illusion persists that it would harm Germany, that it would be unpatriotic to stop this concentration, the press remains silent. It is called a patriotic duty to free Germany from the " yoke of the Dawes plan "; the press feeds the public on a diet of self-pity and righteous indignation. Germany stands appalled before the press picture of the devouring monster, while in all truth the coal and iron trust men and their lesser brothers exploit labour as it is done in native Africa, grow rich and strong on the excess profit between dollar-a-day labour and manufactured goods sold on the world market at standard prices. The German working-man who knows his Shakespeare and Goethe and his Karl Marx, and who has been called the most civilized labourer in the world, has been so broken in spirit by Prussian discipline that apparently he cannot see the conspiracy of big business, political parties and the servile press to pass the whole economic burden of the Dawes plan upon him. Instead of becoming cannon fodder for the Kaiser the German worker today enjoys the delights of industrial serfdom.

In a weak way the socialist press voices a feeble protest now and then, but it too is immersed in political deals because coalitions are always being formed in which the Social Democratic Party participates. There is left only the radical press, the *Rote Fahne* and its offspring, which are paid by Moscow and which print such a mixture of lies and propaganda as to further discredit the already discredited communist movement in Germany.

The news bureau as we know it in America does not exist. The Wolff Agency supplies the *Associated Press* and the German newspapers with a report of what it considers important, chiefly official news and views. It is true though unfortunate that the routine news about Germany comes from the German press. When a big event occurs, real news in the American sense, the American correspondents quite frequently beat the German press by days, so that the German papers have to get their information cabled back from the United States. The Scheer report to the Kaiser on the Battle of Jutland is an ample illustration.

A double example of subserviency to monarchism and German valuation of news was furnished by the marriage of Princess Victoria, the Kaiser's sister, to a Russian adventurer recently. The evening edition of the Ullstein leading newspaper, the *Vossische Zeitung,* sent a few words from Bonn saying the ceremony had taken place. When I asked for the full report which I expected the Ullstein service had prepared for its morning edition, the wire chief informed me he had nothing because Germans were not interested in such trivial events. (The paper contained 30,000 words of political bunkum the next morning.) The Wolff Bureau stooped to soil its diplomatic finger-tips with only a few words, and the entire right-wing or monarchist-nationalist press suppressed all mention of the high event. British and American correspondents, however, had cabled thousands of words about the amazing marriage.

Official censorship in Germany was maintained during the Kapp monarchist revolution with Trebitsch-Lincoln in charge. During the entire period of the republic, however, only one attempt was made to censor us. Some minor general or colonel in the war department gave orders to the telegraph office to return all cables except the official one, which contained the word "Kuestrin."

This fort, dominating Berlin, had been occupied by the so-called "Black Reichswehr" or illegal monarchist soldiers who had smuggled themselves, frequently with the tacit approval of the regular Reichswehr, into the national army. When they seized Kuestrin Germany was in danger. Moreover, if the truth got out there would be a big exposure of monarchist intrigue. So the order to suppress was given, illegally.

The office boys brought the telegrams back with the report that the word "Kuestrin" could not go. A test soon proved that ambiguous dispatches without the word were accepted. Carl Groat of the *United Press* wrote a 500-word description of a ball game between the Black team and the Regulars. His "Home run" was cleverly deciphered as a dash for home by the besieged monarchists, and his four men struck out as four killed. In terms of baseball games, poker games, and just plain American slang it was possible to put over the story the same day, a necessity, because our protest to the foreign office had to go "through channels" and the censorship was not removed until the following day.

Officially the press has remained free in Germany. No Bismarck issues ukases, no Kaiser suppresses editions, and the foreign journalist may print all the facts he can find. But a power stronger than Bismarck and the Kaiser has completely dominated the German press and grows more absolute every day. It is the Dawes-created gold mark.

*   *   *   *   *

The New German Tea-Party Censorship

The armistice marked the end of the old German propaganda machine and censorship. From that day to the present, barring stray incidents like the monarchist revolution in 1920, the battle of Fort Kuestrin and an occasional " disappearance " of telegrams from the post office, Germany has been a land of almost absolute freedom. It is only lately that the big propaganda funds have been revived and that an attempt to control foreign correspondents has been made.

The term " propaganda " has not the sinister significance in Europe which it has acquired in America (due, no doubt, to its conjunction with the adjective " German "). The missionary activities of the Roman Catholic Church come under the heading of " Propaganda Fide," or propagation of the faith, and in European business offices the word means advertising or boosting generally. But the Germans have the acuteness to realize that their propaganda was almost as odious as the Bolshevik, so they leaned over backwards, just after the war, and leaned so far back they must have fallen and hurt themselves. For years they did nothing.

But today there is a secret propaganda fund in every ministry, a total of at least $5,000,000 a year spent at home and abroad. Some of it goes to spreading travel literature, some to subsidizing films, some to entertaining distinguished foreigners, senators, Mayor Walker, Chicago Subway Commission junketeers, visiting journalists and book writers, German-American editors, bankers, Steuben Society leaders, student travel groups, in fact anyone who will say a good word for the country.

About $750,000 a year is spent by Germany to maintain news services and to broadcast news favourably tinged " an Alle," to all who care to listen in. The foreign office alone spends $2,000,000 a year. One hundred thousand dollars a year is spent merely for the transmission of government views on international diplomatic events to the interior newspapers, and the chancellor gets $500,000 annually for domestic propaganda.

These yearly millions are never accounted for in the reports to the Reichstag. Recently there was a considerable scandal when it was discovered that not only were $3,000,000 wasted by the war ministry in subventioning German film companies, but that one company making military propaganda films (The Phoebus) had been influenced by the war ministry to give a decided monarchist-militarist tone to the productions.

From 1920 to 1925 the German foreign office did nothing to influence the American and other foreign correspondents assigned to them. Officials were so chary of being accused of making propaganda that it was really difficult for the journalists to get necessary aid for their work. The foreign office maintained its staff of " referents," one for America, another for Britain, etc., who sometimes listened to a request for an interview with a national minister and who frequently helped in visa and income tax troubles, but while the nation was wailing *" Armes Deutschland,"* " poor Germany," and the public prints were full of propaganda about defencelessness, Polish and French aggression, the dangers of Bolshevik invasion, the futility of the Dawes plan, the necessity of more troops and ships, the plebescite scandals — all these years the gentlemen of the foreign office maintained a cold neutrality in dealing with the foreign press.

But as Germany grew stronger, and jealousy for her sovereignty increased, and she became a member of the League of Nations, and her money hardened and she felt more like her old self again, she began being friendlier and at the same time stricter with her journalistic guests.

In 1924 the Association of Foreign Journalists asked for a weekly meeting with officials of the Wilhelmstrasse, similar to those which President Roosevelt instituted and which his successors have retained, and this was granted. Later on the F. O. announced a few " beer evenings " which were successful. At the Friday noon meetings the foreign minister was present frequently and many questions were answered. Usually some expert from some department would then make a speech giving facts and figures and, naturally, a few points of propaganda.

Nowadays there are teas every Friday afternoon. Between tea and beer and cigarettes it is possible to meet Mr. Stresemann for a little talk, and it is also possible to get a reprimand from an official in the same manner as American newspapermen are diplomatically reprimanded by officials of the Quai d'Orsay and Downing Street.

Returning to Germany recently after a year in the Near East and three months in Mexico, I was surprised by what is considered the miracle of Europe, the economic renaissance of Germany. Simultaneously two obviously foreign office inspired campaigns were started, one against the " *Kriegsschuld Lüge,*" of the alleged lie that Germany was *solely* responsible for the war, the other against the possibility of fulfilment of the Dawes plan. The first was important because the entire Versailles Treaty is based on the supposition that Germany alone, and not Russia or Serbia, is guilty; the second was another effort of Germany's industrial kings to relieve themselves of a terrific financial burden which they have shifted almost entirely on to the industrial labouring classes but which nevertheless cuts into their excess profits.

It was evident that the labour movement in Germany which had been stopped by a flood of blood, then bad paper money, was again beginning to progress. Dissatisfaction was rumored from the coal fields and the foundries. Unemployment, lockouts and threats of big strikes were reported daily. For all these manifestations of unrest the big employers' press blamed the Dawes plan. Duisberg and Hugenberg, heads of manufacturers' associations, trusts and their allied newspaper and news-agency chains, were speaking and writing against the Dawes plan, pleading for revision and prophesying ruin and disaster unless relief came soon.

I made an investigation. From American trade and consular agencies I obtained statistics showing that Germany was prosperous, business was splendid, unemployment was diminishing not increasing, many manufacturers were growing rich and the old international trick of selling high at home and cheap abroad to gain foreign markets was being played with success against Great Britain and the United States.

Manufactured goods were too expensive in Germany; so was food. Oppressive taxes had been put upon the peasants and the old Junkers were treating their tenant farmers with their accustomed pre-war cruelty. Coal miners were being forced to work the ten, eleven and twelve hour day for about $1.60 a day. Labour was angry because wages were lower in proportion to the cost of living than before the war. The docile, disciplined, extremely intelligent German workingman nevertheless had succumbed to the Duisberg-Hardenberg propaganda and the false patriotism which has been fed him since the war.

"You must work ten hours a day," Hugo Stinnes had told labour, "eight hours for yourself, two hours for the Vaterland," and they were working two hours supposedly for the Vaterland while the employers were pocketing the extra two hours' profits.

Councillor Duisberg addressing the National Manufacturers' Association in Frankfurt had said: "Seventy per cent. of Germany's companies are showing no profit this year." Investigation showed that this was a half-truth. The thirty per cent. which did pay dividends were the big corporations, the trusts, which control almost 90 per cent. of Germany's invested capital, and the profits were 11 per cent. gross of which 5½ per cent. was distributed in dividends.

Moreover, investigation, confirmed by American officials, showed that a practise begun during the inflation period has been continued, namely, amortizing plant, offices and machinery, in an unusual way. During the inflation, it may be remembered, big factories and even banks wrote their buildings off at one paper mark when the mark was quintillions to the dollar. Today millions which should go to stockholders go back to the corporation funds and plants worth millions appear valued at one mark. The lack of dividends is blamed on Messrs. Young and Dawes.

By paying $1.60 for a ten hour day German coal and steel

interests are able to sell their products cheaper in Pittsburgh than the mills of the Monongahela and Allegheny can produce them. Because England had refused to join the Steel Kartel of Germany, France, Luxembourg and Belgium, the German interests had no hesitancy in undercutting Brtiain in South America, the East, and sometimes in the British Colonies. But at home high prices are maintained and protected by a tariff wall.

No big estates are being divided in Germany. The Junkers hold them and grow richer, while the British lords who won the war have to sell and divide into small holdings.

The day of the squandering American is gone. In Berlin only the German can afford Berlin prices. The man who puts a spoonful of caviar (at $2. a spoonful) upon each of a dozen oysters (at $4. a dozen) is a German industrial baron, not an American tourist. The theatres, the cabarets, the whole of the new Kurfürstendamm is crowded not by foreigners, as in the old days, but wealthy Germans who spend their money freely because they make it easily, abundantly and frequently dishonestly.

Price American goods in Berlin; allow for 100 per cent. government tax and 100 per cent. profits in handling, and they cost you still more. But many German things made by men getting one fifth the wages of American workingmen, and the materials costing one third as much, raw, as in America, cost twice as much as in New York.

"The Dawes plan is to blame," reply the industrial kings of Germany.

The trade and consular agents think differently. So do newspapermen. And I have found one German industrialist who has confessed.

" We are making excessive profits," admitted Herr Arnold Rechberg to me one day. " We do not pay anywhere near American wages and we ask more than American prices. We made profits by the hundred per cents. during the war and we make them now. Everyone who can is a profiteer. And the profiteers control the government, so all goes without a hitch."

The Dawes plan may have to be revised some day, or it may work out without changing a comma's dot. I do not know. But I do know that up to this present writing the Dawes plan has worked out so well that Germany has become one of the few economically successful nations of the world.

And I also know that big business in Germany is using the Dawes plan as a spectre with which to frighten the little bourgeoisie and big labour.

Industrial exploitation of its workingmen, savage and sinister, and on a scale unheard of under the Kaisers, is the new system in Germany. While the old spirit of revolt which flared up during the week when Ludendorff and Wilhelm fled, and later nobly to save the Republic from Kapp and Ludendorff in 1920, has been tamed by talk of patriotism and Dawes payments. The vast Hugenberg press machinery, all the agencies of propaganda, and all the government powers concentrated largely in the hands of the parties openly admitting themselves political parties owned by the owners of commerce and industry, have succeeded in crushing the new spirit in Germany — all in the name of patriotism and the Dawes plan.

* * * * *

The last, you may notice, is somewhat editorial. Editorials are not entrusted to reporters: he must cable only facts. I cabled some facts, consular statements, figures of profits and wages, figures showing that the Dawes plan was not to blame for starvation wages and the high cost of living. Then a Friday came and I was invited to the foreign office to tea. I do not like tea. Next Friday I was invited with some insistency, and I went.

As I said before, there is no censorship in Germany even though its stepbrother, propaganda, has been revived. But my " errors " were pointed out to me. Diplomatically. Just the way the Quai d'Orsay and Downing Street do it.

I was told my facts and figures were wrong, and that Germany was really suffering because of the drain of money and materials caused by carrying out the Dawes plan. I was told the crisis was coming and that low wages and the high cost of living were due to it. I was told the squandering new German millionaires were exceptions. It was a tea party and all this propaganda was offered in a gentle way.

But sometimes the iron fist can be seen reappearing. For example, a colleague obtained a letter which Hindenburg sent his friend and ex-master, the recluse of Doorn. In it the president discussed the relation of the Kaiser to the new German constitution, the Kaiser's former holdings in Germany, and counselled him to give up certain of his claims so that political peace mght be restored internally.

The Wilhelmstrasse was badly upset by the publication of this letter, and when the Friday tea came around the correspondent who cabled it was told, by an official who tried his best to take the edge off the threat by a smile, that " Germany is again a sovereign nation, and newspapermen can be expelled whenever the government is dissatisfied with their work."

No doubt German sovereignty has been fully restored. Soon it may reach the brilliance of Wilhelm's time. It may even become bold enough to re-establish open censorship.

Chapter IV

" C'EST LA GUERRE "

THEY were going to hang the Kaiser. Lloyd George proclaimed it, the British electorate approved it, France seconded the motion, and America applauded, because hatred of Germany, worked up by years of propaganda, had not yet relapsed. Today there has been such a reversal of opinion in many countries that if one mentions war guilt and war atrocities he is received with incredulous laughter. Were prisoners ever killed? Were wounded ever murdered on the battlefield? Were survivors in open boats ever massacred? By Germans? "Wartime propaganda; newspaper-made hatred," is the reply.

What follows here is legal evidence before the Supreme Court of Germany, without explanation or comment. Almost three years had elapsed since the armistice had been signed, and a fairer attitude was possible. Like many other Americans disillusioned by the peace conference I came to Leipzig prepared to hear Germany vindicated of all charges of cruelty and barbarism in her conduct of the war. The trials were a shock to me. I did my best to report them fully. So did twenty other British and American journalists. But although the Germans did not censor us, our reports had no effect. In many European countries they were not printed. Foreign offices wanted to forget the war for purely political opportunist reasons.

The Allies had prepared a list of 886 names of Entente diplomatic and military leaders whom they had branded as "war criminals." Kaiser Wilhelm's name led all the rest. Ludendorff and Tirpitz followed and various Schultzes and Schmidts concluded it. Once before in history an emperor and generalissimo had been named outlaw and banished. Kaiser Wilhelm was now to pay with his life on the scaffold. (Napoleon had been murdered by climate.)

The German minister of justice made a declaration: "The list has dwindled," he said, "to forty-five cases of which eight have been prepared for trial. But we can call only four cases because of the deaths and disappearances of the accused. The years have gone by, bringing difficulties in obtaining evidence and hatreds have cooled."

The United States, Italy and Serbia had either failed or refused to make accusations. There was to be no Lusitania case nor were Belgian horrors, such as had stirred the hearts of the world in 1914, to be discussed. No Cavell case, no Fryatt case, no Louvain case. We thought at first there would be nothing to write about.

* * * * *

In the magnificent sedate court room of the palace of justice at Leipzig seven judges clad in purple velvet robes entered. They wore purple velvet hats such as artists wear in old portraits of themselves, starched, white, lacy neckwear and stiff white collars and cuffs, like a "portrait of a gentleman" by Van Dyck or Hals. Young men and old. Prussian and Bavarian in type. All dignified and austere.

In German courts justice evidently proceeds with eyes unbandaged and ears alert. The only similarity to an American court proceeding is the administration of the oath. "Do you swear by Almighty God that the evidence you will give in this case will be the whole truth?" the court quotes, and everyone stands. The witness raises his right hand. No Bible is used. The Supreme Court justice then begins a conversation with the witness — it cannot be called cross-examination. He does not ask, he tells the witness his name, age, occupation, to which the witness assents by a shake of the head. Hearsay evidence is taken for what it is worth; anyone's opinion is accepted, and third-hand statements are listened to without protest.

Nobody objects, nobody quibbles, nobody engages in heated arguments about a technicality of law; no law books are consulted for precedent. No attorney rises every minute to denounce evidence as immaterial, irrelevant. No oratory is spilled to impress court or jury. No one thunders for order. No witness is badgered or rocked by cross-examination. There is no excitement, no sentimentality, no emotion.

The president of the court conducts the trial as if it were a private settlement in his own offices. When a witness mentions someone who may be sitting in the audience or among those to be called later, the court asks that person to rise and affirm or deny. Once the accused shouted " liar " to a witness whereupon the judge without objecting to the interruption mentioned the fact that the court room was no place for personalities which might result in a libel suit.

The British and French legal missions completely agreed with this " family affair " manner of interpreting the law and administering justice. But the American lawyer who sat as an observer said it would never do.

Karl Heinen was called.

" This soldier," said a member of the British legal mission, sardonically, " will go down in history as the man who took the Kaiser's place." They had come to try the Kaiser and had to content themselves with a little sergeant, a wine-barrel maker by trade, who had passed the war at a prison camp for British. Heinen was accused of beating prisoners and throwing stones at them. He admitted the charges, saying he had acted under orders. I managed to have a private interview one day with this Kaiser's scapegoat. He said:

"It certainly looks dark for me but I have nothing on my conscience. I acted as a soldier whose highest duty is to carry out orders from his superior. If the court can understand military discipline I will be freed."

Prussian militarism in the person of General Fransecky, commander-in-chief of all war prison camps, rose to defend the brutal system. "The accused was too kind. He should have fired on the prisoners," he testified. He called Heinen a capable, efficient, obedient soldier who carried out his orders faithfully. "The prisoners were at fault — they were collectively disobedient."

Major General Karl Stenger, commander of the 18th Baden Infantry Brigade was the second "war criminal" on trial. He was accused of murdering wounded prisoners. Before a crowded court room which was breathlessly impressed by the fact that a real general was on trial for an atrocity, the scene of the crime was reconstructed. Major Benno Crusius was co-defendant.

The first witness testified that General Stenger had held a council before battle and had given the following order:

"In the coming battle, remember, there is to be no mercy shown, no prisoners will be taken, no wounded are to be left alive on the field."

On August 26, 1914, Crusius (then captain) with Major Mueller and a sergeant making an inspection of the battle field (so ran the evidence) passed a seemingly dead soldier. Major Mueller kicked him. The Frenchman opened his eyes and groaned. " Shoot him " ordered Mueller and passed on. The sergeant shot the wounded Frenchman.

A little further away the party came upon a sight now made familiar by our post-war movies. Two enemies were sharing their scanty rations. The German soldier was pouring coffee into the tin cup of a wounded French soldier who had previously supplied some cigarettes. The two were smiling at their difficulties in conversation. Major Mueller flamed red. " Doesn't he know General Stenger's order to kill all prisoners, " he shouted to Crusius, who repeated to the fraternizing German. The Frenchman understood the tenor of the order and began pleading for his life. " Have this man killed immediately," ordered the major. " Mercy, mercy," cried the French soldier. The Germans waved him away. The Frenchman was on his knees. He clutched the feet of Crusius praying, weeping, hysterical. The Germans shoved him away and ordered the murder. They remained to see it done.

" It was in accordance with orders from General Stenger," said Major Crusius.

Chief Justice Ebermeyer interrupted:

" While the authorship of the murder-order is in question," he said, " there is now no doubt that such order was given and carried out, as reported by the French G. H. Q."

A medical officer testified that Major Crusius in his sleep frequently called out, " God have mercy upon me for what I have done on the battle field." Here was testimony as sensational as a cheap novel and a cheaper movie.

Witnesses testified that General Stenger had used the expression, " Shoot them down like sparrows," referring to French wounded. "Like sparrows," the judges repeated, shaking their heads sadly.

Crusius arose, a feeble, emaciated man dressed in a Prince Albert, speaking in a thin shaky voice. If you closed your eyes you pictured a human wreck. Open your eyes and see what a massive man he must have been. Huge head, partly bald, partly shaved, hawkeyed, hawknosed, thin lipped, two double chins, very flabby, two rows of fat around his neck, like rubber tires, a big square head like a bust of a Roman emperor. Massive. And out of this ancient strength issued a broken voice falteringly. He had nothing to plead except obeying military orders. Duty!

Alsatians, once soldiers of Germany, were the next witnesses. One of them had heard Stenger give the order, "no prisoners, no wounded alive." Once before a German, the All-Highest, had given such a command. When he wished his troops godspeed as they left for China to quell the Boxer Rebellion, Kaiser Wilhelm, history records, had said, "Quarter will not be given, prisoners will not be made." Karl Kleinhaus, now a clerk in Mulhausen, testified the company sergeant major had read the brigade order before the assembled troops: "From today on no more prisoners will be taken. Wounded will be dispatched."

"After the battle," the Alsatian continued, "I saw a sergeant with three prisoners pass by General Stenger. The latter ordered the sergeant to execute the prisoners. The sergeant refused. 'What shall I do,' said the general, 'I can't shoot them in front of the whole staff.' The prisoners were taken behind a barn. Shots were heard."

It was at this point that the general shouted, "The witness is an Alsatian liar," but the taking of the Alsatian soldier's testimony proceeded.

Eugen Oberdorf, bricklayer, of Nettingen, recipient of the iron cross from the Kaiser, "a good German soldier" as the court called him, described the scene behind the barn.

"They were on their knees crying mercy. One said he was married. The sergeant didn't want to shoot them. But Stenger had given the orders direct."

Francis Xavier Schwerer, now a petty official in Strassbourg, testified: "I myself saw Major Crusius himself kill a wounded Frenchman lying on the field near the road." Joseph Dietsch of Tagsdorf, Alsace, swore that Colonel Neubauer addressed to his officers the order: "No prisoners will be taken. Shoot the Frenchmen down as swine."

General Stenger was found not guilty and Major Crusius was sentenced to two years' imprisonment. The French legal mission quit Leipzig. The court then took up the subject of submarine frightfulness, the result of a policy openly announced by Tirpitz.

Lieutenant Boldt and Lieutenant Dithmar of the U–86, off the coast of Ireland in June, 1918, sank the hospital ship *Llandovery Castle*. They refused to testify, saying that the officers and men of the submarine had taken an oath never to speak about the atrocity.

Second Officer Thapman of the British ship was the principal witness. He testified there were eight American doctors on board who were probably mistaken for military by the Germans. After the ship sank the personnel took to the life-boats. Lieutenants Boldt and Dithmar then gave the order to murder all the survivors. Fourteen three-inch shells were fired against Thapman's life-boat. When German sailors attempted to help the wounded, Thapman testified, the German commander, with two revolvers, fired on his own men to prevent rescue.

The U–86 was ordered to ram the life-boats which were filled with women nurses, the American doctors, and many wounded. Five boats were sunk and all on board drowned. Several life-boats which escaped shell-firing and ramming were attacked by the submarine in a series of narrowing circles, at one time coming within twenty-four inches of Thapman's boat. Still he escaped.

German witnesses declared the U–86 was commanded by Captain Patzig.

"Where is Patzig — why isn't he on trial?" the court asked.

"Because he is hiding probably in Danzig," the witness replied.

Lieutenant Johann Boldt then spoke up. "Captain Patzig," he said, "sank the American transport *Cincinnati,* thereby preventing the landing of an additional 32,000 American troops monthly, and earning the gratitude of our fatherland. I am proud I served under Captain Patzig. If every U-boat commander had been as good as Patzig, the war would have ended differently."

German sailors then testified they received the order: "*versenket spurlos,*" — sink without trace, after their officers realized they had torpedoed a hospital ship. They were guided by the proverb "Dead men tell no tales." "Unmindful of the cries of the wounded and the appeal for mercy from the women, the officers ordered us to fire shells into the life-boats until all human beings were dead. We did not want to do this dirty work for our officers. Dithmar and Patzig had a dramatic interview which amounted to mutiny but Patzig dominated."

"After the slaughter was over — we did not realize we had missed a boat — Captain Patzig called a meeting of the crew.

" ' You know what has happened,' he said, ' I order silence. I take responsibility. I alone shall answer before my God.' "

Thus did German sailors weave a fine hangman's noose for their former officers. But in the afternoon a remarkable incident occurred, made possible only by German court procedure — or rather lack of procedure rules. Twenty German officers and seamen appeared to testify to British naval atrocities. They concentrated on the famous *Baralong* case. The *Baralong,* they said, was a British war-ship, disguised as a freighter, and flying the American flag. It sent out fishing vessels as decoys and trapped the U-31. Officers and men testified the *Baralong* refused to rescue the Germans in the water.

The British legal mission made no protest to the introduction of this case.

Admiral von Trotha, chief of the naval staff, was called as an " impartial expert." He defended Boldt and Dithmar. " I honor the German submarine officers," he said, " and place them higher than myself."

Chief Justice Ebermeyer: " Why did the two officers refuse to give testimony? "

Admiral von Trotha: " They are pledged to obey and remain silent. I honour their keeping their word to their superior officer." Furthermore, testified the chief of the naval staff, the two officers had acted in " fatherlandish fashion " when they torpedoed the *Llandovery Castle*. He described the " terrible life " aboard submarines. " Our U-boat officers were under great mental strain," he concluded.

Another witness said: " Lieutenant Boldt was an excellent officer, a student of philosophy and the Christian religion."

The Chief Justice in summing up the case said:

" Where is this Captain Patzig who boasts he did the fatherland a great service by torpedoing the American transport
Cincinnati? Why doesn't this brave man appear? Why does he
leave subordinates to face the charge of sinking a hospital
ship? Why doesn't he come out of hiding? "

The next day the court decided the two lieutenants were to
serve four years in jail. Dithmar was cashiered. Boldt was forbidden to wear the naval uniform again.

The two officers arose like two pieces of military clock-work,
heard the verdict, and sat down.

The court called the sentences severe. The British mission said
they were trifling for proven murder. As the court adjourned a
deputation of naval officers rushed into the room, surrounded
the convicted officers, cheered and congratulated them on
their keeping silent about the atrocity.

* * * * *

So ended the world-heralded war criminals cases.

The Kaiser remained in Doorn getting his three square meals
a day and writing childish defences of himself; Hindenburg
became president of Germany; Tirpitz went to the Reichstag
amidst the hooting of naval whistles; Ludendorff blamed his
defeat in successive years on the Socialists, the Jesuits, the Jews,
the Freemasons, the Protestants and tried to re-establish the
religion of Wotan and Loki; General Hoffman who forced
the peace of Brest-Litovsk tried for years to organize an army
of German soldiers, French guns and American money to conquer Russia, and, failing, died. Patzig was never found.

Napoleon, you see, was not a royal person — not even a nobleman. He was exiled. But the Hohenzollerns are a ruling
family closely connected with every court in Europe. The dip-

lomats who started the war, of course, enjoy traditional diplomatic immunity. "Hang the Kaiser," was Lloyd George's slogan for campaign purposes only. It would never do to hang a king. So after all, none of the kings of Europe nor the old diplomacy were greatly excited when Lieutenants Boldt and Dithmar escaped from prison a few months later.

Chapter V

Censorship by Circumstance or the Revolution in Vienna

THE amazing revolution of July 15 and 16, 1927, in Vienna, produced for the American newspaperman a new problem: how to fight the censorship of circumstance.

Ever since the division of the old Empire into the Succession States, Austria had been free from press control, in fact a haven for those coming from the white terror in Budapest or the Bratianu terror in Bucharest or the green terror in Sofia. But at seven o'clock on the evening of the July uprising, a general strike was called, the radio, telegraphs, mails, trains, automobiles — every means of international communications ceased to function, and while blood flowed and men died we were held *incommunicado*.

The morning of July 15 saw thousands of men and women marching cheerfully into the Ring. The night before, a verdict had been given by the court in the case of three men accused of firing into a parade at Schattendorf, in the Burgenland, that small piece of Hungary which was awarded Austria when the former nation was turned into an international allotment. In Schattendorf, the preceding January, labour had held a demonstration. As it passed an inn someone fired a rifle, killing a child and wounding an already wounded war veteran.

Three men were arrested and admitted the shooting. But the case had its national and international complications. The Socialists demanded revenge because they had organized the

446

parade and the murderers were acknowledged reactionaries. The Burgenland, however, has been a weak spot in the Austrian national entity, and as the trial had become the big political event of the day the government was faced with a possible uprising if the verdict went against the three citizens of Schattendorf.

Accordingly pressure was brought on the courts to free the accused, one of whom undoubtedly was the murderer. The government, it seems, preferred trouble in Vienna to trouble in the new province. So the court gave the decision " Not guilty."

Not much tinder and flint for revolution, so it seemed to the foreign representatives of the press who contented themselves with a dozen-word cable giving the verdict merely as a matter of record because they had previously sent sensational descriptions of the shooting. Yet the next morning, spontaneously, without even the usual orders from organizations or the distribution of broadsides or banners, the revolution was on. The mob had fermented. The mob, which Victor Hugo says is " the human race in misery," had come out of its hovels and its workshops, and flung its misery in the face of law and order.

*   *   *   *   *

From a window of the Grand Hotel I saw them endlessly marching. They had no leaders and carried no flags. But they shouted:

" *Nieder mit die Hure Justizia, Nieder, nieder nieder.*"
" *Nieder mit die Hure Justizia, Nieder Huren Justiz.*"

At the Opera there was a turning. From my balcony I could see crowds converging on the Parliament Palace. I walked on the outskirts of the loosely formed line. How good-natured this mob was. So different from German mobs which I had seen time after time engage in demonstrations and rioting ever since the day of the revolution outside the railroad station in Cassel during the week of the armistice. There were pleasant Austrian faces, sweet Viennese faces. None of that Prussian brutality, it seemed, but more of the universal kindliness of Southern people. Some ate sandwiches and many a joke was passed along the line.

At Parliament a thin green row of police kept the mob off the incline leading to the main portal. As the mob had no leaders the police argued with the men and women nearest them, and sent groups circulating. So hours passed. July heat, excitement and empty stomachs began their work. Soon three ambulances were brazenly pushing through the loose twenty thousand and gathering those who had fainted. This added a small intensity to the morning, hundreds milling around the ambulances. Street vendors appeared with cold drinks and cheap ice-cream — 10 groschen, 1.4 cents, for a teaspoonful of ice-cream handed out on a piece of paper or a pastry container. The vendors did a grand business.

At 10:30 o'clock it was a picnic, not a revolution.

But there was tension in the air. You felt it instinctively. I actually heard men say, " Something will happen — something must happen," ominously. Just to look at thirty thousand men and women pushing around and yelling, " Down with the prostitute, Justice," was to realize that danger impended.

Then two or three men began to run. Who they were, why they ran, is a mystery; they themselves probably could not explain; but immediately there was a rush of at least 5,000. It was like an ocean wave which threatens for a while to beat

Stresemann (then Chancellor of Germany) saying to the author: " Sometimes you think you hear the voice of Almighty God, and it is only that of a Privy Councillor."

The Vienna Revolution. Barricades erected by the peaceful citizens after Moscow agitators had gained power over the mob.

down ships or rocks but dissipates itself and hardly troubles the peaceful beach far away.

At exactly eleven o'clock about two hundred mounted police could be seen riding up a side street towards Parliament. Immediately the crowd was all in movement. No one wanted trouble. The nearer the horses came, the more agitated grew the mob, the quicker the movement was away from Parliament.

And then a handful of Moscow's trained men took hold of the crowd and tightened it. Revolvers and knives appeared in their hands — they were no more than 200 but they had the words of leadership. A shout went up.

" Death to the police."

Men in green uniform, unprotected by numbers, became the victims of the communist-led mob. As I walked up the Ring and turned into Bellariastrasse, where the museum is, I saw five or six men beat down and trample a white moustached, elderly policeman, tear off his green coat, hang it on an electric light post, and kick their heels into the middle of his sword until it bent. Far up Bellaria street the mounted police were riding faster.

They came down hill towards the Ring in a clattering fury, each man drawing his sword and waving it over his head like a Bedouin on the war-path. The spurred horses, crowded by sidewalks and fences, huddled and flew like a dark stream through a broken dike. A cry of fury and despair, inarticulate, mingled with the surge and crash of descending cavalry; the mob turned and fled, dividing into equal streams, one up, one down the Ring. A dozen communists launched stones and knives at the police then tried to join the fleeing.

The two hundred cavalry poured into the Ring. They rode so fast they could not rein their horses as they faced the iron fence of the royal park which is at the foot of Bellaria street. Horses barged into each other. Horsemen had their feet crushed and yelled in pain. The sword fell from one police official's hand. There was confusion.

I had fled with the mob down Bellaria street, taking refuge in a door-way of a house on the Ring to the left. The mounted police saw the mob running both to the right and to the left. They turned right and rode towards the Opera. One horseman remained behind, his animal injured, limping. He was attacked by at least a hundred, his clothes torn from his body and his horse led in triumph through the mob, like an emblem of a conquest through the streets of Rome.

I went up Bellariastrasse to view the havoc of the charge. But there was none. Not a shot had been fired nor had a single head been cut by a sabre during the charge. A few stones lay on the sidewalk and in the museum's hedge was the bent sword of the first victim of the revolution. I was dressed in a new suit of clothes, newest cut, grey with a blue stripe, and wore the straw hat I had just brought from New York. To these clothes I owe my life.

Four or five Communists seized me, cursing and yelling at me. Before I could utter an astonished " What " one of them had placed a sickle around my throat. They yelled at me as if I was an audience the size of a Yale-Harvard game. Then as suddenly the sickle was pulled out of the hand of the man who held it by another who outshouted him with, " Can't you see by his clothes that he is a foreigner. Leave him alone."

Led by a girl with wild eyes, wild hair, a wild voice and wild gestures, another crowd, unmindful of the police which were engaged in dispersing the mob near the Opera, moved towards the Palace of Justice repeating the " Nieder mit die

Hure Justizia." A few policemen stood outside the door trying to argue. But the crowd began pushing furiously, the yelling increased, stones were thrown, and as the police were driven into the building, the girl leader and some companions, all under twenty, followed them through the door.

Hundreds overran the police. Windows were raised or smashed by the hasty. A score of little officials, grey and bald and docile, disturbed at their work among two millions of legal papers, pushed their fearful way through the delirious crowd and escaped. Soon the girl leader appeared at a window. She held in each hand a bundle of documents, probably mortgages or deeds, fixed with seals and tied with red tape. These she threw to the mob.

Again she appeared, this time her face contorted as with anger or laughter, and, undoing the red tape, she threw the loosened documents to the wind. Some fell heavily; light papers fluttered and cut airplane figures while men and women fought on their toes for them.

Someone struck a match and lighted a bundle of documents on the marble steps of the Palace of Justice. A thin smoke pillar arose and a cheer went up. From five or six windows other girls and boys began throwing bundles of legal papers, which were added to the small blaze, so that flames could now be seen all the way to the museum. A wind arose and scattered thousands of flaming papers, thousands of half-charred ones, throughout the neighbourhood. They rose and fell and filled the air. Smoke and an acrid smell spread to all the streets.

The fire on the steps now climbed the pillars. As the flames mounted so did the passion of the mob. The girls who came to the windows with more and more packets became more and more frenzied as they beheld the flames grow until at last they just stood at the windows with bundles in their arms, hair dishevelled, clothes torn, waving their hands at the mob, leading it as a drunken conductor a crazy orchestra.

Then one by one the figures disappeared from all the windows and for a few minutes the roaring mob saw nothing but it heard the sound of splintering wood and falling objects. The mob yelled for more legal papers. It was rewarded by a burst of flame from several windows, while the communist girl and boy leaders emerged from the main door-way. They had set the archives on fire.

Suddenly horns tooted and bells clanged. Firemen came with ladders and engines, pulling furiously at their bells while the thin mob on the outskirts reluctantly made way. They tried to push through the thick mob but the leaders at the fire on the main stairway gave them orders to disband because they intended to destroy the Palace and contents that day.

The firemen parked their machinery. The flames gained window after window. The mob near by shouted. Further away from the fire it was just a spectacle. Not only was ice-cream sold by street vendors but also hot Frankfurter sandwiches with mustard and horse-radish.

At 1:30 a few hundred men clad in light green and carrying a sign, "Workingmen's Police Guard," marched up with canes, saw the size of the mob, scented its temper, and marched away again.

A little later, however, a motor-cycle came up a side street, was stalled by pedestrians, started again, and backfired.

It banged once, twice, and again. A panic followed. At least five thousand of the fifteen thousand engaged in destroying or watching the destruction of the law courts, rushed headlong away from the backfiring motor-cycle, shrieking and elbowing for dear life.

It was apparent to anyone who could stand there and escape mob hysteria, that the mass was enjoying the beginning of the revolution, but was unwilling to share in any violence, which was entirely the work of the few communist leaders. The mass did not care to risk bullets. The mass was ready to fly even when it mistook backfiring for a machine-gun.

At exactly two o'clock the sound of a salvo was heard from the direction of the Parliament building. It was followed by salvo after salvo. With the exception of the leaders and a hundred or two whom excitement had won over to them, the entire 15,000 at the Palace of Justice joined with the 25,000 or 30,000 in the Ring and around Parliament, in flight in any direction which promised safety from bullets. The police rode after this fleeing mob and shot men and women down. Where there was resistance there was a battle; where it was merely overtaking them it was a massacre.

A wheel chair with a legless veteran was upset. Women ran so fast that they dragged their children almost off the ground. The ice-cream man was caught and forced to abandon his cart, which was overturned. Oranges and apples were sent rolling away and crushed underfoot.

Still the shooting continued. It was easy for the men on horseback to catch up with the mob which was filling every street, and to shoot into it. In one instance a squad was driving a crowd into a street from one end while another squad came up from the other. The two crowds collided and halted. The police suspected resistance. They opened fire. Eighteen of the hundred and one dead and more than a hundred of the seven hundred wounded were taken from this street.

I ran with the rest. Up near the Opera I made a detour of two miles and came to the Parliament buildings and the Palace of Justice. Outside Parliament I saw men lying in the middle of the street in little huddles. The wounded were stumbling along. As one man passed me I noticed blood was dripping from his clotted hair. He held his hand to his head and drew it back to look at the blood streaming on his fingers, sickeningly. Up and down the street mingled blood and dung and dirt and the overturned fruit and food, ice-cream and crushed oranges.

That night the revolution became earnest. The day had been spent on entirely unnecessary bloodshed. The holiday mob, temporarily in the hands of keen, quick Communists was ready to disperse at the sight of mounted policemen, but the latter had taken their revenge for injuries or the death of two or three of their number by indiscriminate slaughter of fleeing people. But the resistance grew. In the industrial workers' wards the police stations were stormed and police killed. Barricades and battles were reported from many parts of Vienna.

* * * * *

It was at this period of the day, when the force of the revolution could not be judged, when the possibility of the establishment of a red régime was actual, that we discovered ourselves cut off from the world. We had witnessed an amazing spontaneous uprising but there was no way of sending a word about it out of Vienna. It was worse than any kind of official censorship, which can always be met by compromise or evasion. For our enterprise it was a dead city.

Five years earlier, during a railroad strike, I had succeeded in leaving the country by taking a street-car to Pressburg or

Bratislava as the Czecho-Slovaks now call their frontier city. Now there were no street-cars nor automobiles for hire; but a colleague, Navarre Atkinson of *The New York Times,* had just bought an automobile. It was so new it should have been driven at thirty that night. But we put on the limit.

It is less than a hundred good miles from Vienna to Bratislava. We started without dinner thinking to dine well before midnight. But troubles began before we left the city limits. Stones were thrown at the car. Mobs blocked us with their bodies and cursed us. We tied the American flag to the motometer and it helped in the city. But scarcely had we entered the suburbs before armed guards stopped us and insisted that we return.

"Nothing must move — absolute order of the Labour Unions," the leader of the first outpost of revolution said, and many times that night it was repeated.

"This is the American ambassador and his aide," I replied to each in turn and exhibited the red passport with its gold seal impressively. As Austria no longer has an American ambassador it was not really false pretence — just plain swindle.

"I'll let you through — but you'll not pass beyond the next town," each revolutionary group leader said in turn.

Count the villages between the capital and the frontier, multiply by two, and you have the number of our encounters with armed forces. Not all of them were reds. Frequently we found the regular militia in control of one town and another in the hands of the Heimwehr, the peasant reactionary, illegal, secret, armed body which was eventually to quell the revolution.

At one place an officer in green asked for a lift. We took him a few miles, when he asked to get off and sank into a ditch mysteriously. At the next cross-roads some reds at the point of bayonets questioned us about our passenger and then started up the road to shoot or capture him.

So it went until midnight. To those who claim it was a local Vienna revolt, not a national revolution, I offer the foregoing testimony to which can be added similar experiences of newspapermen who drove in *via* Lenz and other main roads. All Austria was up in arms.

At the frontier the Czechs refused to let our automobile in but were kind enough to telephone for a taxi. We rode to the telegraph office and filed dispatches. Press privileges were refused us so the cost was enormous. We then tried to telephone to Berlin and found that one hotel porter had a monopoly on long distance calls and he was out of town. We returned to the post office to see how our telegrams were faring.

"I've got 40,000 words ahead of you now, all from local editors writing in German," said the official, "and when Prag sends me relief tomorrow I will be able to move your telegrams in three or four days."

Bribery did not avail.

Another impasse worse than censorship.

Then another little accident from which world scoops are born. On the street we asked directions from a little Hungarian-Jewish clothing shopkeeper. He seemed sympathetic and we were glad to pour our tale of woe into any willing ear. This man had missed his calling. If ever there was a born reporter it was this shopkeeper whose name we never learned and whose kindness we never repaid. He leaped into the fray. For hours he fought for us, precious hours narrowing quickly to the zero American press time. He overcame the recalcitrant Czeckish central with threats and promises — and he got us three minutes on the Berlin wire.

Then a new struggle began. In three minutes it was not possible to dictate more than ten words. To get another three minutes we had to put in another call which was granted us when the Prag-Berlin line was not busy.

Between one and four in the morning Atkinson and I were able to get twenty-two calls, sixty-six minutes, in which time by spelling every word at the top of our lungs while sweat and tears ran down our faces and our voices grew hoarse or cracked or turned to a whisper, we were able to telephone less than 1,000 words.

This is how we beat the censorship of circumstance.

We did this four nights. Each night it meant fighting the red and green guards and the Heimwehr, the telegraph and the post office officials of Czecho-Slovakia. We went without sleep and food most of the time. On the fourth night, returning to Vienna when the frontier reopened at five in the morning we both fell asleep in the car — Atkinson was driving — and rolled off the road into a ditch.

A week later, when the revolution and the general strike had been broken, due to the Heimwehr from all the anti-socialist country-side marching on Vienna, when the telegraph functioned again, each of us got a radio from our American offices. Mine read:

" Good work. Thanks."

Chapter VI

D'Annunzio, or the Bow-Legged Napoleon

FANFARE. Alarums and excursions. Drums. Silence. Stretching of necks. A crowd surges forward. Up the street comes the conventional tramp, tramp, tramp of feet, an old sound forever filled with tight joy. Only the Fiume children, Italian and Yugoslav alike, elbowed out of the way by their elders, unable to see or enter into excitement, make sacrilegious sounds while they play in the public square behind the solid human line.

Heading the procession, an imperial twelve feet in front of generals and admirals, marches a little man in the grey-green uniform of a field marshal. He wears a monocle and white kid gloves. There is a squinty smile on his face. He marches like a soldier but his feet stick out to the right and left; he is terribly bow-legged and ridiculous but his haughty head disregards his amazing toes. Sometimes he salutes superciliously.

Master of *mise-en-scene,* Gabrielle d'Annunzio, commandant and dictator of Fiume, coming to review the Dalmatian Legion, men who had taken his romantic oath to fight and die for Fiume.

" Ayah, ayah, ayah! Alala! "

A group of black-fezzed boy soldiers near the reviewing stand shout a greeting like an Indian war whoop. Youth applauds.

'Viva d'Annunzio! 'Viva 'Italia! 'Viva d'Annunzio!

Patriots, mostly freshly imported Italians in the Piazzo Dante Alighieri, raise a shout.

458

The spiritual father of a later Fascismo and the reviver of yells and salutes and other dead Roman claptrap, salutes again, bows, deepens his mechanical smile, and walks bow-leggedly on inspection. It is all very perfunctory. It is a holiday in Fiume, where nearly every day is a holiday because trade and sea commerce are dead, and all that can be celebrated is their funeral. But the crowd wants to hear brass music, to see uniformed men walk in rows, to hear the rhythm of discipline.

D'Annunzio, his inspection over, mounts the grand stand to show his full glorious self to the mob and bask in its plaudits. The crowd pushes forward more fiercely, the guards push back more fiercely, the band in the square strikes up one of Sousa's old marches, and the parade is on.

First comes a colonel, with a company from a famous regiment. The crowd recognizes both, recognizes them three times a week in fact, and shouts:

" 'Viva! 'Viva! 'Viva! "

Back in the square, glum Yugoslavs do not applaud or shout. They dully flatter themselves that they for once have not succumbed to mob psychology. They whisper treason.

" Does he want to frighten us with his tri-weekly soldiery? " says one. " Now that even the pro-Italian city council has voted against his staying any longer, and the last plebiscite has gone against him three to one, he brings out more and more of his black-shirted Arditi."

" A wise man," says another behind his hand, " to keep his soldiers always on the alert, for they are his sole supporters nowadays. Every civilian is against him."

The troops march. The children, groping their way through forests of feet, gain the street before their elders.

" Sinistra," snap the commanders of companies.

As every company goes by all eyes turn to the left and fix on the chief. When d'Annunzio is not saluting he is adjusting his monocle.

Ayah! Ayah! Ayah! Alala!

This time the marching companies, full throated, take up the yell and it is repeated up and down the corso.

The little Arditi regiment comes along, shock troops in black fezzes and black shirts, boys who are later to engage in riots and disorders, the administration of castor oil to Socialists and the establishment of Mussolini. They carry a regimental banner and an Italian flag. Military salutes. I take off my hat, and looking about, find I am the only civilian who has done so. It is a mystery.

There is a long break in the line. Then comes the Bersaglieri band. The men are not marching, they are running at a good speed, but they keep time as they run and they play music as they run. Even the Yugoslavs cannot remain outside psychology, they too applaud and their tongues stick in their mouths as they try to join the Italians in a shout.

Full three companies of Bersaglieri follow on a rhythmic run. Their officers, beautiful cock feathers waving in their helmets, pirouette like so many Mordkins and Nijinskis. They actually seem to dance. They run, whirl about in step, shout the " eyes left! " and whirl back in step, saluting as they whirl by.

Alpini, cyclists, machine-gun companies with equipment, infantry, Red Cross, artillery, follow, then the armoured cars, a lieutenant with four bravery medals and a wooden leg, a cyclist with only one arm, another who frees both hands and makes a flowing salute, an old Garibaldi soldier wearing a blood-red shirt and a beard a foot long, a long panorama of grey-green men and occasional touches of wild colour.

They shout to him, they play to him, they salute him. The whited sepulchre which once housed the soul of a poet and genius is filled with egotistic satisfactions. He stands to the salute, a pale, ruined Napoleon with bow-legs.

*   *   *   *   *

The room was crowded with things. Pictures, statues, hangings, purple drapings, pillows, a couch, too many chairs, a small carved table, miscellaneous small furniture. He wore no monocle nor the field marshal's cap. He was almost obscenely bald.

I asked him many questions in bad French and he replied, apparently, in dactylic hexameters. He discussed the poetry of Dante. I asked him about the commerce of the port. Would he blow it up if the Allies came to take it. He would, and so give his bones a magnificent and romantic finale in flame and explosion. He spoke of Ireland and India, Russia and Egypt, all the revolution and strife in this world, but he never raised his voice or made a wild Italian gesture. His voice was poetry, but there was no fire left in the old purple poet.

" Fiume to be divided? Fiume to be a free city? " (he replied to a suggestion) " Fiume would soon become a nest of traffickers, brokers, usurers and political grafters. Her beautiful face carved by passion and worn by tears would be abased like one of those faces that ape out upon her civilly from the left shore of the Eneo. Her masculine hand, held towards her country in the act of perpetual giving, would be drawn back to the bag of thirty pieces of silver. She would betray herself."

He beheld himself not merely as the dictator of Fiume but

the Messianic leader of all the downtrodden peoples of the earth; he was sure the banner he had raised in this small corner was rallying all helpless and hopeless humanity from pole to pole.

"What if we perish in the ruins of Fiume," he said softly. "The spirit of our resistance will leap forth watchful and active. From the dauntless Sinn Fein of Ireland to the red banner which in Egypt unites the Crescent with the Cross, all the insurrections of the spirit against the devourers of raw flesh, and against the exploiters of weaponless peoples, will catch flame anew from our sparks which fly afar.

"Our cause is the greatest and the most beautiful that today is opposed to the dementia and to the vileness of the world. It extends from Ireland to Egypt, from Russia to America, from Roumania to India. It gathers together the white races and the coloured races, reconciles the Gospel with the Koran, Christianity and Islam; rivets in one sole will as many peoples as possess, in their bones and in their arteries, salt and iron sufficient to feed action.

"We shall always be victorious. All the rebels of all races of mankind will gather under our banners. And the weaponless shall be armed. And violence will oppose violence. There shall be a new crusade of all the poor and impoverished nations, of all poor men and all free men, against the nations which usurp power and accumulate riches, against predatory nations, against the caste of usurers which yesterday made the profits of the war and today profits by the peace, and we shall re-establish the true justice which a cold and foolish man with a hammer borrowed from a former German chancellor, crucified with fourteen nails."

And so on.

This is how he spoke for an hour, and I could not hope to catch word or rhythm, so I had his secretary prepare me a copy from d'Annunzio's dictation, and the poet must have known how good his stuff was, for he used the same paragraphs in a public oration later, and included some of them in a volume published in Fiume.

In parting d'Annunzio suggested that I interview Dr. Anton Grossich, president of Fiume, who would state the case of a native son in favour of Italy. I replied that I would do so, providing that I coupled the interview with that of the leading native Yugoslav son. This offended and puzzled the commandant because he shared, with most Continental Europeans, the thought that pure objectivity by a neutral foreign journalist meant giving only his own side of the case. However he promised me immunity from his censorship bureau — a promise which was not kept.

My visit to President Grossich led to a lot of trouble.

*   *   *   *   *

He was a nice, sweet, kind, aged man who didn't know what in the world he was saying. He made enough damning admissions to ruin the cause of d'Annunzio. Out of pure humanity I was easy with him. But there was one actual fact I could not suppress. Grossich had described to me the plebiscite in favour of d'Annunzio and the Italian rule upon which all the military and the politicians were trumpeting Italy's claim to the disputed port.

"We won," said Grossich. "It was a fair election. All the good citizens were allowed to vote. Just before plebiscite day we cleared out all the unfit elements, all the Socialists, workingmen, trouble makers. We deported about five thousand of them."

By a strange coincidence it seems that all the trouble makers, Socialists and workingmen were the bulk of the possible Yugoslav voters. With 5,000 deportations of the opposition the Italian forces had put through an election under military terror which they claim they had won by a small margin and which the Yugoslavs claim they lost by a large margin.

Despite the censor, I was able to smuggle this fact through.

To obtain a Yugoslav spokesman was a difficult matter. I found many but all feared bodily harm and imprisonment. One day, however, my interpreter found a man who began by saying:

"My name is Timotheus Marinkovich. I am seventy-four years old and have not long to live. Good. I will take the risk of dying in d'Annunzio's prison and let my name be used for a statement of the Yugoslav case in Fiume."

What he then said mattered much once, but nothing now.

I smuggled this interview through. Grossich's plea for Italy and Marinkovich's plea for the S. H. S. Kingdom were printed side by side.

My interpreter came and said: "Get out of the town at once. D'Annunzio will shoot you if you don't. He knows all about your visit to Marinkovich, Marinkovich is in jail."

I took the night train for Trieste. At a little half-way stop three of d'Annunzio's soldiers came searching for me. They insisted on my returning to Fiume. I refused to go. Three of them punched me, then seized my arms and legs and carried me and my baggage off the train. The Italian travellers complained that the fuss had caused a delay in schedule. (Trains in

Italy could run on schedule even before the *deus ex machina* Mussolini.)

At the police station near the depot I stayed all night while they sent a courier to Abazzia with the news of my arrest. Meanwhile I had insisted on telegraphing to friends and the American consul in Trieste. I also spoke menacingly of the American fleet blowing up Fiume although every American in that part of the world knew that America had been insulted and the consuls chased from Fiume by d'Annunzio's forces without much protest from the State Department.

At dawn a courier arrived and whispered. My belongings and passport were returned to me. A train came along and I took it to Trieste.

There, a day later, I read the testimony in the trial of my Yugoslav spokesman, my friend Marinkovich:

"I am seventy-four years old and have not long to live," he told the court. "Why should I take the risk of dying in d'Annunzio's prisons by letting my name be used for a statement of the Yugoslav case in Fiume? I never saw the journalist in question. . . ."